W9-AQA-644

The Handbook of Foreign Student Advising

Revised Edition

Gary Althen

Saint Peter's University Library

Withdrawn

The Handbook of Foreign Student Advising

Revised Edition

Gary Althen

Intercultural Press, Inc.

For information, contact:
Intercultural Press, Inc.
P.O. Box 700
Yarmouth, Maine 04096 USA

© 1995 by Gary Althen

All rights reserved. No part of this publication may be reproduced in any manner whatsoever without written permission from the publisher, except in the case of brief quotations embodied in critical articles or reviews.

Book design and production by Patty J. Topel
Cover design by Lois Leonard Stock

Printed in the United States of America

00   99   98   97   96   2   3   4   5   6

Library of Congress Cataloging-in Publication Data

Althen, Gary.
       The handbook of foreign student advising / Gary Althen. — Rev. ed.
              p.   cm.
       Includes bibliographical references and index.
       ISBN 1-877864-34-X
       1. Faculty advisers—United States—Handbooks, manuals, etc.   2. Students, Foreign—United States—Handbooks, manuals, etc.   I. Title.

LB2343A39   1995
378.1'94—dc20   95-3433
                                                                     CIP

B
343
439
1995

Table of Contents

Acknowledgments

Inspiration for continuing to work in the field of foreign student advising, and to seek to do it better and write about it, continues to come from David Hoopes, Josef Mestenhauser, Richard Brislin, and Roberto Clemente, all of whom were acknowledged in the first edition of this *Handbook*. To their names should be added those of Tim McMahon and Kay Thomas. Tim, formerly the "king of schmooze" at the University of Iowa, drew my attention to many helpful and stimulating books and joined in fruitful discussions of them. Kay, my partner in a number of professional undertakings, consistently offers perspectives that I have overlooked.

Several colleagues in the University of Iowa's Office of International Education and Services make it possible for me to write and carry out other professional development activities. OIES director Stephen Arum gives unqualified support to his staff's efforts at professional development. The competence of my colleagues John Rogers, Lisa Dings (now moved on to a new phase in life), and Margaret ("Maggie") Brooke enables me to give at least some attention to matters other than daily office operations. John, Lisa, and Maggie were good enough to read the entire manuscript of this book and offer their suggestions for its improvement. So were two former University of Iowa colleagues, Maureen Fitzgibbon and Virginia ("Ginny") Gross. I am particularly grateful to these individuals, because I know how much effort is involved in reading and commenting on someone's manuscript.

Colleagues who read and commented on part of the draft include Stephanie Becker, Alisa Eland, Marcus Fang, Karen Klopp, and Parandeh Kia. For their comments, too, I am grateful.

OIES graduate assistant Nonhlanhla Makwakwa hunted down references for me. Chris Walters of the University of Iowa Library was also helpful and efficient in reference-seeking.

Mary Peterson, formerly of the NAFSA staff, has been supportive and helpful over many years, as have Janet and Milton Bennett of the Intercultural Communication Institute.

Many readers of the first edition whom I've encountered in conference hallways and meeting rooms have acknowledged the helpfulness of that book, inclining me to undertake this revision.

Finally, some words of appreciation to my wife, Sandy, who has supported my working on this enterprise on private time. Without that support, a project like this would never be realized.

It goes without saying that the people named above do not all agree with each other or with me about what is in this book. Ultimately, responsibility for any misstatements or misguided notions is my own.

Gary Althen
Iowa City, Iowa
1995

Introduction

In the introduction to the first edition of this *Handbook*, I wrote that foreign student advising is the most interesting job on the campus. I still believe that, as do any number of my colleagues. "I can't imagine doing anything else," I've often said, and heard other FSAs say. What makes the job so interesting? Many things, including the array of people FSAs encounter, the diversity of tasks they carry out, and the opportunity to learn new things each day.

And not just interesting, but rewarding. Few people get the opportunities FSAs do to help other people accomplish constructive tasks, to teach useful knowledge and skills, and to learn firsthand about the contributions of cultural diversity to creative problem solving and a rich life. Few people hear words of thanks from others as often as FSAs do.

But foreign student advising is not an easy job, at least not if it is done well. This book, like its predecessor, is intended to help FSAs gain a deeper understanding of the job and improve their ability to carry it out.

This edition of the *Handbook* retains the organization of the first. The earlier chapters are more theoretical and the later ones more practical. Chapter 1 discusses the practical and conceptual setting in which FSAs work. Chapter 2 concerns the nature of the foreign student adviser's position. Chapter 3 discusses the personal characteristics of successful FSAs, and chapter 4 examines some general attitudes and ideas that inform an FSA's work.

The fifth chapter catalogues the various areas in which FSAs are well advised to develop knowledge. Chapter 6 treats the skills they will want to develop, and chapter 7 concerns various aspects of an FSA's daily work. Chapter 8 offers some brief concluding remarks.

While the organization of this edition is the same as that of the first, the content is substantially different. This edition alludes to many of the changes in the international, national, and educational environments that have taken place since the first edition was published. It refers to dozens of publications that have become available. It reflects ten years of additional experience, reading, and thinking on my part.

And it is a more personal book. The first edition strove to be descriptive, objective, rather impersonal. This edition, by contrast, makes clear what some of my biases are. Readers will thus be able to respond not just to ideas and theories, but to particular points of view on issues that FSAs confront.

While writing this, I have been acutely aware of the Americanness of it. So much of my professional life involves interpreting and explaining human behavior in cultural terms that by now the cultural underpinnings of my own behavior—including what I write in this book and the way I write it—are continuously near the forefront of my consciousness. I employ what the Iranian-born observer Ari Siletz refers to as the "you-are-here organization" in American English writing, frequently telling the reader what is going to be discussed next, or what is being discussed now, or what we have just finished discussing. I seek to get right to the point, make the point clear, and then summarize it. I avoid using unnecessary words. Frequent subheadings mark the way. All this goes with my understanding of "good" American English writing. I write this way with an acute realization that people raised in other cultures, using other languages, might find it tedious, unintelligent, and even insulting, assuming, as it seems to do, that a reader needs a map and a large number of signs to keep from getting lost, as does a tourist on an unfamiliar interstate highway.

I think it is an occupational hazard for foreign student advisers to sometimes feel hindered, if not paralyzed, by the realization that they are operating on the basis of values and assumptions that are essentially arbitrary and that other people cannot be assumed to share.

But we must begin somewhere. We must employ some style and approach. I am reminded of a training session in which small groups of participants were discussing what I know as "The Parable,"[1] a tale

---

[1] This tale, or variations of it, has various names, including "Alligator River." One version is in Margaret Pusch (ed.). *Multicultural Education: A Cross-Cultural Training Approach*, 138-40.

in which a sailor named Sinbad offers to take a maiden named Rosemary across an alligator-infested river where her betrothed awaits her, but only on the condition that she first spend the night with him. There are other characters and other complications to the short tale, at the end of which participants in the training are organized into small groups and asked to rank the various characters in the tale, indicating whose behavior they most approved, whose the least, and whose in between. As it always does, the task provoked heated discussion. Participants argued various points of view, and the groups were unable to agree on rankings. Then we discussed the values that underlay various participants' viewpoints and the possible genesis and relative arbitrariness of those values. Participants seemed to get the point.

I then asked, "Now, setting values aside, which of the characters in this story *really* did exhibit the best behavior?" After a long silence, one participant spoke up: "Wait a minute! You can't make a decision like that without basing it on *some* values. You *always* have values."

Indeed. And you always have a cultural background, and you always work within a given cultural framework. So it is with this book. While it discusses a field in which value differences (and cultural differences in general) are a key aspect, and while it urges continuous awareness of the cultural presuppositions of other people, this book is written mainly for foreign student advisers who work in the United States. Most of them are themselves Americans. Thus, it uses a style that is presumably comfortable and accessible for them, and it urges on them a point of view that would not fit in other cultural contexts. It assumes an individualistic orientation, a fair measure of control over situations, and a belief in the efficacy of self-improvement.

In operating on the basis of these typical American assumptions, I risk conveying the impression that I see no problems associated with them, when indeed the problems seem numerous and grave. Such books as *The Pursuit of Loneliness* (Philip Slater), *The Culture of Narcissism* (Christopher Lasch), *Habits of the Heart* (Robert N. Bellah and others), and *Care of the Soul* (Thomas Moore) are among the many that raise serious questions about the nature and direction of contemporary American society. Those questions are not reflected in this *Handbook*, despite my belief in their importance.

Some of the colleagues who critiqued drafts of this book suggested that it makes unrealistic assumptions about people's commitments to their jobs and to self-improvement. Most FSAs, I was told, won't take up any more than a few of the suggestions this book offers, if indeed they take up any at all. Perhaps that is true. I hope it is not. Just as I do not think patients should have to go to doctors who do not remain informed about current developments in prescription medication and surgical treatment, or that homeowners should have to rely on plumbers who are unaware of advances in pipe fittings, I do not think foreign students or institutional faculty and staff should have to rely on foreign student advisers who are not continuously seeking to remain abreast of developments in their field and to improve their knowledge and skills.

This is not to say that FSAs should expect to advance quickly in all the areas this book addresses. More than twenty-five years of work and thought have gone into the compilation of ideas and suggestions offered here. New FSAs ought to regard this book as a basis for many years of learning and practice. Becoming and remaining a good foreign student adviser is a lifelong enterprise, full of hard work and occasional difficult times, but ultimately quite rewarding.

1

The Setting

In 1982, the American Council on Education projected that the foreign student[1] population in the United States would number 1,000,000 by the year 2000. That projection was evidently ill-founded. The foreign student population explosion that preceded the projection ended, at least temporarily, shortly after the projection was published and widely quoted. The number of foreign students continued to grow, but only at a gradual rate.

Even so, foreign students moved more into the public eye than they had been before publication of the first edition of *The Handbook of Foreign Student Advising*, and the work of foreign student advisers (FSAs) got increasing attention. These changes resulted from a variety of often interrelated developments at the international, national, and institutional levels.

INTERNATIONAL DEVELOPMENTS

Changes in international political and economic relationships, as well as political developments within individual countries, impinge on the work of foreign student advisers. The most dramatic of such events over the past ten years have been the opening of China, the Tiananmen Square protests in that country, and the collapse of the Soviet Union and the Soviet bloc.

---

[1] Some people prefer the euphemism "international students" to the more precise "foreign students." Despite heavy lobbying to the contrary, I continue to believe the more precise term is better, and use it throughout this book. "The notion that you change a situation by finding a newer and nicer word for it emerges from the old American habit of euphemism, circumlocution and desperate confusion about etiquette, produced by fear that the concrete will give offense," Australian-born journalist Robert Hughes writes in his analysis of contemporary American society, *Culture of Complaint: The Fraying of America*.

Rapid increases in the number of students from China accounted for much of the growth in the U.S. foreign student population in the early and mid-1980s. By the time of the 1989 Tiananmen Square shootings, Chinese students were the largest group of foreign students in the United States. A scant ten years earlier, almost none were here.

With the demolition of the Berlin Wall and the dissolution of the Soviet empire, more and more students from Eastern Europe and Russia were coming to the United States. Some came as refugees, but more came as a result of personal or professional ties to people in the United States. FSAs found that they had yet another new group of students about whose educational and cultural backgrounds they needed to learn more.

Other international political developments that impinged on FSAs over the past decade were the Persian Gulf War (which left Iraqi, Kuwaiti, and many Palestinian students in difficulty of various kinds) and booming economies in Korea, Japan, and Taiwan. Legions of Japanese came to the United States, many of them for short-term English and culture programs. Many Koreans came too, confronting FSAs with representatives of a culture they often had trouble comprehending.

While the economic fortunes of some Asian countries contributed to increases in the number of students from those countries, economic misfortune in other areas brought declines. The number of students in the United States from African countries (except perhaps South Africa, which was a special case) diminished, as did the number from Latin America.

Foreign student flow into the United States is frequently affected by U.S. government policy. The U. S. government has invested in financial aid for some of the Russian and Eastern European students mentioned earlier and for students from South Africa and the Caribbean basin.

A final international political development that impinged on the work of FSAs was the explosion in the number of refugees. Hundreds of thousands of people fled turmoil in many different countries. While only a relative handful of them reached U.S. campuses, their presence and the special issues they presented often made FSAs reconsider their traditional focus on nonimmigrant students. Refugees, asylees, beneficiaries of the mid-1980s amnesty program, and people in new immigration statuses called "temporary protected status" (TPS) and "deferred enforced departure" (DED) joined the traditional F-1 and J-1 students in seeking assistance from foreign student advisers.

Two other international developments that began to affect the work of FSAs were the AIDS epidemic and the resurgence of tuberculosis. Both of these health problems brought up issues regarding testing of foreign students' medical conditions, health education, treating diseases, and the confidentiality of medical information.

NATIONAL DEVELOPMENTS

Other changes in U.S immigration law and regulations, beyond the new TPS and DED statuses, impinged significantly on the work of FSAs. The Immigration Reform and Control Act of 1986 (known as IRCA) in effect made American employers into agents of the INS (Immigration and Naturalization Service) by requiring them to complete a particular form (called the I-9) for every new employee, showing the employee's identity and authorization to work in the United States. On many campuses it was FSAs who, because they had long been responsible for dealing with immigration matters, became responsible for the I-9 procedure, at least for noncitizens.

President George Bush's 1990 executive order protecting Chinese students in the United States after Tiananmen Square, and the subsequent (1992) Chinese Student Protection Act (CSPA), brought FSAs an enormous quantity of work related to Chinese students. An entire book could be written about the political, administrative, educational, social, and psychological impact of the Chinese students and scholars who came here in the 1980s and early 1990s.

The CSPA made it possible for thousands of Chinese students and scholars to adjust to permanent resident status at a time when the American public and the American government faced major issues concerning the general issue of immigration. While some in academe and elsewhere argued that both academic tradition and the need to develop or maintain competitiveness made it necessary to seek the best minds available for educational and research enterprises, no matter where those minds came from, others argued that it was dangerous to become reliant on people whose ultimate allegiance might be to some other country and whose employment in the United States might displace U.S. workers.

One by-product of this debate was an increasing public realization of the degree to which American universities had become dependent on foreign-born students and young faculty to carry out their teaching and research missions.

The situation of Chinese students and scholars and the debate about immigration forced FSAs to confront their traditional assumptions about their clients, whom they had long conceived of and treated as people who were in the United States only temporarily and who would eventually return to their own countries. Many in fact did not go back, and FSAs themselves were often called upon by their institutions to do the paperwork necessary to enable them to remain in the United States to pursue their academic careers.

The nature of federal regulations affecting foreign students and exchange visitors (people in J-1 status) also changed dramatically during the past decade. Responding to (among other things) the efforts of NAFSA: Association of International Educators, the INS promulgated new regulations intended to deregulate foreign students, removing many decisions from INS hands and placing them in the hands of foreign student advisers, called "designated school officials" (or DSOs). In addition, the U.S. Information Agency in 1993 published new exchange-visitor regulations, which also enlarged FSA (or "responsible officer") responsibilities.

A lesser national issue that brought considerable attention to foreign students, and thus to FSAs, was what came to be known as "the FTA issue." Complaints from American students—and their parents—about foreign teaching assistants at universities led to the establishment of FTA training programs on many campuses and, in several cases, to state legislation mandating efforts to insure FTAs' oral effectiveness.

Nationwide concerns about sexual harassment and multiculturalism (however defined) also came to be reflected in the work of foreign student advisers, as did concern about escalating costs of medical care. Many FSAs found themselves involved more and more in discussions about health insurance and the question of mandatory health-insurance policies for students from other countries.

INSTITUTIONAL DEVELOPMENTS

Perhaps the most dramatic on-campus development related at least indirectly to foreign students has been the widespread adoption of the rhetoric of internationalization. For years FSAs, other international education practitioners, and their faculty allies felt themselves rather in the wilderness as they called for the internationalization of their campuses and curricula. Probably more because of the increasing interpenetration of national economies and academic disciplines than because of the power of international educators' rhetoric, campus leaders have joined the call for internationalization. Whatever that vague term means, it normally includes "more foreign students" and "better utilization of our foreign students for the purpose of educating our domestic students."

Academic leaders have begun openly to acknowledge their reliance on foreign teaching and research assistants and also on foreign-born teachers and researchers. When the Berlin Wall fell, academics in many disciplines eagerly sought what they regarded as well-prepared students and scholars from Russia and Eastern Europe. Meanwhile, many students and scholars from China continued to awe American faculty with the quality of their intellect and their willingness to work.

FSAs have been called upon more and more to assist with the foreign student- and scholar-related aspects of this internationalization—to find financial aid for promising students from China and the former Soviet empire, to do the paperwork needed to hire both temporary and permanent foreign faculty and staff, and to help remedy "cultural problems" that arise when noticeable numbers of foreign students and scholars come to the campus.

Certain management trends swept the country, affecting many campuses and many FSAs. Chief among them were strategic planning and total quality management.

In sum, an array of interrelated developments at the international, national, and institutional levels has drawn ever increasing attention to foreign students and foreign student advisers. FSAs now face heavier and more diverse demands for knowledge, thought, sensitivity, and operational effectiveness. If it could be said in the first edition of this book that the conceptual framework in which FSAs operate was inadequate to account for the complexity of their work, that conceptual framework is all the more inadequate now.

THE CONCEPTUAL SETTING

There are at least two ways in which FSAs are helped by having a clear rationale for their work. First, the solution to many a practical conundrum follows directly from the possession of a clearly conceived general goal. For example, what should an FSA do when asked to advise a sponsored student who wants to marry an American citizen and remain in the United States rather than honor a contract with a sponsor to return home and teach? There are several possible responses to that question. One would follow from the assumption that the purpose of international educational exchange is to foster economic and social development in countries less prosperous than the United States. Another, and quite different, answer would follow from the assumption that educational interchange is intended to enable individual participants to realize their personal development to the maximum extent possible.

Second, a clear rationale helps in the continuing effort to explain oneself and enhance one's own prospects when competing for institutional, state, and national resources and influence. Why should the institution support an FSA? Why should the state not establish policies that discourage foreign students from studying within its borders? Why should U.S. immigration policy be as lenient as possible toward students from abroad? Different answers to these questions flow from different concepts of the nature and purposes of international educational exchange.

Inadequacy of current concepts

Contemporary discussion and debate about foreign students in the United States and elsewhere is marked by incoherence, inconclusiveness, and a measure of prejudice. One way to examine how we think about foreign students is to consider the *metaphors* we use, explicitly or implicitly, when we talk about students from other countries. Some of these metaphors are incompatible with each other, while others address different aspects of the foreign student situation and can be complementary. What becomes clear when we look at these various metaphors is that we rarely use the same one or ones consistently. Rather, we jump from one to another. Often, discussions about foreign student policies are inconclusive and even contentious because the discussants are using different metaphors.

Here are several metaphors that emerge from noticing what people say about students from other countries:

- *Foreign students are students.* According to this view, foreign students are students like any others, not in need of or deserving any special attention or effort. "They came here and joined our game," adherents of this view will say, "and they can play by our rules."

- *Foreign students are students, but they have some special needs.* When viewed this way, foreign students have some distinguishing characteristics that warrant special handling by the institutions they attend. Those characteristics have to do with language background, cultural differences, educational habits and expectations shaped by some other educational system, and of course the limitations U.S. immigration law and regulations place on their activities.

- *Foreign students are pains in the neck.* Some see foreign students as causing more trouble than they are worth, given their difficult-to-understand English, their need for additional time in test taking and academic advising, and their initial inability to demonstrate the intellectual skills of analysis and synthesis that are rewarded in the U.S. academic system.

- *Foreign students are guests.* According to this metaphor, Americans are hosts to students who are in the United States for a visit. As hosts the Americans are presumably expected to be sensitive and attentive, but not to meddle. The guests are expected to be grateful and polite and to keep their complaints to themselves.

- *Foreign students are valuable educational resources.* Students from other countries bring different cultural backgrounds and perspectives to nearly any issue, according to this metaphor, and educators ought to take advantage of that fact by admitting reasonable numbers of such students and making arrangements—through housing, programming, and instructional devices—to assure that domestic students learn from them.

- *Foreign students are potential contributors to economic development abroad.* This metaphor supposes that significant numbers of foreign students are from relatively poor countries and that, upon completion of their U.S. studies, they will return to their own countries and do work that applies what they have learned in the United States in ways that will improve the general lot of their compatriots.

- *Foreign students are potential contributors to domestic economic development.* According to this view, foreign students, at least ones in technical or "hard science" fields, can contribute to economic competitiveness at the local, state, and/or national levels in the United States. Indeed, they may be crucial to that competitiveness, as the number of domestic graduates in these fields continues to be too small to meet the demand.

- *Foreign students are potential political capital.* This metaphor assumes that most foreign students will have positive experiences in the United States and will develop an appreciation for the political and economic institutions that prevail here. When they go home (presumably as leaders) they will remain sympathetic to this country, supporting its policies and perhaps working to promote the development of U.S.-style institutions in their own countries.

- *Foreign students are potential customers.* Not only will they come to appreciate U.S. institutions and ways of thinking, but they will become accustomed to certain products while living in this country. When they go home, they will still want those products.

- *Foreign students are bearers of wealth.* In an era when the bottom line gets great attention, foreign students commonly get credit for bringing thousands or millions (depending on the size of the geographical area under consideration) of dollars into American educational institutions and their surrounding communities. Those who see foreign students as bearers of wealth consider their goodwill worth courting.

- *Foreign students are a threat to national security.* Some people see foreign students as a threat to national security, given their presumed access to information about up-to-date technology. Those who see foreign students in this way express fear that they will return home and help develop military weapons or techniques that could someday be used against the United States, or that they will use their knowledge to aid overseas businesses that are competing against American businesses.

Amidst this plethora of metaphors and derivative arguments, coherent discussion aimed at agreement on policy and practice is unlikely to emerge. The problem, as Josef A. Mestenhauser puts it,[2] is that the old paradigm for international educational exchange no longer serves well, but has yet to be replaced by a new one. Mestenhauser's promising line of thought derives from Thomas S. Kuhn's analysis in *The Structure of Scientific Revolutions.* Kuhn's general idea is this: At any given time there prevails a general theory, concept, or paradigm which satisfactorily explains a particular phenomenon or set of phenomena. As knowledge and thought advance, the accepted paradigm is found wanting and is finally dislodged by a new paradigm that better explains the phenomena in question. One

---

[2] In personal conversations.

of Kuhn's examples has to do with the replacement of the earth-centered theory of the solar system by the sun-centered theory—the so-called Copernican revolution.

Mestenhauser argues that the current paradigm of international educational exchange developed in the post-World War II era, when (1) the United States was clearly ahead of all other countries in economic and technical strength, (2) foreign students were comparatively few in number, carefully selected, mature, and affiliated with a small number of major U.S. universities, (3) the idea prevailed that people everywhere would benefit from exposure to U.S. education and technology, (4) it could plausibly be argued that a noticeable portion of returned foreign students would achieve leadership positions in their own countries, and (5) the idea that international person-to-person contacts promoted world brotherhood was widely accepted. These circumstances led to the general idea that international educational exchange was a good thing, with political, economic, and humanitarian outcomes which most people regarded favorably.

These circumstances no longer prevail. Not only that, but new complications have arisen. First, American higher educational institutions have fallen on hard economic times. Second, they have come to place high priority on recruiting and retaining nonwhite domestic students. These two changes have brought about competition for money and administrative support. Who should get scholarships and other forms of financial aid? What student service office is most in need of support? Don't those who work with foreign students and those who work with domestic minority students have enough in common that they can be merged into the same office or at least work closely together in providing services and educational programs?

Third, to further confound the already confounding issues of foreign versus minority students, recent years have seen significant increases in the number of immigrant and refugee students. Their concerns have elements in common with both foreign and domestic minority students, but their particular combination of these concerns makes their situation unique. How do they fit into our institutional structures? Who is to help them overcome their particular obstacles to educational success?

A fourth change is the increased willingness to acknowledge the fact that in some fields of study, foreign students have become integral parts of graduate study and research. Far from being oddities or burdens, foreign students are now indispensable in many science, engineering, mathematics, computer science, and business departments. Most foreign students are not in the United States as a result of this country's charity or generosity. Rather, they are here because this country's educational institutions offer something they or their sponsors are willing to pay for, or because the institutions themselves need the labor foreign students supply.

Fifth, graduating foreign students have become crucial components of the labor pool in several fields of endeavor. FSAs and other practitioners in international educational exchange can no longer easily assume that all foreign students will or should go home.

No new paradigm has arisen to accommodate these new circumstances. The frustrating debates continue and, in an era of diminished resources, perhaps even intensify.

Toward a New Concept

In their daily lives, FSAs will not be actively involved in developing a new paradigm for international educational exchange. But, whether they are aware of it or not, policy decisions in their own offices or elsewhere in their institutions, in their states, and in their national capital are being made on the basis of some paradigm or other. FSAs who want to influence those policy decisions cannot ignore the need for a more adequate set of guiding concepts for their work.

2

The Nature of the
Foreign Student Adviser Position

In *Absence of Decision,* their 1983 report on the international education policies of American colleges and universities, Craufurd D. Goodwin and Michael Nacht observed that

> the foreign student adviser was often the least influential figure in the entire organizational structure. Buffeted by events and conscious of impending change in one direction or another, advisers often were powerless to make their views known to higher-level policy makers or to have a voice in the planning process...(8).

This was the case even though, in Goodwin's and Nacht's view, "...the foreign student adviser is an unusual, well-informed resource who should be used as a catalyst, source of information, and accumulator of campus wisdom far more frequently than is presently the case"(8-9).

One of the factors that makes FSAs unusual is that their duties bring them into contact with people in all categories and at all levels in the institution—students from freshmen to postdoctoral researchers, faculty from instructors to deans, staff from custodial workers to heads of administrative offices, and administrators up to the chief executive officer. In addition, FSAs often have important off-campus relationships not just in the local community but at the state, national, and, increasingly, the international levels.

With all these contacts, it is little wonder that the FSA is at least potentially a well-informed participant in discussions of institutional policy on foreign students and on broader international education matters as well.

Why, then, does the FSA generally remain a low-level figure with little power and influence in the institution? Part of the explanation is no doubt the fact that FSAs lack access to the sources of greatest power in educational institutions. Those sources are money (especially money from external agencies that confer large grants) and high-level positions that bestow power on their incumbents.

Another part of the explanation for their low status and relative lack of power and influence (these terms will be elaborated upon later) is the jumble of responsibilities they have and the conflicting expectations people have of them. Let us now examine those factors more closely.

RESPONSIBILITIES

Despite the fact that there are now two educational institutions[1] offering degrees in foreign student advising, people can and usually do enter the field without any formal preparation. Unlike physicians, lawyers, psychologists, or other recognized professionals, FSAs do not need licenses or certificates to enter the field.[2] Lacking mechanisms to assure standardization, FSAs have no established answers to the two main questions about their responsibilities: To whom are they responsible? And, what are they responsible for doing? These questions are easier for licensed professionals to answer.[3] Compared with members of the recognized professions, FSAs face a greater array of complaints, problems, issues, possibilities, and expectations, and their work gets the attention of an audience with sharply divergent views as to what they should be doing.

To whom are FSAs responsible? Different FSAs, in different situations, offer various opinions. So do their clients, their supervisors, and others who have an interest in their work. Among those to whom different people consider FSAs to be responsible are these:

1. their own conscience, as influenced by ideas of what is good for international educational exchange, what standards in their field ought to be, personal values, and other factors

---

[1] Lesley College in Massachusetts and the School for International Training in Vermont.

[2] Discussions about certification for FSAs and other international educational exchange participants are under way within NAFSA, but they are not expected to reach fruition any time soon.

[3] This is not to say that members of the licensed professions face no daunting issues. Indeed they do, as the media inform us with their coverage of such issues as euthanasia and the confidentiality of information about AIDS patients.

2. their supervisors

3. their institution's chief executive officers

4. one or more people in the institutional hierarchy between their supervisors and the CEO

5. the agencies (state or other) that employ them

6. their foreign student and scholar clients

7. the foreign students' parents

8. faculty at their institutions

9. administrative staff members at their institutions

10. members of the community

11. colleagues in the field of international education

12. the U.S. Immigration and Naturalization Service and, for FSAs who are responsible for exchange-visitor programs, the U.S. Information Agency (USIA)

13. organizations that sponsor foreign students

14. the U.S. government

15. foreign governments, especially Third World

16. a supreme being

17. a "higher law"

What are FSAs responsible for doing? Again, there are assorted opinions, given here in no particular order:

1. carrying out procedures specified in federal regulations related to foreign students and exchange visitors

2. enforcing U.S. immigration law and regulations

3. assuring that foreign students behave decorously

4. handling crises involving foreign students

5. helping foreign students adjust to a new culture

6. helping foreign students realize their educational objectives with the least possible difficulty

7. relieving institutional colleagues of the burden of dealing with students from abroad

8. helping institutional colleagues deal constructively with students from abroad

9. monitoring foreign students' academic and perhaps social conduct on behalf of the institution, sponsoring agencies, foreign governments, and/or the students' parents

10. helping U.S. students, staff, faculty, and/or community members learn from foreign students about other societies and/or about intercultural relationships

11. helping foreign students achieve the maximum feasible amount of self-development

12. helping poor countries advance politically and economically, by aiding students from those countries and assuring their return home

This array of things to do and of people to do them for gives rise to a bewildering array of tasks for FSAs. Participants in a workshop for new foreign student advisers produced the following list of tasks they sometimes felt expected to perform—whether they actually performed them or not:

- administer
- advise on taxes
- advise student organizations
- admit foreign applicants
- advocate
- advise, in general
- baby-sit
- be a diplomat
- be a dumping ground
- be a friend
- be an intermediary
- carry out DSO[4] responsibilities
- carry out RO[5] responsibilities

---

[4] Designated school official. At the time of this writing, U.S. Immigration & Naturalization Service regulations on foreign students (more precisely, F-1 and M-1 students and their F-2 and M-2 dependents) used this term to refer to institutional officials responsible for signing documents related to an array of procedures. As these regulations change, the term used to designate school officials who do the pertinent paperwork may change also.

[5] Responsible officer. At the time of this writing, the U.S. Information Agency used this term to designate the person registered with the agency as having main responsibility for carrying out certain provisions of the U.S. *Code of Federal Regulations* (CFR) with respect to exchange visitors at the RO's particular institution. An ARO is an alternate responsible officer. The term is subject to change, as the regulations evolve.

- change community attitudes
- consult
- counsel
- empathize
- enforce laws
- facilitate
- liaise with community organizations
- liaise with the media
- liaise with sponsoring agencies
- mediate
- mentor
- monitor
- network
- perform magic
- professional development
- program (cultural, social, and educational activities)
- provide information
- recruit
- refer
- solve problems
- teach
- train students, staff, and/or faculty
- write and edit

These responsibilities and tasks are sometimes complementary, sometimes incompatible. (Most FSAs would say they are always incompatible with the number of hours in the day!) Some ideas about choosing among them will appear in chapter 4 and elsewhere in this book. Meanwhile, let us look more closely at some of the factors that influence the set of responsibilities an FSA carries out.

FACTORS INFLUENCING THE FSA'S JOB DESCRIPTION

In the real world of colleges and universities, many people do not have a formal job description, or at least not one that indicates what they actually do. Here, the term "job description" is used in a generic way, to refer to the set of responsibilities a given FSA assumes.

Many factors influence those job descriptions, including mandates, what the boss wants, history, research, various stakeholders' perceptions and expectations, and the FSA's own characteristics and proclivities.

Mandates

Several years ago my institution, like many others at the time, undertook strategic planning. As part of that exercise we looked first at our mandate, that is, at what we were legally required to do. We realized that, amidst all the programs, activities, and services we offered, the only thing truly required of us was to sign Forms I-20 and IAP-66 and carry out certain record-keeping and reporting requirements stated in federal regulations concerning F and J status. Everything we did beyond that—orientation programs, counseling and advising, host-family programs, spouse programs, speaker programs, intercultural training, predeparture programs, newsletters, handbooks, information sheets, etc.—we had inherited or devised ourselves.

Most FSAs would probably find that the same is true of their operations. Only the immigration-related paperwork is truly required. The rest of it is devised locally, for reasons discussed below.

What the boss wants

Many FSAs operate independently of their supervisors. In fact, many FSAs complain that, as far as they can tell, their supervisors know little and care less about what they do. But on some level most supervisors do care at least somewhat. At a minimum they want to be kept informed so there are "no surprises," and they want their FSAs to be sure the institution's foreign students do nothing to create unfavorable publicity. Even these minimal expectations set a tone and direction for the FSA's job.

Beyond this minimum, particular bosses might want, for example, an exemplary orientation program, or a resolution of the perceived problem of foreign students' limited English proficiency, or a periodic international festival that will presumably create goodwill and favorable publicity. Some supervisors are quite knowledgeable about the problems and prospects of international educational exchange and expect sophisticated educational and training programs to be part of the FSA's job description.

The FSA's job description will be influenced by whatever the particular supervisor wants.

History

These days, few FSAs are the first incumbents of foreign student advising offices in their institutions. Most are assuming a predecessor's place or joining people already on the staff. In either case there is a history behind what the staff does and how it does it. Whether a new FSA is expected to continue on a course already set or to change course, the office's history is a powerful determinant of an FSA's job description. History tells the FSA "what this office has always done."

Research

Mitchell Hammer, in "Research, Mission Statements, and International Student Advising Offices," argues that "there are four major lines of sojourner adaptation research that are particularly relevant to the formulation of mission statements in international student advising offices" (219). They are (1) the problems foreign students face on arrival and later during their stays, (2) the students' psychological reactions to their new setting, (3) the influence of social interaction and communication on the students' adaptation, and (4) the concept of the students' adaptation as a culture-learning process. Hammer's essay provides what amounts to an historical overview of the evolution of foreign student office missions, from the early "help foreign students solve their problems" approach to the more contemporary focus on culture learning (219-229).

While most FSAs have probably not read more than a small portion of the books and articles Hammer includes in his bibliography, their job descriptions have likely been influenced by research findings or at least trends in social scientists' interests.

Stakeholders' perceptions and expectations

The occupant of any role is influenced by other people's perceptions of the role and of the person who occupies it. FSAs are constrained by their image in the eyes of many stakeholders, including foreign students, institutional colleagues, and external agencies.

Foreign student views. Foreign students' perceptions (or conceptions) of the FSA are influenced by at least five factors. These include (1) their past experience with employees of organizations (bureaucracies), (2) their experience with student service offices (particularly offices serving foreign students) in their own countries, (3) their experience, if they have had any, with FSAs at other American institutions, (4) their own experience with the FSA or foreign student advising office at their current institution, and (5) the reputation of the FSA or foreign student advising office at their current institution.

1. The manner in which people understand and deal with bureaucracies varies greatly from country to country. Some foreign students come from countries in which all employees of educational institutions are in fact employees of a central government, perhaps one dominated by a single political party. Others come from countries where people get jobs in the bureaucracy on the basis of personal or family connections, rather than on the basis of competence or aptitude. There are many other variations. The result is that FSAs and other college and university staff members cannot assume that foreign students share their assumptions related to the workings of the bureaucracy. Among the assumptions not necessarily shared are these:

   - The office and organization have truly legitimate reasons for being.

   - The office's procedures are logically related to its reasons for being.

   - People who work in the office had to have certain qualifications to get their jobs.

   - Fair (that is, impartial, impersonal) procedures are not only possible and desirable, but are supremely important.

   - Important rules, regulations, deadlines, procedures, and official information are written down and taken seriously.

   - The ability to perform well in a job is not necessarily related to age or gender.

   - Females can have positions of authority.

   - An institution would indeed hire and pay someone whose job it was to try to minimize the problems facing students from other countries.

2. American colleges and universities offer a far wider range of student services than do postsecondary institutions elsewhere. Thus, most foreign students have had little if any experience with educational institutions that furnish health care, counseling, job placement assistance, recreational programs, or, certainly, foreign student advising. So most foreign students have no foundation, in their own educa-

tional backgrounds, for understanding what a foreign student adviser is.

3. Some foreign students transfer from one U.S. institution to another and bring with them impressions of FSAs based on their experience at the previous institution. Here is what one such student said to me about the foreign student office at his previous school: "Students went there only as a last resort, and only when absolutely necessary."

    On the other hand, I heard a student express this view of his institution's FSA office: "This [office] is the one place on campus where I can be sure I will be listened to and given whatever help is possible."

    Clearly, transferring foreign students bring a wide range of perceptions of the FSA.

4. Even before they arrive at an FSA's institution, foreign students normally have some experience with the FSA's office, through the vehicle of prearrival information and perhaps additional letters, faxes, or e-mail messages through which the student sought additional information. These various messages might or might not convey a sense of helpfulness, empathy, and administrative competence. They might emphasize warnings, cautions, and threats, or hopefulness and a glimpse of benevolent possibilities.

    After their arrival, the students, of course, have their own experiences with the FSA and develop their own ideas and expectations about that person.

5. Newly arriving foreign students often quickly find veteran foreign students at the institution, particularly if there are such students from their own countries. From those students they will hear about the FSA—what sort of person the FSA is and what they can expect of the FSA's office.

The sum of all this can be at any point along a continuum. At one end of the continuum is the view that the FSA is essentially an agent of law-enforcement or intelligence organizations and has no sincere interest in assisting students. The law-enforcement agency with which FSAs are most commonly associated is of course the INS. Some students assume that FSAs work for the FBI and/or the CIA as well. I have encountered students who believed FSAs were affiliated with other countries' intelligence agencies.

The conception of the FSA as law-enforcement agent might not be altogether inaccurate. Some FSAs do indeed behave as though they are deputies, to use a term that is elaborated upon in chapter 4.

In their orientation program they stress legal do's and don'ts. They set up systems to monitor students' levels of enrollment and their employment status. They often warn students about what the law and regulations do and do not allow, and they report students who they believe have run afoul of the legal restrictions.

At the other end of the continuum are those students who view FSAs as utterly benevolent figures who will at least attempt to resolve any difficulty the students face. These students, in contrast to those discussed above, are likely to visit their FSAs willingly and perhaps frequently.

Between these extremes is a range of views on the matter of FSAs' allegiances and abilities.

Wherever their views fit on this continuum, foreign students, for reasons discussed later, are likely to overestimate the amount of power FSAs possess. An FSA is well advised to try to assess the conception among the foreign students and scholars on their own campuses of the FSA's role and his or her competence.

Institutional colleagues' views. Faculty and staff perceptions of the FSA are most strongly influenced by their own attitudes toward foreign students and by the FSA's reputation for competence. If a new FSA assumes office after another person has held the position for a number of years, the predecessor's reputation and image are likely to exert a sometimes remarkably durable influence on institutional colleagues' perceptions of the FSA's role and responsibilities. This can be a problem for a new FSA if the predecessor was held in either unusually high or unusually low regard. The new FSA may disappoint colleagues who have come to expect a consistently outstanding performance from the foreign student adviser or encounter resistance if the predecessor was deemed ineffective or misguided.

Faculty and staff who are favorably inclined toward foreign students are likely to have a positive view of FSAs, or at least to give them the benefit of the doubt. The opposite is true of faculty and staff who are unfavorably disposed to students from other countries.

The FSA's place in the institutional structure is another factor that influences colleagues' perceptions of the FSA's role. Many FSAs are in the student affairs branch of the administration. While at some institutions student affairs personnel are generally held in high regard, at others they are not. An FSA's effectiveness can be affected by the general image of the part of the institutional structure in which the FSA position is located and by the amount of power and influence the FSA's superior holds.

It is mainly through competent performance, however, that FSAs can enhance their influence among institutional colleagues. The subject of an FSA's influence is discussed at greater length later.

External agencies' views. FSAs deal with so many external agencies that it is nearly impossible to generalize about the agencies' views of them. The agencies include the INS and other federal bodies, sponsoring organizations, the education sections of foreign embassies, and assorted community organizations. Their perceptions of FSAs are shaped by, among other things, individual staff members' attitudes toward foreign students, the agency's corporate experiences with FSAs, and the nature of the agency's business with foreign student advisers.

It is probably safe to say that INS staff members have a very wide range of views of FSAs. Some are seen as softhearted, amateurish do-gooders inadequately devoted to upholding the immigration law. Other FSAs are seen as stern and strict, eager to do all they can to help enforce the immigration law. "Some of these foreign student advisers are far more strict than any immigration officer I know," remarked one INS official at a NAFSA conference.

Staff members at sponsoring agencies and embassies tend to deal fairly frequently with the FSAs at the schools under their jurisdiction, so they have the opportunity to become familiar with individual FSAs. According to interviews I have conducted with sponsoring agency staff members, some FSAs are seen as helpful, well-informed, and reasonable; some are seen as negligent or even hostile to their foreign-student clients; still others are seen as excessively parental in their outlook.

Community organizations' perceptions of FSAs also vary widely, depending on the viewpoints of the various individuals involved and on the history of the interactions between the FSAs and the organizations. Some FSAs are perceived as competent, helpful, and willing or even eager to cooperate. Others are viewed less positively— as, for example, not very competent, not able to get along with other people very well, and/or more concerned with matters of territory and control than with fostering beneficial community-student interactions.

SAINT PETER'S COLLEGE LIBRARY
JERSEY CITY, NEW JERSEY 07306

The FSA's characteristics and proclivities

It is not only mandates, history, what the boss wants, and stakeholders' perceptions that help shape the FSA's job description. It is also the FSA's own ideas, perceptions, and personality. FSAs are not interchangeable.

The first point to consider may be how an FSA initially got the foreign student advising job. Some people actively seek FSA positions. Others have the job thrust upon them in what veteran FSA Bill O'Connoll calls the *"ZAP*, you're the foreign student adviser" phenomenon, in which a person is suddenly and unexpectedly assigned the FSA responsibility. Presumably, people in the former group have a better understanding of what the job might entail and deem themselves suitable for the work. FSAs who have been zapped into their positions may have little if any understanding of what the post entails and may not want to be doing it.

This brings us to a major concern, that of an FSA's *motives* in carrying out the position's responsibilities. Three basic human motivations, according to a frequently used typology, are *power, achievement,* and *affiliation.* People motivated by a need for power are ones who enjoy being dominant over others. People motivated by a need to achieve feel rewarded when they can carry out discrete tasks or reach clear objectives. People motivated by a need for affiliation are happiest when they have harmonious relationships with large numbers of people.

Of course, all three of these basic motivational patterns are to be found among the ranks of foreign student advisers. But individual FSAs are likely to give their work a slant that reflects their particular motivation. FSAs seeking power are likely to emphasize those parts of their work that have the potential for dominating or controlling other people, for example, enforcing immigration regulations. Those moved by a need for achievement are likely to emphasize programs or administrative arrangements they can set up and perhaps things they can write or otherwise create. Those motivated by a need for affiliation will emphasize the parts of the job that entail talking or socializing with other people, not just foreign students but institutional colleagues and others.

Other personality variables besides motivation are reflected in the way various FSAs approach their work. In *Neanderthals at Work,* Albert J. Bernstein and Sydney Craft Rozen offer a useful typology of personalities that includes *believers, competitors,* and *rebels.* Many

FSAs are believers, that is, people who have a relatively unquestioned faith in the rightness or goodness of the system, and who believe that if they work hard and follow all the proper rules and procedures, their efforts will eventually be recognized and things will work out as they should.

FSAs are less often competitors. Competitors seek positions of power and tend to become bosses, Bernstein and Rozen say. Such people are not likely to be attracted to foreign student advising since FSAs, as Goodwin and Nacht noted in the passage quoted at the outset of this chapter, are typically rather low in the institutional hierarchy.

Nor are rebels likely to be well represented in FSA ranks. Rebels, in Bernstein's and Rozen's typology, are impatient with rules and routines and generally believe that it is their energy and inventiveness that really make the organization function.

Whatever their basic personality type, FSAs often seem, as Goodwin and Nacht suggest, to view themselves as separated from the centers of decision making on their campuses. More than that, they often see themselves as outcasts or underdogs, operating on the fringes of the organization. They are convinced that their work is important but unappreciated. They work hard, as believers often do, with the faith that someday the higher-ups will recognize the intrinsic value of their contributions.

In *Neanderthals at Work,* Bernstein and Rozen argue that hard work and loyalty are usually not enough to gain stature in an organization. They discuss other matters that organizational employees must attend to if they wish to rise in the hierarchy or at least get more respect.

AN ANALYSIS OF THE FSA POSITION

We have already observed that the FSA normally occupies a rather low position in the institutional hierarchy. Some FSAs are deans or directors, but most are not. Most FSAs have little power. They may, however, have considerable influence. An understanding of the concepts of power and influence is important to an understanding of the FSA position, so the next several paragraphs will be devoted to those concepts as they pertain to FSAs.

Power and influence

Definitions. Power is customarily defined as the ability to induce others to behave in certain ways, usually through the dispensation of rewards or punishments. Power in an institutional setting arises from control over resources (money, mainly, and sometimes space and information) that are in short supply and from occupancy of roles officially vested with authority. The more powerful positions in an organization are the higher-level ones whose occupants dispense money and jobs. They establish mission statements, institutional policies, and job descriptions for lower-level employees.

In an institution, then, power is based mainly on position in the hierarchy. Influence, by contrast, is the ability to induce others to behave in certain ways by means other than the dispensation of rewards or punishments or the exercise of formal authority. A powerful person may or may not be influential; a person without power may have considerable influence. Influence can arise from many things, which we will see below.

FSAs and power. Most FSAs have little if any power. They can give or withhold signatures on immigration forms and assorted certification forms (a power which some FSAs use to induce foreign students to behave or not behave in certain ways), but otherwise they are rarely in a position to work their will through the dispensation of rewards or punishments. Unless they are deans or directors (and sometimes even if they are), they are not high in the chain of command. They rarely have the authority to allocate funds in any significant amount or to control jobs other than clerical ones. They usually cannot assign residence hall rooms, design courses that suit foreign student interests, grant exemptions from institutional rules, or offer academic credit to induce students to participate in programs they might organize. At smaller institutions, the FSA responsibility may be only one of many vested in an already overworked administrator. If such people have power in their institutions, it is usually because one or more of their other responsibilities holds higher status within the hierarchy. Their power is likely to be in their own chain of command only, however, and not in other parts of the institution.

The fact that FSAs have little power is not obvious to everyone. Foreign students, in particular, are generally unfamiliar with American-style bureaucracies and the job descriptions, chains of command, and emphasis on "objective" decision making. Foreign students are likely to interact more with the FSA than with any other member of the administration. They know the FSA has some relationship with immigration regulations and procedures. From all this, foreign students may erroneously infer that FSAs have more power than they actually do.

FSAs are, in fact, best viewed as *intermediaries*, people who, while lacking power, work to bring different people together in the pursuit of common aims. To function effectively, intermediaries need influence.

FSAs and influence. While they usually lack power, FSAs may have influence. They may therefore be able to accomplish a great deal on behalf of their clients even though their formal status in the hierarchy is not high. In the absence of real possibilities for obtaining power, FSAs who want to be effective need to work conscientiously at enhancing their influence. That means paying attention to these factors[6]:

- Acknowledged competence
- Articulateness
- Intelligence
- Knowledge
- Ability to write well
- Informal relationships with powerful or influential people
- Sociability
- Ability to get along with disliked people
- Physical attractiveness
- Thick skin

Many of these factors will receive further consideration later in the *Handbook*. The point to be stressed here is that an FSA's effectiveness is usually much more a function of influence than of power. Influence, of course, is not a physical entity. It is subjective and is therefore perceived differently by different people. This reflects one of the most interesting aspects of the FSA position—its many audiences.

The FSA's numerous audiences

When we raised the question, "To whom is the FSA responsible?" we saw that there are many possible answers. The effective FSA has

---

[6] Here and in many other places in this book, I draw on Richard W. Brislin's *The Art of Getting Things Done: A Practical Guide to the Use of Power*. Brislin often uses the word "power" where I would use the word "influence," but, whatever the vocabulary, his suggestions deserve any FSA's attention.

influence among foreign student and scholar clients, faculty and staff throughout the institutions, INS and other governmental officials, sponsoring agency personnel, people in the community, and other FSAs. The problem is that an action which may raise an FSA's stature in the eyes of one of the audiences may diminish it in the eyes of another. Some FSAs, for example, will take the position of advocate for virtually any foreign student who is in any sort of difficulty, no matter how irresponsible or even devious the student may have been. Such an FSA might be held in high regard by foreign students (although even that is unlikely), but cannot expect to have the respect of faculty or of the INS.

Other FSAs are viewed with suspicion by foreign students who are skeptical about their motives and mistrustful of what they say. Such FSAs, even when they feel they are properly meeting the expectations of other constituencies, cannot hope to have influence with their foreign-student clients. FSAs, like everyone else, cannot please all of the people all of the time.

The balancing act

Faced with diverse and sometimes incompatible expectations and standards of evaluation, FSAs must continually seek a balance among competing wishes, interests, demands, and viewpoints. This implies taking all pertinent viewpoints into account and then applying defensible standards to the exercise of judgment. This is the essence of a foreign student adviser's job. Those who do it well will gain the respect of their various audiences and will accrue influence among them. Those who act on the basis of inadequate information, faulty assumptions, prejudices, or inappropriate standards will lose respect and influence.

The so-called "Iranian student crisis" of the late 1970s and early 1980s presented many foreign student advisers with extreme challenges to their ability to maintain a balance. When Iranian students began coming to the United States in large numbers in the second half of the 1970s, they were not especially popular on many campuses or in many communities. They were seen as aggressive, hypocritically obsequious, and untrustworthy. FSAs who seemed sympathetic to them risked incurring the disrespect of their institutional colleagues. As the revolution progressed in Iran, some Iranian students participated in political demonstrations that became violent, and the reputation of Iranian students and FSAs who seemed to sympathize with them suffered further.

Then came periods in which funds from Iran were cut off. Some Iranian students had enough savings to see them through. Others did not. Many of the latter turned to their FSAs for help. These FSAs knew it was their job to try to help these foreign students who were in financial difficulty because of circumstances beyond their control, but the students were widely disliked and resented. FSAs were caught in the middle. How far could they go in trying to help them?

The taking of the American hostages in Tehran evoked strong anti-Iranian sentiment throughout the United States. Iranian students here were sometimes victims of hostile acts. They began, on the other hand, to gain the sympathy of some FSAs and others who saw them as victims, as people being punished for an action in which they had no role. FSAs were again caught between their wish to assist their clients and public hostility toward those clients.

Then the U.S. government, through the Immigration and Naturalization Service, set out to identify and interview all Iranian students in the country. Many INS district offices sought educational institutions' cooperation in this undertaking, usually by asking FSAs to aid in arranging the interviews. This caught FSAs between their need to retain reasonable working relationships with the INS and their desire to show some allegiance to their students. Should they cooperate with the INS? If so, to what extent? What could they do to provide Iranian students with the documents they needed for the interviews?

When the Khomeini regime took over in Iran and instituted sweeping restrictions on the remission of dollars abroad, FSAs on many campuses were faced with needy students on the one hand and tight budgets and sometimes unsympathetic institutional colleagues on the other. How far could they press the students' cases? Many of the students did not want to return to Iran, given what they perceived to be the repressive and anti-intellectual nature of the Khomeini government. But the U.S. government was generally not sympathetic with this attitude. What were the FSAs to do?

Volumes could no doubt be written about the manner in which the Iranian student crisis was handled on different campuses. These volumes would show FSAs ever in the middle, caught among competing and incompatible pressures, hopes, demands, and expectations. Some FSAs emerged with heightened influence. Others were less able to find a workable balance and their influence declined.

The next major episode that affected FSAs throughout the United States involved students and scholars from the People's Republic of

China. Until the early 1980s, there were no such students or scholars in the United States, or in many other countries outside the PRC. But China opened in the early 1980s. At first there was a trickle of visiting scholars. Within a few years there was a torrent of students. By 1988, as has been mentioned, there were more students from the PRC in the United States than students from any other country.

From the beginning, PRC students and scholars placed heavy demands on FSAs. Part of the reason they called on FSAs so often was probably an outcome of their upbringing. Their U.S. school (usually a university rather than a college, because most were visiting scholars or graduate students) had taken the place, in their conception, of the "work unit" they had left behind in China, and they were in the habit of seeing the work unit as the source of official information, guidance, permission, and assistance. They had come to what was to them a very strange land ("It's like I just came here from the moon," a recently arrived PRC student once said to me), and they needed considerable information, guidance, and assistance.

Furthermore, there were several distinctive aspects of the PRC students' and scholars' immigration situations that compelled them to seek FSA services. They had single-entry visas, so trips outside the United States meant they had to get documents to acquire new visas. Their spouses could not accompany them when they first came, so they needed documents with which the spouses could get visas to come later. The spouses, once here, often became students and needed documents and assistance with the procedures. Many Chinese who came in the early years were wrongly categorized as scholars and later needed immigration documents to change to the student category. Then, following the Tiananmen Square incident and President Bush's executive order that was intended to help PRC students in the United States, nearly all the students wanted to change from J-1 status in order to free themselves from the two-year foreign residence requirement. Thus, more visits to the FSA were necessary. And finally, when the Chinese Student Protection Act became law, many Chinese students sought their FSAs' help in understanding the relevant INS procedures and in preparing their documents.

Through all this, the Chinese evinced certain behavior patterns that galled many Americans, including some FSAs. They were remarkably persistent in seeking what they wanted. Like the Iranians, they would not take no for an answer. They would just keep coming back, but on the return visits would often have a slightly different version of the "facts" that underlay their requests. Their accounts of their situations would often leave out important information that would come to light only later. They insisted on giving gifts in circumstances in which most Americans would regard the giving of gifts as inappropriate. In many quarters, then, Chinese students came to be regarded as nuisances, as devious and self-promoting.

On the other hand there were many, especially on the faculty, who wanted everything possible done to help their intelligent, hardworking Chinese students. They were captivated by the Cultural Revolution stories the older students and scholars had to tell and fascinated by what they learned from the Chinese about their ancient, and very different, culture.

In all of this the FSAs were caught in the middle, pressed on the one side by the persistent requests of the numerous Chinese, and on the other side by those who either disliked the Chinese or thought their own interests were being slighted when the Chinese got so much attention. Many FSAs as individuals were emotionally caught up in the Chinese student situation, whether they were generally sympathetic or unsympathetic toward that group. Maintaining impartiality was not easy.

Again, some FSAs were able to find a judicious balance and emerged with the respect not only of the Chinese students and scholars but also of faculty and administrators on their campuses. Others were unable to find that balance.

The Iranian and Chinese situations were extreme cases, given their duration, the strong emotions they evoked, and the large number of students they involved. But FSAs can expect to encounter more and more situations requiring a delicate balance as long as the number of foreign students remains large and conditions within and among so many countries remain volatile.

The use of influence: FSAs as leaders

FSAs have a comprehensive view of their institution's foreign student-related policies and procedures. They can see when foreign students suffer from deficiencies in the prearrival information, the orientation program, housing policies, financial aid arrangements, academic advising, and so on. While they may see things that need to be changed, FSAs usually lack the power to bring about changes through their own efforts alone. If they want to improve the foreign student programs at their institutions, FSAs need to assume a leadership role and develop the influence needed for effective informal leadership.

What has been said here about the FSA's position is rather theoretical. Some more practical observations come in chapter 4, under the heading, "The Role of the Foreign Student Adviser."

3

Personal Characteristics

Many faculty and staff at my institution have said to me, "I certainly wouldn't want your job." The remark usually comes in the context of a discussion of a particularly difficult foreign student situation that I am trying to resolve.

But I do want my job, and I know many other longtime foreign student advisers who share my allegiance to this field. It seems to me there is a set of personality characteristics to be found among FSAs who enjoy their work and do it well. Those characteristics include intelligence, patience, nonjudgmentalness, interest in cultural differences, respect for others, tolerance for ambiguity, sociability, self-awareness, kindness, and decisiveness.

This is no doubt an arbitrary list.[1] Another experienced FSA might choose a somewhat different set of characteristics or make a longer or shorter list. In discussing these characteristics I will try to explain why I consider them especially important to FSAs and how some of them can be cultivated. Basic personality characteristics probably cannot be modified significantly, but some changes are possible on the margins. People who are considering a career in foreign student advising can judge whether they see themselves in the list above or the commentary below.

INTELLIGENCE

It is not the purpose here to enter the debate about the meaning of "intelligence," or of any of the other concepts on this list. The term

---

[1] In *The Art of Getting Things Done,* Brislin offers a list of "personality traits" derived from his survey of powerholders. His list overlaps in part with mine, but has some differences too. His list includes energy; balance ("mid-range between strident and dull"); congeniality; a thick skin; imperturbability; sense of humor; loyalty; self-insight; and charisma.

"intelligence," as used here, refers to several abilities: to learn relatively quickly; to retain large amounts of information; to discern relationships among various ideas, facts, or events; to solve problems creatively; to reason clearly.

FSAs encounter a wide variety of personalities, situations, and kinds of problems. Being able to apply extensive knowledge in constructive and creative ways is clearly an asset to them. Intelligence, too, contributes to influence, particularly in a higher-education community. While intelligence itself (whatever it is) may not readily be fostered in an adult, some habits of mind closely related to intelligence can be fostered. These include exposing oneself to a wide range of information, learning to focus attention, and exercising self-discipline.

PATIENCE

Anyone who has been a foreigner knows that the most welcome trait among the host people, when it is found, is patience. Foreigners anywhere appreciate people who calmly take the time to listen, clarify, and respond.

Without the ability to be patient, FSAs cannot hope to interact constructively with clients who often speak English less than perfectly and who, being out of their element, might require explanations—sometimes repeated explanations—of situations or procedures with which local people have been familiar since childhood.

It is sometimes harder for FSAs to be patient with fellow Americans than with foreign students. An American FSA expects to maintain a pleasant disposition in interactions with people whose English proficiency is limited and whose backgrounds have not prepared them to understand local customs, institutions, and techniques. An FSA hears many "simple" questions from foreign students and scholars, and may have to work long and hard to give a comprehensible reply. It is easy to understand why this is so. Remaining patient is part of the job.

Some of the questions and comments of one's fellow Americans seem harder to endure with equanimity. "Do you speak all their languages?" I have been asked countless times. (That would be thirty or forty languages.) "Don't they all have a lot of money?" (Some do and some do not; I have known some who could afford to eat but once a day.) Since it is one of the FSA's tasks to enhance institutional and community receptivity to foreign students, the Americans' naive questions and sometimes offensive stereotypes (about foreign students' body odors, for example) are best treated with patience and tolerance.

Most people know when they are becoming impatient. Accelerated breathing, heartbeat, and speech are common symptoms. People who desire to be more patient (or who have been persuaded that more patience would be valuable, whether they want to be patient or not) can learn to recognize these symptoms and pause, or momentarily withdraw, into themselves when they appear.

Nonjudgmentalness

Most students of intercultural relations—and of interpersonal relations in general—acknowledge the importance of nonjudgmentalness in functioning constructively in intercultural situations. "Things in the other culture are not right or wrong," the cliché goes, "they are just different."

Long before we become interested in intercultural relations, we are cautioned not to be judgmental. "Judge not, lest ye be judged," says an admonition from a highly respected and often quoted source. "Let the one who has not sinned cast the first stone," says another. And, with an intercultural bent, "Do not judge another man until you have walked a mile in his moccasins."

The validity of these warnings is reinforced by our own experiences with judgmentalness in others. We try to avoid people who we know will judge or evaluate us. If we cannot avoid their presence, we avoid discussion topics we suppose will evoke their judgments of us. And we know how much we welcome the presence of people who do not judge us, people who accept us as we are and do not convey the idea that we ought somehow to be different in order to have their approval. We can relax in the presence of such people and speak as we wish about what we will, without fear.

Yet nonjudgmental people are rare. Most of us emerge from childhood with our heads filled with "shoulds" about other people's ideas and behavior. When other people fail to act the way they "should," as they inevitably do, we judge them negatively. FSAs have to resist this tendency to evaluate others because it is in no way constructive and because their clients, having been raised with sometimes radically different ideas, will frequently behave in ways that will force FSAs to disapprove if they insist on judging. As James Bostain, formerly with the Foreign Service Institute, put it in one of his lectures,

"People act the way they were taught to act, and they all have different teachers."[2]

It is far easier to agree that judging others is destructive of human relationships than it is to stop judging them. To stop judging, one has to convince oneself completely that *it is not necessary to judge others.* To put it another way, FSAs do not need to have an opinion about how foreign students should be and what they should do. FSAs might have well-founded views about the likely outcomes of certain of their clients' attitudes and behaviors, and they can certainly describe those views to the clients. But they need make no judgments of other people's value as human beings. To the degree that they can rid themselves of "shoulds" and accept others as they are, they will become more approachable, more respected, and more effective.

None of this is to say that FSAs are not expected to make judgments of any kind. Certainly they are, but with respect to their own and others' behavior, not with respect to other people's value as human beings.

If being nonjudgmental helps FSAs operate constructively in intercultural situations, it does likewise for foreign students and scholars. So FSAs do their clients an important service if they help them become less judgmental. One way to do that is to expose them to the "D.I.E. Formulation," described in Appendix A.

INTEREST IN CULTURAL DIFFERENCES

One of the fascinations of foreign student advising is seeing the manifold ways in which cultural backgrounds affect people's perceptions, ideas, and behavior. Beyond that is the interplay of cultures as foreign students and scholars interact with each other and with the natives. FSAs work in a living laboratory for studying intercultural relations, and those who are interested in that topic will encounter an endless supply of incidents about which to think, write, and teach others. One example of an outcome of such thinking is an essay, "The Intercultural Meeting," reproduced in Appendix B.

People who are not interested in the subject of cultural differences and intercultural relations, or who consider cultural differ-

---

[2] I heard this in a surreptitiously circulated videotape of a Bostain cross-cultural training presentation at the Foreign Service Institute. For me it captures an attitude that is crucial to success in intercultural relations.

ences to be inconveniences and impediments to the proper functioning of things, are not likely to enjoy working as FSAs. Some FSAs seem interested in cultural differences, but only insofar as they produce examples of quaint or novel human conduct. People with this outlook usually behave in a condescending way toward foreign students. Foreign students sense that, of course, and respond negatively. The dislike of being condescended to seems to appear in all cultures.

It is not just for reasons of personal or professional satisfaction that successful FSAs are likely to have an intense interest in cultural differences. It is also because so much of their work entails helping foreign students and members of the host institution and community understand cultural differences and cope with their effects. Whether through orientation or other types of educational programs, workshops, public speaking, advising and counseling, general problem solving, or the preparation of written materials, FSAs are trying to help others understand how cultures shape people's ideas, perceptions, and behavior, and how cultural differences can be confronted constructively.

RESPECT FOR OTHERS

To say that FSAs need to have a respectful attitude toward other people may seem redundant, since related points have already been made. Yet the topic deserves some specific treatment.

Respecting other people requires a constant struggle against the tendency to evaluate others and to see our own behavior as natural and others' as unnatural. We might acknowledge the importance of feeling and displaying respect for others, and we may feel and display such respect on most occasions, but there are always situations in which true respect does not seem to be present. Often these situations have to do with male-female relations (for example, the custom of arranged marriages or the manner in which many Middle Eastern and African men treat women—including their own wives) or with status relationships (for example, Oriental formality and obeisance toward older or higher-status people). American cultural ideas about male-female relationships and relationships among people of different status are so deeply set that respecting diverse ideas about them requires constant and concerted effort.

The other point to be made here is that respecting differences among Americans is often more difficult than respecting differences manifested by people from other cultures.

People who are generally open-minded and accepting of the cultural differences reflected among foreign students and scholars may become self-righteous and intolerant in their responses to institutional colleagues whom they regard as racist, sexist, or chauvinistic. The psychodynamic roots of the foreign students' and the institutional colleagues' values and attitudes may be identical, but the former may be accorded respect and the latter not. It sometimes seems to be easier for human beings to accept others who are comprehensively different from themselves than to accept those who resemble them in many ways but are different in some others. Our institutional colleagues "should" think and act properly (that is, the way we do), we seem to tell ourselves.

FSAs have to work constructively with colleagues throughout their institutions, so they need to challenge any tendency they find in themselves to judge and condemn colleagues who have different values and viewpoints.[3]

TOLERANCE FOR AMBIGUITY

An ambiguous situation is one lacking a clear genesis, a set of boundaries, a set of cues for expected behavior, and/or a certain expected outcome. In an ambiguous situation, one cannot be certain what is happening or how one ought to behave. Ambiguous situations frequently occur in intercultural relationships, promoting anxiety and feelings of insecurity.

Some people have a low tolerance for ambiguity. They insist, at a psychological level, on explicitness and clarity. They react with impatience and sometimes anger when things are not made clear for them. They may supply their own clarity by closing out alternative explanations and insisting that they know *the true nature* of a situation.

Because FSAs are working with people who have differing worldviews, values, and assumptions, they will inevitably become involved in ambiguous situations. I well remember, for example, an agitated

---

[3] This is not to say that FSAs must *accept for themselves* behavior that is not in accord with that to which they are accustomed or which they believe is proper. FSAs might, and probably will, encounter behaviors they find distasteful and even plain wrong. They can respect it, though, in the sense that they can understand how it came to pass. For more thoughts on this, see the section on cultural relativism in the closing chapter of *Learning across Cultures* (edited by Gary Althen), "Recurring Issues in Intercultural Communication."

student coming to me and insisting that I help resolve a problem that involved him and his wife and child, on the one hand, and another couple who lived in the same apartment complex, on the other. According to the student, his infant son was persistently ill because the other man's wife was practicing witchcraft on him. It was my job, the student said, to right this wrong.

Unless one happens to know just how to handle interfamily conflicts centered on witchcraft, a situation such as this is, from the FSA's view, ambiguous. What is really happening? Indeed, how can one even find out what is happening? What is one to do? What possible resolutions exist? Only with patience and respect can one proceed to inquire into the various participants' views of the situation, their own suggestions about solutions, and eventual mediation.

In this instance, the mediation was not successful. A first mediation session did produce an agreement that the disputants would avoid each other and try to prevent any escalation of their conflict. The agreement held for several months. Then it broke down and another session became necessary. That session ended in a screaming, hitting, scratching melee that five campus security officers came to quell. The conflict between the families was never resolved. It disappeared when the students graduated (three of them with doctorates) and moved away. I never did understand what was happening.

Signs of intolerance for ambiguity combine the signs of impatience with a spoken or unspoken insistence that the situation has certain specific characteristics. "What is at issue here is thus and so," for example, or "If Person X would only do or understand such and such, everything would be fine." Another sign of intolerance of ambiguity is a feeling of uncertainty about what one's own role in a situation ought to be, coupled with a feeling of discomfort resulting from that uncertainty.

Upon recognizing these signs an FSA can pause and say (internally), "This is one of those ambiguous situations I will inevitably encounter. I need to be patient, try to understand it better, and recognize that I may never understand it at all."

SOCIABILITY

In *Cross-Cultural Encounters*, another book of great value for FSAs, Richard W. Brislin makes these comments about sociability:

Some people are warm, make others feel comfortable in their presence through choice of topics in conversation, are able to communicate an interest in people, are considerate enough to listen to others rather than to talk at them. Related traits are respect for others with different points of view, an interest in topics to which a person may not have been exposed but which are important to others, a willingness to sacrifice one's own desires in favor of someone else's (selflessness), and an ability to be nonjudgmental when observing unfamiliar behaviors or hearing different opinions (59).

This definition contains many elements already discussed. Brislin includes sociability among the variables he says bear on a person's success in intercultural situations. For FSAs, sociability contributes not just to success in intercultural relationships, but to influence in general. Elsewhere,[4] Brislin notes that

> meeting people quickly, putting them at ease, finding topics of conversation which others can readily discuss, being interesting so that the others will have memories of any interactions six months later can help a person obtain useful information or develop beneficial relationships (51).

Encounters with foreigners or strangers can be uncomfortable because of a lack of agreement as to what discussion topics and styles of interaction are appropriate.[5] A sociable person can reduce this discomfort and help people find a satisfactory means of relating.[6]

Influential people, Brislin says, can keep other people's goodwill, and they make as few enemies as possible. These too are aspects of sociability, and they are keys to long-term success in an organization.

Self-Awareness

FSAs can benefit from self-awareness on both cultural and personal levels.

---

[4] In *Understanding Culture's Influence on Behavior.*

[5] See Dean C. Barnlund's comparison of American and Japanese communicative styles in *Public and Private Self in Japan and the United States.*

[6] My colleague John Rogers observes that sociability can lead to difficulty in intercultural situations if it is not combined with self-awareness (the characteristic discussed next). What is regarded as highly sociable behavior in one society might not be so regarded in another. For example, the cheerful, outgoing chattiness sometimes associated in American society with fraternity members, politicians, and salespeople may be deemed highly offensive in cultures where people are normally less demonstrative.

From the viewpoint of their foreign student and scholar clients, FSAs (unless they are natives of other countries) are representative Americans. FSAs need to know what it is about themselves that their clients are likely to consider exemplary of the host culture.

FSAs will have countless occasions to explain aspects of the host culture to foreign students. For this reason, too, an awareness of the culturally-based aspects of their own ideas and responses is beneficial. The characteristics of American culture that seem to draw the most consistent attention of foreign students are the emphasis on the individual, informality in interpersonal relationships, and action orientation. On these and related topics, FSAs will probably want to digest my book *American Ways* and Edward C. Stewart's and Milton J. Bennett's *American Cultural Patterns: A Cross-Cultural Perspective.*

Another source of cultural self-awareness for FSAs is conversations with foreign students and scholars. Their observations about American society can be most instructive.[7]

Personal self-awareness cannot come from books as readily as cultural self-awareness can. It is more likely to come from introspection and from hearing other people's relatively uninhibited response to one's ideas and behavior. It is an interesting commentary on American society that many people here do not have friends or acquaintances who are willing to speak openly with them. Many Americans have no one to tell them what sort of impression they are making, what their nonverbal behavior reveals about their feelings, what their characteristic responses to typical situations are, or how they might improve aspects of their behavior toward other people in order to make it more constructive.[8] To get this feedback, as it is termed in the jargon of counseling, Americans may be compelled to join some sort of encounter or self-improvement group, go to a counselor or therapist, or take a course in group dynamics or interpersonal communication.

If joining a group, going to a counselor, or taking a course is what FSAs must do in order to gain some self-insight and some perspec-

---

[7] Observations from a number of foreign scholars are brought together in Philip R. DeVita's and James D. Armstrong's *Distant Mirrors: America as a Foreign Culture.*

[8] Americans seem to have the idea that they should not tell their friends negative things about them because it will hurt their feelings and perhaps cause lasting damage to the relationship. Instead they tell "white lies." In some other societies, people *will* tell their friends negative things about them because they believe their friends need to know these things and will not hear them from anyone else.

tive on the way they seem to others, then they ought to do it. They will want to be able to answer such questions about themselves as the following:

1. What impression do I generally make on other people?
2. How do other's perceptions of me jibe with my perceptions of myself?
3. How am I feeling right now? (Asked at any given time.)
4. What is happening in this conversation right now? (Asked at any given time.)
5. What topics or situations do I typically handle less well than I would like?
6. What typical behaviors of mine are commonly misconstrued by others?
7. What typical behaviors of others do I commonly misconstrue?
8. What are my tendencies in dealing with situations that involve tension? Anger? Conflict?
9. Do I commonly make unwarranted assumptions about other people?
10. What are my prejudices about various categories of people (defined not just by nationality or ethnicity, but by gender, occupation, and other category labels I use)?
11. What are my "buttons," that is, what behaviors or comments set off an automatic positive or negative reaction from me?
12. What modifications in my outlook and behavior might make me more able to contribute constructively to the human situations of which I am a part?

Effective FSAs are self-aware enough to have answers to questions such as these and to be able to keep such questions at some accessible level of consciousness during most of their interactions with others. This self-awareness enables them to monitor their interactions as they take place and to modify their approaches when modifications seem necessary to keep the interactions constructive.

KINDNESS

Kindness, we can say, complements what Carl R. Rogers, the noted humanistic psychologist, called "unconditional positive regard," a combination of positive feelings and expectations about other human beings. Kindness also implies concern, empathy, and caring.

FSAs are often called upon to help people. They also see many situations in which people could use help whether they seek it or not. Foreigners anywhere often need help because there is, by definition, so much they do not know about the local scene. It is not just foreign students who can use an FSA's help, however, but also local people who interact with foreign students. This might include U.S. students, faculty, institutional staff, landlords, merchants, the local police, and many others. Effective FSAs are the sort of people who have a natural impulse to help others.[9] Their kindness is reflected not just in actions they might take to ameliorate unpleasant situations, but also in the respectful and sympathetic way they respond in conversations with others.

DECISIVENESS

My colleague Martin Limbird, who works in an international education office, often gives this response when asked about his occupation: "My job is to change the world." That is a big job, of course. People with such big jobs always have more than enough work to do. Effective FSAs are nearly always very busy because they have many demands on them and so many things they want to accomplish.

People who want to accomplish a great deal benefit from being decisive. Decisive people are those who recognize that decisions need to be made, that many decisions must be made on the basis of inadequate information, that most choices have both positive and negative consequences (often unforeseen and unforeseeable), that the negative consequences of most decisions can be endured, and that most decisions, if their outcomes turn out to be unacceptable, can be changed.

Having all these premises in mind, decisive people, once they have gathered what pertinent information and viewpoints they can and have reflected on them for a reasonable amount of time, make their decisions and move on.

Decisiveness is a characteristic that can be cultivated. Fostering it mainly entails convincing oneself of the validity of the premises

---

[9] As we will see in the next chapter, under the heading of "problem ownership," there are limits on the help an FSA will offer.

given above. Albert Ellis's chapter "Enhancing Decisiveness" in *Executive Leadership: A Rational Approach* offers useful suggestions to people who would like to become more accomplished by reducing their tendency to postpone making decisions. "Make Good Decisions Quickly," in Jimmy Calano's and Jeff Salzman's extremely useful book, *CareerTracking,* also offers useful suggestions.

4

Attitudes and Ideas

People who work with people approach their jobs with some set of ideas and attitudes concerning their clients and their own role vis-à-vis those clients. Those attitudes and ideas shape the way they carry out their responsibilities. They help people decide what situations they should enter, how they should treat clients, what outcomes they should seek, and what actions are considered appropriate, ethical, and moral.

This chapter examines some of the attitudes and ideas FSAs bring to their work.

CONCEPTIONS OF FOREIGN STUDENTS

Can and should foreign students and scholars be treated with respect? No doubt nearly all FSAs would say their answer to the question was yes. But if you listen to some FSAs talk, or listen to some foreign students and scholars talking about FSAs they have known, it would be clear that for some FSAs the answer is really no or perhaps, well, maybe sometimes.

The question of whether foreign students and scholars deserve respect can be seen as having several subquestions, each of which is amplified below. Those questions: (1) Are foreign students respectable human beings? (2) Are they engaged in an estimable enterprise? (3) Is their behavior acceptable? (4) Are their requests and expectations reasonable? (5) Can they be trusted?

Are foreign students respectable human beings?

If you ask foreign students how Americans treat them, nearly all, except perhaps those from Canada and Northern Europe, will say Americans condescend to them. FSAs (at least those who are American-born) often do that too, whether they intend it or even realize it. Americans, including those who might eventually become foreign student advisers, are continually exposed to the idea that theirs is a superior country and way of life. (It is common but not universal for people to believe in their own culture's superiority.) Foreigners come to be seen as somehow less human, intelligent, and sensible than people in the United States, less able to solve life's problems, and less emotionally complex.

It is not unusual to hear foreign students being discussed, gossiped about, or spoken to as if they were children. Americans frequently believe that foreign students don't need or deserve the confidentiality of treatment or the procedural protections that U.S. students receive. They are said to "chatter" when using their own language among themselves, whereas if they were using English they would be "talking."

School officials will talk about "our internationals" in ways they would never talk about "our Arizonans" or "our Floridians." (For example, "Our internationals are so good about participating in our programs.") FSAs will begin a question or a tale with, "I have a foreign student who...," suggesting a sense of ownership or control. Administrative offices will keep foreign students standing in line or subject them to complex, unexplained procedures that would never be inflicted on domestic students. Administrators and faculty members commonly assume that all students from a particular country will know and like each other and will willingly give assistance to and receive help from each other. There is also a common assumption that foreign students who are members of a particular family (sisters, cousins, etc.) will have harmonious relationships. These are not assumptions Americans make about themselves, however. It would be considered ridiculous to suppose that all Americans will like each other just because they happen to be compatriots or that all family relationships among them are harmonious.

The subtle feeling that foreigners are inferior persists even among FSAs (who are the ones most often heard to talk about "our internationals"), and it certainly persists among institutional colleagues, within the student body, and in our communities. If you don't believe it, ask some foreign students.

On the other hand, there are FSAs who patronize foreign students by investing them with a nobility they as individuals probably have not achieved. Just as individual differences among foreign students are obscured when they are all regarded as inferior, so are differences obscured when students are categorically regarded as highly intelligent, courageous, and pure of heart and deed.

There is an additional response to the question of whether foreign students deserve respect, a response heard mostly from FSAs who have lived abroad. Such FSAs may have a fairly balanced view of students who come from countries where they themselves have lived, seeing the individual differences among them and recognizing that all have their strengths and weaknesses. But they are not so able to be respectful of individuals from countries with which they are less familiar.

This discussion is intended to emphasize the difficulty Americans face in escaping the better-than-thou attitude toward foreigners that pervades their society. Respecting foreign students—seeing them as individual human beings, treating each with appropriate consideration—is not easy to do. Successful FSAs generally do it, at least more often than unsuccessful FSAs.

Are they engaged in an estimable enterprise?

If you ask foreign students why they came to the United States to study, you will get an array of answers: to get a better job in their chosen profession; to improve their English; to be able to earn more money; to contribute to improvements in their own country; to learn about life in another culture; to get a postsecondary degree; to study with a particular faculty member or in a particular department or school; to gain access to knowledge and facilities not available at home; to satisfy parental wishes; to escape some undesirable situation at home; to comply with an employer's or a government's plan; to be closer to a loved one already here; to get a green card and remain permanently in the United States (or some mix of two or more of these, a mix that might change as time passes).

Most FSAs probably consider some of these motives more worthy than others. Students with motives an FSA considers more worthy are more likely to get respectful treatment than are those whose motives the FSA deems less estimable.

Is their behavior acceptable?

The most common stereotypes of foreign students are probably these: They are intelligent, cliquish, inadequate in their command of English, less than adept in using their hands in the laboratory, traditional or sexist in their attitudes and beliefs about women, slow to grasp and employ the concepts of analytical and creative thinking, and sometimes odoriferous.

Most FSAs will have refined stereotypes of specific nationality groups, as will many college and university staff and faculty members.

Granting that there may be some substance behind these stereotypes (if there were not, they would not be so common), we turn to the question of whether we consider foreign students' behavior acceptable. Some FSAs would generally say yes. Others would say no. Successful FSAs—those who, among other things, have generally positive interactions with the foreign students on their campuses— would say yes. They would believe Bostain's dictum, "People act the way they are taught to act, and they all have different teachers." They would accept the cultural differences foreign students and scholars embody, even as they try to help the students and scholars modify certain culturally-based behaviors that cause them difficulty in their host country.

Are their requests and expectations reasonable?

On November 1, 1991, a Chinese who had recently earned a doctorate from the Department of Physics and Astronomy at my university murdered five people, including three faculty members and a fellow Chinese who had also recently graduated. The latter, an academic rival of the killer's, had been a very popular young man— highly intelligent, generous, and energetic. In the aftermath of the shootings, it became clear that many of the victim's friends and former classmates from China now studying in the United States would be coming to Iowa City for his funeral. With that in mind, one of the officers of the Chinese students' and scholars' organization asked me whether the university would furnish housing for the visitors.

Was this an outrageous request from a student seeking to milk the system and the situation for all they were worth? Or was it an understandable request from a person who, based on a Chinese upbringing, viewed the university as the students' work unit, responsible for all aspects of their welfare and certainly the appropriate place to turn for assistance in a time of trial?

I chose the latter interpretation and explained to the student that, given its charter as a public university, my institution could not appropriately provide for the housing. The student expressed appreciation for the explanation and turned to the task of finding volunteer hosts among the student organization's membership. It seemed clear to me that the student simply did not know what could reasonably be expected from the university and made a request that would have been perfectly appropriate in the country where she had spent most of her life.

Some FSAs might have settled on the first possible interpretation of the student's request, though, and seen it as yet another example of a foreign student trying to play on people's sympathies in order to get undeserved special treatment. (If I had been younger and less experienced, or if I had not been somewhat familiar with the work unit and other aspects of Chinese culture, I might have settled on the first explanation myself.) Certainly many FSAs and other school officials have the general view that foreign students are out to exploit us, taking advantage of our technology, facilities, services, generosity, and our gullibility.

No doubt some students do so. The question is what is our general view of our clients and their requests of us? Do we generally consider their requests reasonable or at least understandable, or do we think they are seeking to abuse us and the system? Successful FSAs are more likely to hold the former view.

Can they be trusted?

Faculty and staff members sometimes telephone FSAs, recount something a foreign student has told them—usually an explanation for a deficient performance or inadequate behavior—and ask the FSA if the student is telling the truth.[1] Without going into the complex questions of what constitutes truth, whether indeed there always *is* a truth, or how important telling the truth might be compared with other values, we can say that FSAs vary in the degree to which they are inclined to be trusting or skeptical, or even cynical, when assessing what their clients say. There is probably no ideal place on this continuum. Clearly, though, FSAs on the extremes will be less than effective.

The sum of any FSA's answers to the set of questions discussed above serves to define that FSA's conception of foreign students. Effective FSAs will be self-aware enough to realize that they face these questions almost every day and that, from somewhere or other, they have their own answers to them.

---

[1] When I first became an FSA, I was struck by the number of faculty and staff who seemed to suppose that, as a foreign student adviser, I had special insight into the mental workings of everyone from the ninety-odd countries represented by students on my campus.

THE ROLE OF THE FOREIGN STUDENT ADVISER

In chapter 2 I argued that FSAs have little or no power and must cultivate influence in order to be effective. I went on to suggest that this influence will be enhanced to the degree that FSAs find an appropriate balance in meeting the various responsibilities and expectations they face. I will now offer some more specific ideas about the FSA's role, beginning with a description of a minimal set of responsibilities for an FSA and then discussing additional responsibilities that some FSAs undertake. Finally, I will suggest that, beyond what they do in compliance with their job descriptions, FSAs serve as role models for participants in cross-cultural interactions.

The minimal job description

The one universal element in advertisements for vacant FSA positions seems to be *knowledge of the F-1 student regulations.* Federal regulations regarding F-1 students and J-1 exchange visitors require institutions to have "designated school officials" for F-student matters and "responsible officers" for J matters. Some FSAs do little other than *immigration advising and paperwork.* This can happen for several reasons: (1) Their institution expects nothing else of them. (2) Their institution is understaffed in the FSA area, and responding to the demand for immigration advising and procedures fills all available time. (3) In the name of immigration responsibilities, they carry out procedures, such as monitoring students' levels of registration, that the immigration regulations themselves do not require.

Orientation for new foreign students is a second component of the minimal job description. Even if foreign students are generally mainstreamed into the orientation program for domestic students, there are topics of unique significance to foreign students, including immigration regulations and procedures, the American academic system, and the American approaches to health-care delivery and health insurance.

A third component of the minimal job description is *dealing with crises,* usually in the form of deaths, serious injuries and illnesses, and arrests that involve foreign students. FSAs may assume some role in spouse and child abuse situations.[2]

---

[2] For a helpful introduction to the phenomenon of spouse abuse and the "cycle of abuse," see Lenore E. Walker's *The Battered Woman.*

Additional components of the minimal FSA job description relate to *admissions* (either making admissions decisions, contributing to those decisions, or liaising with those who do make the decisions); *housing; financial aid; advising* (giving information and suggestions); and *general problem solving*.

Finally, most FSAs are expected, at least implicitly, to orchestrate institutional procedures concerning foreign students, to liaise with sponsoring agencies if the school enrolls sponsored students, and to support community-related programs such as host-family programs and organizations for spouses.

See chapter 7 for more information and ideas about all the activities in the minimal job description.

Additional areas for FSA work

Culture learning. To the FSA job description, some people would add responsibilities in what John E. Walsh of the East-West Center calls "culture learning." This term refers to the idea of learning about culture and cultural differences in order to become more self-aware and knowledgeable, more empathetic, and better able to function in multicultural situations. At some institutions it is part of an FSA's responsibility to foster culture learning, not only among foreign and American students but in the institution as a whole and among members of the community. My opinion is that work in the area of culture learning is inseparable from work in most of the minimal areas of FSA responsibility. Prearrival information, orientation programs, handbooks or other printed materials, individual advising, and work with nationality organizations and international housing units are among the culture-learning formats FSAs routinely employ.

While it seems clear that foreign students and scholars need to engage in at least a modicum of culture learning in order to realize their academic objectives while living in another country, it is less clear, at least to some, that the natives stand to gain from interacting with culturally different people. Some in the international education field argue that FSAs need not be concerned with culture learning among the host population because it is not relevant to their jobs. In my view, FSAs ought to be concerned with the hosts' attitudes and treatment of foreign students *for the sake of the foreign students*, if for no other reason. A receptive campus and community will make the foreign students' experience in the United States easier to manage and more beneficial for all parties.

Chapter 7 contains more comments on work FSAs can do in the culture-learning area.

Internationalization. The catchall term "internationalization" (as in "internationalization of the campus") is more and more often a part of an FSA's job description, at least implicitly. The term is regrettably vague and may manifest more the influence of a fad than a lasting commitment to identifiable changes in institutional policy and practice. Nevertheless, FSAs, under the rubric of internationalization, might be expected to help recruit larger numbers of foreign students; seek ways to incorporate foreign students into the mainstream of campus life; and/or help students, faculty, and staff interact more constructively with students from other countries.

Globalism. A term that is perhaps even more vague than internationalization, and is somewhat related to it, is "globalism." In an FSA job description it may be phrased as global awareness, global education, or perhaps awareness of interdependence. The general idea is that the world's countries are involved with and mutually dependent upon each other, and the people of the United States need to be more adequately prepared to participate in a world of interdependent nations. Foreign students are seen as vehicles for fostering a more global outlook among the natives. They are asked to serve as panelists, make presentations, and/or give interviews on such world issues as hunger, pollution, and human rights. FSAs are often expected to organize these activities.

Development. Some FSA job descriptions embrace the notion that foreign students, at least those from "Third-World countries," are vehicles for economic and social improvements overseas and that specific attention needs to be paid to the development enterprise while the students are in the United States. The idea that FSAs should promote professional integration[3] of foreign students is related to a concern with economic and political development abroad.

The FSA as a role model

Whatever the details of their job descriptions, FSAs are likely to be the focal points of intercultural interaction on the campus. They are

---

[3] NAFSA has a publication called *Professional Integration: A Guide for Students from the Developing World*, edited by Mary Ann G. Hood and Kevin J. Schieffer, which suggests ways in which foreign students can employ lessons from their U.S. experiences in their professional lives back home.

the "experts" in dealing with people who are different. Veteran FSAs will attest to the number and variety of phone calls they get from faculty, staff, and sometimes other students that begin, "You know a lot about dealing with foreign students. I want to know what you think I should do in this situation." Then they will recount a perplexing set of circumstances involving someone from another country.

FSAs do not always have specific answers for questions such as these, but they can convey—just as they routinely can be seen to embody—a constructive attitude toward intercultural interactions. The components of this attitude are well summarized in the seven lessons Craig Storti draws from his *Cross-Cultural Dialogues:*

1. Don't assume sameness.
2. What you think of as normal or human behavior may only be cultural.
3. Familiar behaviors may have different meanings.
4. Don't assume that what you meant is what was understood.
5. Don't assume that what you understood is what was meant.
6. You don't have to like or accept "different" behavior, but you should try to understand where it comes from.
7. Most people do behave rationally; you just have to discover the rationale.

So far in this chapter we have discussed varying conceptions of foreign students and the role of foreign student advisers. Continuing our consideration of some attitudes and ideas with which FSAs approach their responsibilities (however they or their institutions portray those responsibilities in job descriptions), we turn to the topic of the FSA's position in relation to foreign students.

THE FSA'S STANCE VIS-À-VIS FOREIGN STUDENTS

Josef A. Mestenhauser, in an essay entitled "Are We Professionals, Semi-Professionals, or Dedicated Good Guys?" raised the question of the stance FSAs assume toward their clients and their work. To me his title suggests labels that designate two alternative positions, *professional* and *good guy.* I would add some others: *educator/student developer, monitor, deputy, avenging parent,* and *God.*

A typology of FSA stances

Professional. A professional person strives to keep personalities out of a case as much as possible, to be objective in determining facts and drawing conclusions, and to make decisions based on standard practices and accepted ethical guidelines. Judges, for example, are expected to disqualify themselves from cases in which they have a personal interest and believe they cannot impartially apply appropriate laws and precedents. Some FSAs prefer this stance. They believe it is appropriate to maintain a certain detachment from clients, lest their judgments be unduly influenced by personal relationships.

NAFSA, under Mestenhauser's leadership, developed a code of ethics (about which more is said later in this chapter) and is discussing certification of people who would work in the educational exchange field, seeking to make their actions and decisions more professional. A professional stance on the part of an FSA would entail not just the application of a code of ethics but of a set of education-oriented principles and practices consistently applied in the many contexts in which FSAs carry out their work.

Good guy. Many FSAs assume the stance of the good soul who is doing wholesome work in the name of a noble cause. They tend to be open, trusting, accepting people who enjoy relationships with others, including those who are culturally different.

An issue that confronts all FSAs, but particularly the good guys, concerns the degree to which it is appropriate to be friends with foreign students and scholars. This question can be particularly thorny for younger female FSAs, who are likely to find themselves subject to the attention of male clients. Many factors might impel foreign students and FSAs toward the development of close personal relationships. Are FSAs wise to encourage this, or even permit it? I would say not. FSAs run risks when they become friends, at least close ones, with their clients. They can lose their objectivity (to the degree that objectivity is possible in human relationships) and their credibility if they are closely affiliated with certain students. Other foreign students are more likely to see the FSA as one who plays favorites if he or she has (or is thought to have) close friends among the students. Institutional colleagues are likely to have doubts about an FSA's professional competence if the FSA's intimate friends include students from other countries. Experience suggests that involvement in romantic relationships with foreign students is especially likely to damage an FSA's stature. Difficulties may also ensue from having known enmities with particular foreign students.

This is not to suggest that FSAs ought to be cold, aloof, or detached. Nor does it suggest that FSAs will not have more affinity for some students than for others. FSAs can certainly be warm, cordial, and relatively open. They are likely to find that some particular students are drawn to them personally and to the kind of work the FSA's office is doing. That does not necessarily cause difficulties.

I am inclined to believe that it is unwise for any regular employee of a foreign student office to become intimate friends with clients. Such proscriptions as these are unlikely to prevail over the mysterious forces of love and romance, however. When they do not, those staff members who have close affiliations with clients will want to exclude themselves from official situations involving those with whom they are involved.

Educator/student developer. FSAs are often encouraged to see themselves as educators, not as mere bureaucrats who spend their days filling out forms and issuing documents certifying one thing or another. Janet M. Bennett, for example, writes that

> ...true professionalism in international education requires a proactive position on student development, calling for the conscious planning, facilitating, and evaluating of development opportunities in the context of the international experience. We must go beyond our administrative...role to see ourselves primarily as educators, as facilitators of learning rather than merely as gatekeepers of knowledge, rules, and regulations.... [A]t each crossroad, the question is not merely what form to file and what rule to apply, but how the learner is best educated, and how the international experience can contribute to that (107-8).

FSAs are not often teachers in the formal sense, but they have ample opportunity to educate by example, in face-to-face sessions with clients or others, or in training programs. The student development approach inclines its adherents to see their interactions with clients as opportunities to promote learning or personal growth. As people who are living in another culture, foreign students and scholars can learn much about their own and the host culture and about the dynamics of intercultural relationships. They have countless opportunities to develop insight, personal flexibility, and world-mindedness. FSAs can be catalysts for that learning.

Student development theory has contributed a concept that can provide a frame of reference for many FSA-client interactions, the concept of "challenge and support." The idea is usually attributed to Nevitt Sanford, who, writing in the days before the sensitivity to sexist language, said, "The institution which would lead an individual toward greater development must...present him with strong *chal-*

lenges, appraise accurately his ability to cope with the challenges, and offer him *support* when they become overwhelming" (46, emphases added).

An FSA's clients are being challenged by the mere fact that they are studying or doing research in a foreign culture. FSAs who use the student development approach need to appraise each client's ability to cope and to find ways to provide appropriate support. This can be difficult for FSAs, given the wide array of clients and situations they encounter and the time pressure under which they often work. FSAs must ask themselves, "What are the challenges this client currently faces? Does the client have enough support to confront these challenges constructively? If not, what can I do to provide the support that could make this a developmental experience?"

Some FSAs are trained in the field of college student personnel and have been formally exposed to the student development approach. They have studied research and analysis carried out in the United States with young Americans. Katheryn E. Story, writing in the *Journal of College Student Personnel,* rightly argues that the theories underlying the student development approach as it is generally taught in U.S. universities are a product of U.S. cultural assumptions that do not apply to many foreign students. Story's main point is that the student development theories place a high value on individual autonomy and self-reliance. Americans tend to assume that these are valuable traits. Many foreign students, and probably most people elsewhere in the world, have been taught to assume that maturity entails considerable concern for the well-being of others and for intragroup harmony. The rugged individualists that Americans admire are likely to be viewed as selfish and inconsiderate in many other societies. So student development professionals may need to modify their assumptions and approaches in order to work effectively with students from other countries.

Monitor. When I was in elementary school, the teacher would appoint students to be monitors in the hallways, lunchroom, and sometimes the lavatories (as they were called in those days). Monitors were responsible for watching over the other students and reminding any miscreants to correct their behavior.

Similarly, some FSAs assume the stance of the monitor, watching for misbehavior among the foreign students and urging violators to step back onto the correct path. For example, monitor FSAs will routinely keep track of the number of hours for which foreign students are registered each term or the number of hours they work on the campus. Should students transgress regulatory requirements in these areas, monitors will send them a letter or speak to them personally, pointing out their transgressions and encouraging them to follow the rules.

Some FSAs attribute their monitoring behavior to the INS regulations, but those regulations place course-load requirements and employment restrictions on foreign students, not on FSAs. The INS regulations do not require FSAs to monitor foreign students' conduct.

Recent and still controversial USIA regulations for the Exchange-Visitor Program require people in J status to have certain health-insurance protection. The regulations also oblige responsible officers (usually FSAs) to inform exchange visitors about the insurance requirement. Some responsible officers, though, have taken it upon themselves not just to inform people in J status about the insurance provisions, but to monitor their compliance with it.

FSAs who assume the monitor stance will come to be seen by foreign students and scholars less as supporters, advocates, or potential allies in culture learning, and more as representatives of an unfriendly authority.

Deputy. FSAs who assume the deputy stance go beyond monitoring clients' behavior to actively working on behalf of a law-enforcement agency. One of the most alarming documents I have seen in my career as an FSA was a mission statement of a foreign student office at a small school in the north-central United States. "The foreign-student office," the statement began, "is essentially a branch office of the United States Immigration and Naturalization Service." The statement went on to explain not just the immigration procedures the office carried out, but the types of information it routinely collected from or about its foreign students and sent to the INS. The statement said that the school's own policies on the confidentiality of student records did not restrict the school from submitting any requested information to the INS, the FBI, or any other law-enforcement agency

If they learn of a foreign student who is working without authorization, deputies generally see it as their duty to report that student to the INS. They may also take the initiative to report students whose registration drops below the full-time level, or who otherwise violate the immigration regulations. Despite a NAFSA code of ethics provision to the contrary,[4] deputies are likely to support and help carry out institutional policies that bar admission to out-of-status aliens.

FSAs who assume the deputy stance will be viewed as enemies by the foreign students and scholars they are ostensibly meant to serve.

One impetus for adopting the deputy role was the Immigration Reform and Control Act of 1986. IRCA makes all American employers deputies of the INS by compelling them to assure that all new employees can legally work in the United States. At many colleges and universities the responsibility for getting this assurance, at least from noncitizens, has been given to foreign student offices, where expertise in interpreting immigration documents presumably lies. The step from complying with IRCA to becoming a deputy can be a very small one.

Avenging parent. The Internet is proving to be an ever better window on the foreign-student advising business, as more and more FSAs subscribe to what is known as "Inter-L"[5] and use it to ask their questions. One FSA recently asked, over Inter-L, what other FSAs do about foreign students who request a new I-20 to replace one they have allegedly lost, when in fact experience shows that most students can find their I-20s if they would just take the time to look for them.

After receiving forty-six replies to the inquiry, this FSA posted a summary on Inter-L (emphases added):

> Almost everybody acknowledged that they had had similar occurrences. The vast majority advises that when students come in and ask for an I-20 in replacement for one that was lost or could no longer be found, *they should be made to understand that this is not a routine affair, but that instead, they'll have to pay a price.* About half said that they require new financial documentation. Others require that students complete a "request for replacement of lost I-20" form, which

---

[4] The provision reads, "Members [of NAFSA] with admissions responsibilities shall...employ only criteria relevant to a candidate's academic potential, level of language proficiency, educationally relevant special abilities and characteristics, and availability of financial support, in determining admissibility."

[5] Inter-L is an electronic bulletin board, where subscribers can post information for all (or specified categories of) other subscribers to see, and post questions that all (or categories of) subscribers are invited to answer.

can be designed in many ways, *depending on how strongly you want to encourage your student to "go back home and look some more."*

The majority of respondents also added that—*as an extra penalty*—they make students wait several days before the I-20 is issued. Others (eight respondents) tell students that their I-20s will be mailed to them (I assume that is told to those who come in just when they are ready to go back home for vacation or whatever). Among those eight, five said they make the student pay the shipping cost in advance.

Finally, a small number of advisers suggested asking for a fee (suggestions were made ranging from $5 to $30). Some of those recommending this action had some misgivings about the legality of such an action, but they felt that it would be effective.

An FSA operating from the avenging parent stance is concerned not just or mainly with promoting students' education and maturation, as a student developer might be, but with inflicting punishment along the way. Many times, the urge to inflict punishment seems to come less from a concern with the student's learning and maturation than from the adviser's wish to exact retribution for having been inconvenienced.

Avenging parents, like deputies, are unlikely to be seen as students' allies in the culture-learning process.

God. A former FSA at a Big Ten school reportedly told a student from India that if he did not stop dating an American woman he would be barred from the institution's international center. While that might be an extreme case, it does exemplify the God role, in which the FSA presumes to have superior moral judgment and ultimate power over any and all aspects of foreign students' lives. FSAs assuming the God role are likely to hold—and express—firm opinions about whom foreign students should marry ("their own kind"), where they should live after they graduate ("they should go home"), and what kind of occupation they should follow (ones that will "help people in their country have a better life"). Such FSAs foreclose entire areas of conversation with foreign students, who, like anyone else, are not interested in hearing other people's ideas about what would make them better human beings.

To get a glimpse of the practical outcomes of the various stances FSAs assume, let us look at a lengthy Inter-L message that conveys not just the substantive responses to one FSA's question but also something of the stances of those who replied. The question was posed by a part-time, small-school FSA. She asked Inter-L subscribers whether F-1 students can legitimately enroll for less than a full course of study if they do not have enough money for full-time tuition.[6] "There was much unanimity amongst the twenty-six responses received," the FSA reported (emphases in the original).

Almost all agreed that allowing students to go part time because of financial difficulties was entirely unacceptable. (Suggestions here were: (1) "allow" student to be part time, or not attend at all, for a quarter and then apply for reinstatement when ready to attend again; (2) apply for off-campus work authorization based on economic necessity, if eligible; (3) go home!)

Almost all also agreed that depression or other extreme mental or emotional anguish would fall under "medical." Most everyone said that they have had cases like this and *have usually* required a letter/note from either a doctor or counselor to document and have in [the] student's file. A few mentioned that they would only OK this kind of situation *if* the note from the doctor/counselor indicated that there were ongoing therapy in place and that there was a good/excellent prognosis for the condition to be improved or "cured" in the near future....[7]

Almost all also agreed that a student's uncertainty with major or direction was *not* a reason to exempt her from full time. A comment was made that in this situation it would be more appropriate to have the student take *more* classes, not fewer, in order to check out various areas and come to some conclusion as to direction of study.

A few people said that they approve just about anything (within reason and *excluding financial reasons*) if the student's academic adviser recommends in writing that he or she feels the student would benefit by taking part-time for a term or two. Reasons given here were difficulty with English or reading assignments; difficulty with cross-cultural adjustment; difficult schedule; academic probation; sequential course required and course not offered that term; misadvising or misplacement.

One person said he was *very strict* in interpreting the full-time regulations. He said, "To do otherwise would be tantamount to my being instrumental in attempts to erode this important F-1 rule...."

Another person made some interesting comments about the term

---

[6] INS regulations at 8 *CFR* 214.2(f)(6) do *not* include financial limitations among the acceptable reasons for an F-1 student's being enrolled for less than the full course of study specified in the regulations. A careful reading of 8 *CFR* 214.2(f)(6) would presumably answer the FSA's question. The next chapter discusses the matter of knowledge of the immigration regulations.

[7] Notice that there is absolutely no such requirement in the regulations. A God or an avenging parent is at work here.

"exempt." He said it's not our position as advisers to "exempt," "require," or "reinstate" students, that it is their choice as to what they do and how they proceed with the whole issue of full-time and part-time and everything else as a matter of fact. *If* they chose to go part time, for whatever reason, it is their choice to make. *If* they later come to us for any F-1 benefits, it is then *our* responsibility to request that they apply for reinstatement. But we cannot even "require" them to do that. All we can do is *advise....*

The comments reveal a mixture of stances. No FSA is likely to operate entirely from any one stance, but each is likely to incline toward one or another. Each stance is more likely to achieve some results and less likely to achieve others. Effective FSAs pay conscious attention to the question of their stance, examining what ideas and assumptions lie behind their decisions and what results are likely to flow from them. To help with that examination, we now look at some of the factors that influence an FSA's role relative to clients.

Factors influencing an FSA's stance

For purposes of this *Handbook*, detailed analyses of the factors mentioned below is not necessary. What follows is a listing of factors, with a few comments about some of them.

Following the American custom, I will first mention *legal mandates*. The IRCA, the Immigration and Nationality Act (usually referred to simply as "the Act"), as amended, the federal regulations concerning F-1 students and, in some cases, the federal regulations concerning J-1 exchange visitors, all impose certain responsibilities on educational institutions that enroll foreign students and that hire employees. As should be clear from discussion earlier in this chapter, these responsibilities are not always clearly defined. They leave room for interpretation. While they might provide boundaries within which a particular FSA makes judgments, the nature of those judgments is likely to be influenced by other factors mentioned in this section.

Professional standards might influence an FSA's stance. These are discussed in the next section of this chapter.

Institutional culture influences the way an FSA's responsibilities are construed. Some institutions assume a laissez-faire attitude toward their students, while others watch and guide them more closely. To some degree this reflects a large school–small school difference, but even among small schools there are major differences in the degree to which the school stands in loco parentis.

Institutional history also plays a role in shaping the FSA's job. One experienced FSA wrote this on the Internet:

> To a certain extent, the campus community and the local community define the role of the FSA. I think that in large part, FSAs in small communities or in college towns are pressured to keep the foreign students in line, and are told to check on the full-time status, work permission, etc. [of foreign students]. Having worked at a university where there was not much support for international students and where the university was quite concerned about conflicts between the campus and the city, I was often asked to do things which should never have been asked of me. I often had debates with my director, who always took the side of the city over the rights of the international student.

Part of the institutional history that is salient here is the stance assumed by an FSA's predecessor. If a given person holds an FSA post for a significant period of time, students and institutional colleagues come to expect certain attitudes and behaviors from that person or that office, and they learn to behave accordingly. A new FSA cannot readily break out of the predecessor's mold.

The *FSA's personal and professional history* also influence the stance that the FSA will take. Again, from the Internet:

> ...[T]here are many new people in the field and I think they will tend to be careful in the beginning for fear of doing something wrong and for fear of putting a student in jeopardy for some future benefit.

An FSA who is new to one school, but has experience at another, will naturally carry over some outlooks from the previous school and may or may not change them in the process of accommodating to the new job.

FSAs who have been burned in previous dealings with foreign students, or at least certain categories of them, are likely to take a particular point of view toward other such students whom they encounter later. An FSA might decide, for example, that no student from Country X can be trusted. (On the other hand, a strong positive experience might lead to the point of view that all students from Country Y are marvelous human beings.)

Finally we turn to the complex matter of the *FSA's personality,* which is of considerable consequence in shaping the way the job is carried out. FSA personality elements that are salient in this context include motivation, authoritarianism, and nurturance.

Motivation was discussed earlier, in chapter 3. The power and affiliation dimensions probably do most to explain an FSA's personal stance toward foreign students. High affiliation needs are associated with the good guy and perhaps the student developer stance, and high-power needs with the God and other more authoritarian stances.

The authoritarian personality syndrome is not unrepresented among FSAs. "…[P]eople who behave according to this syndrome," Richard W. Brislin explains in *Cross-Cultural Encounters,*

> enjoy both using their authority and accepting it from others who are higher in status. The expression of authority on both levels leads to an unquestioning acceptance of the commands a person receives and passes on, and an acceptance of the system which permits the communication of orders (50-51).

Authoritarianism probably underlies the monitor and the God stances, most likely to be found in people who like to lord it over others.

"If I want someone to nurture students," said the director of a foreign student office at a large university, "I'll hire a nurturer." This director, whose personal proclivities lead him to be more interested in administration than in working with individual students, was acknowledging the fact that some people are more nurturant than others. They generally feel sympathy with other people and are inclined to want to help them. They are comfortable dealing with the expression of strong emotions. People high on the nurturance scale are more likely to play the nice guy or the student developer roles, and less likely to be avenging parents, deputies, or monitors.

Two special cases

Two categories of FSAs face special complications with respect to the issue of stance. One is those whose sexual orientation is other than heterosexual. The other is those who are foreign-born.

Gay, lesbian, and bisexual FSAs face not only the conventional difficulties that confront nonheterosexual people in this society,[8] but also the confounding fact that their clients come from societies with a wide range of attitudes toward gays. Should gay, lesbian, or bi-

---

[8] For discussion of issues confronting gay, lesbian, and bisexual students and student affairs personnel on contemporary American campuses, see Nancy Evans's and Vernon J. Wall's *Beyond Tolerance: Gays, Lesbians, and Bisexuals on Campus.*

sexual FSAs "come out" to their clients? Should they show any particular concern for clients who might not be heterosexuals?[9]

Foreign-born FSAs must walk a line between identifying with their clients, on the one hand, and with their institutional colleagues, on the other. One way foreign-born FSAs can enhance their credibility with clients is to emphasize the commonality of their situation as foreigners. That can have advantages for the FSA, but it risks alienating them from institutional colleagues, who might come to see the FSA as more closely allied with the clients than with the institution. Foreign-born FSAs face the realities of ethnic and race relations in the United States in a way Caucasian Americans do not, giving this issue an intense personal as well as professional dimension.

PROBLEM OWNERSHIP

"Problem ownership" refers to one's notion of the locus of responsibility for a problem. To own a problem is to be in a situation in which one's needs are not being met or where one is dissatisfied with one's own behavior. (Thomas Gordon discusses the concept in all of his effectiveness training books. Stephen R. Covey's concept of a circle of concern, from *The Seven Habits of Highly Effective People,* is closely related.) FSAs can save themselves considerable psychological stress and clarify possible courses of action by paying close attention, when presented with a problem, to the question of whose problem it is. Many people, including some who are attracted to foreign student advising because it offers a chance to help others, cause difficulty for themselves and others by failing to consider the question of problem ownership.

Take, for example, the not uncommon situation of a newly arrived foreign student who tells the FSA that he does not have enough money to enroll and that he needs financial aid. Whose problem is this? Many FSAs assume it is theirs, because the student who has the problem is foreign. Certainly the student can be expected to try to induce the FSA to buy into the problem. But who caused the problem? The student did, unless the institution understated the amount of money the student would need, something institutions rarely do. And who suffers if the problem is not solved? The student

---

[9] Indeed, should they even come out to their fellow FSAs? Gay, lesbian, and bisexual members of NAFSA report numerous instances of rejection from their own professional colleagues.

does. Who owns this problem? The student does. Should the FSA take action on this student's behalf? We will consider that question in a moment.

Applications

The concept of problem ownership has three important applications in foreign student advising: as a tool for economizing effort, as an aid in maintaining mental health, and as a device for helping students gain perspective.

Economizing effort. FSAs (unless they are lacking influence) generally have more than enough work to do. This means that they must choose from among many possible activities. In making those choices, problem ownership is an important consideration. Should the FSA in the previous example take time to seek money for the student who arrived short of funds? Probably not, unless there is not enough other work to do. The FSA might suggest that the student find a less expensive school or postpone registration, but the FSA would be unwise to enter the time-consuming effort of raising money to solve this student's self-made problem. Time and anguish saved by clarifying the ownership of a problem enable FSAs to better provide their services to foreign students in general.

Helping maintain an FSA's mental health. There are too many problems in the world—and even on any particular American campus—for one individual to solve. People who take all the world's problems as their own probably lack adequate insight into that fact. They work for a while on this problem and for a while on that, all the time worrying about all that is left undone. They render themselves exhausted and distracted, unable to work consistently and effectively even on those problems they are in a position to affect. People in the so-called "helping professions" are especially susceptible to this malady, because they sympathize with troubled people and want to help them.

An effective FSA needs a clear mind and an adequate supply of mental and physical energy. Effective FSAs know they cannot solve all the problems students experience on account of such things as civil war in Eastern Europe, currency devaluation in Africa, death in families in Hong Kong, Professor X's unfair grading system, the irrationalities of the American health-care system, or a student's failure to buy automobile insurance or employ a reliable method of birth control. Effective FSAs know that unfortunate things happen to people and some of those unfortunate things will require their victims to make radical changes in their plans. Some foreign students might, for example, have to delay graduation, or sell some durable goods they would rather keep, or take a job they would prefer not to take, or ask an unsympathetic cousin for a loan, or even abandon, at least temporarily, their academic objectives.

FSAs are in a position where they can cripple themselves by worrying about and working on problems they do not own and cannot solve. They will be mentally healthier, and therefore more capable of being effective, if they take care to determine which of the problems they encounter are their own and which they are in a position to do something about.

Helping students gain perspective. Like FSAs, foreign students (and nearly everyone else) can gain perspective on their own circumstances and thereby improve their own mental health if they incorporate the concept of problem ownership into their outlook. FSAs may have opportunities, in the course of their advising and counseling, to help students do so. One student came to me very upset because a group of his compatriots were making fools of themselves, he said, by parading in front of a principal campus building every day in the name of a certain political cause. Not only were they making fools of themselves, he said, but they were conveying an embarrassing image of people from his country. This was disturbing him to the point where he was not sleeping well or studying effectively.

I offered this student an explanation of the problem ownership idea. I then asked him to explain to me how the problem he presented could be considered his problem. He could not do so, of course, because the problem was not his. If his compatriots wanted to make fools of themselves, that was their prerogative. If the natives were unwise enough to generalize too much from the demonstrators' example, that was their problem. The student saw that, and went away, he said, relieved of a large burden.

Many students' problems essentially vanish when the students learn to distinguish between their own and others' problems and realize how pointless it is to expend their mental energy on problems they did not create, are not really victims of, or cannot remedy.[10]

The final topic of this chapter, professional standards, is a more general one than problem ownership, which can be clearly and spe-

---

[10] For more discussion of the problem ownership idea, and examples drawn from administrative situations, see Thomas Gordon's *Leader Effectiveness Training.*

cifically put into operation on a daily basis. Professional standards in foreign student advising, on the other hand, are more nebulous, although less so than they were before NAFSA's recent and continuing efforts to develop and implement a code of ethics.

PROFESSIONAL STANDARDS

NAFSA's early 1980s formulation of professional standards for educational exchange was spurred in part by well-known instances in which American educational institutions were essentially selling admissions to foreign applicants who, it was thought, could contribute needed tuition income. What emerged from arduous discussions within NAFSA were two publications, *Standards and Responsibilities in International Educational Interchange* and *NAFSA Principles for International Educational Exchange.* All FSAs should own and be familiar with these two publications.[11]

Both *Standards and Responsibilities* and *Principles* concern expectations of institutions that participate in educational exchange.[12] They do not focus on individual conduct. NAFSA's Code of Ethics, developed in the late 1980s and early 1990s, does have that focus.[13] The desirability of having a code of ethics emerged as it became clear that individual practitioners, even those operating in a supportive, enlightened, and sensible institutional framework, face questions for which they wish to have some guidance. The NAFSA code contains many elements that are common in the codes of ethics of American professional organizations, relating to such matters as truth in advertising, confidentiality, and respect for diversity. Other provisions of the NAFSA code are probably unique to NAFSA's concerns, for

---

[11] Like NAFSA's code of ethics, the *Principles* are printed in the *NAFSA Directory.* And both appear, along with several other NAFSA policy statements, in *Standards and Policies in International Educational Exchange: A Guidebook for Policy Development, Professional Conduct, and the Continuing Growth of International Education.*

[12] For example, the *Principles* state that "an institution that enrolls foreign students...should provide...an orientation program that introduces students to the physical environment [of the institution], registration procedures, academic policies, housing, counseling and health services, visa requirements and INS regulations, financial services, and social and intercultural activities...."

[13] For example, the code says that "in relationships with students and scholars, members [of NAFSA] shall...recognize their own cultural and value orientations and be aware of how those orientations affect their interactions with people from other cultures."

example those having to do with immigration regulations, religious proselytizing in the context of community hospitality programs, and accepting gifts in the context of working with clients who come from societies where gift-giving customs are far different from those that prevail in American society.

All FSAs should be closely familiar with the NAFSA code of ethics, copies of which are available free from the organization. (See Appendix C for the address of NAFSA and of other organizations mentioned in this *Handbook*.) NAFSA seeks to disseminate its code as widely as possible. The full text appears in the membership directory, and is given away at conferences. New members routinely get a copy. The NAFSA code of ethics is referred to and quoted at several points in this book, reflecting its importance to FSAs.

Like any such code, it is revised from time to time. FSAs should attend to that fact and get a copy of each new version.

No code of ethics, though, provides clear guidance for all cases. The popular phrase "ethical dilemma" reflects the fact that many situations call for choices between two or more possible courses of action, both (or all) of which have advantages and disadvantages. Individual FSAs are still left to draw a judicious balance among assorted possibilities.

5

Knowledge

Knowledge might or might not be power, but it certainly is influence. An FSA's store of knowledge is called upon to aid in understanding and explaining a remarkable array of situations. The more FSAs know, the more influence they can have. This chapter discusses knowledge with which FSAs will want to be familiar, using these arbitrary categories: self-knowledge, institution, community, professional colleagues, external agencies, clients' backgrounds, applied linguistics and contrastive rhetoric, current affairs, intercultural communication, international education, and immigration regulations.

SELF-KNOWLEDGE

We have already (in chapter 3) discussed self-awareness as a valuable characteristic for FSAs. That, of course, is an aspect of self-knowledge. The two terms can be distinguished by saying that self-awareness pertains to a moment-by-moment consciousness of what is happening within oneself and with respect to others in a given situation. Self-knowledge is a more inclusive idea, referring to a general familiarity with one's own enduring characteristics and proclivities. Here, the important aspects of self are personality characteristics, strengths and weaknesses, values, "buttons," and stereotypes.

Personality characteristics

In the preceding two chapters we have mentioned several personality characteristics and related them to the manner in which the FSA job is conceived and carried out. Mention has also been made of motivation, whether to power, affiliation, or achievement. FSAs will want to know how much of each of these motivations they themselves embody.

Some additional traits figure into the way an FSA copes with the daily pressures of the job. These include the FSA's usual responses to stress, conflict, displays of strong emotion, and the behavior (or even the mere presence) of people in authority.

One need not take personality tests to gain the self-knowledge and understanding desirable for FSAs, though that is one approach. Simply noting the patterns in one's behavior and responses, especially in contrast to those of other people, can provide insight into one's personality.

Strengths and weaknesses

FSAs ought to know what job-related functions they do well (for example, remember detailed matters such as immigration regulations, think on their feet, or remain calm under pressure) and what they do poorly (write reports, meet deadlines, conduct meetings, etc.). Then they can delegate to others the necessary tasks they know they cannot do well or work to improve in their areas of weakness, or both.

Values

As used here, "values" refer to preferences and to convictions about what is right and wrong. Different people have different values, of course, and it helps to know our own and to have an idea how ours compare with others'. I find it helpful to remind myself, for example, that I place a high value on verbal articulateness and on being organized, while others may rank sociability higher than I do. By being as aware as I can be of my own values, I can better understand my own reactions to other people and theirs to me.

Buttons

"Buttons" is not a scientific term, but it conveys the common-sense notion that we all have certain kinds of events, topics, situations, or people that set us off into a predetermined, automatic response. When our buttons are pushed, we are not usually able to be attentive to others, to be as self-aware as we might otherwise be, or as able to behave rationally or constructively. Buttons that commonly get pushed in foreign-student advising work include those related to perceived sexism, dishonesty, pushiness, or ingratitude; prejudice among the natives; and foreign students who want to immigrate.

Good FSAs know what their buttons are, and they work consciously to reduce the number and sensitivity of them. When they realize that one of their buttons has been pushed, they try to stop talking, regain a constructive attitude, and request help if they think they could use it.

Stereotypes

All of us have stereotypes, no matter how much we preach about their undesirability. I have heard FSAs talk in very stereotypic terms about Iranian students, Chinese students and scholars, Arab and Latin-American males, foreign athletes, wealthy Korean ESL students, foreign students who want to remain in the United States, faculty members, INS officers, consular officials, and no doubt other categories of people as well. I might even have taken part in one or two such conversations myself. The point for FSAs is to *be mindful* of their stereotypes and to welcome opportunities to have them challenged.

INSTITUTION

FSAs work in organizations. To get things accomplished, they have to work constructively within those organizations. That requires knowing their institutions' missions, procedures, and personnel. It also requires knowing something about organizational behavior, particularly the behavior of academic organizations.

Missions

Different educational institutions have different overall objectives or missions. Small, private colleges do not have the same missions as large, research-oriented universities. FSAs should know the raison d'être of their own institutions, so they can make plans or design programs in harmony with the institution's overall direction and help foreign students understand (which they often do not, at least at first) what sort of institution they are attending.

The most obvious place to look for an institution's mission statement (whether or not it is explicitly labeled as such) is in the institution's catalogue. Other statements about an institution's general directions can be found in planning documents and in the speeches of the chief executive officer. FSAs are wise to be familiar with such things.

FSAs should realize that there may be discrepancies between an institution's stated mission and the objectives actually being sought, and that an institution's mission might somehow be or become incompatible with their own values or interests, making it appropriate for them to seek employment elsewhere.

Procedures

Even small educational institutions in the United States have detailed procedures for many matters concerning students, for example, gaining admission, getting transfer credit, proficiency testing in languages and mathematics, paying tuition, checking out library books, registering for classes and making changes in registration, getting health insurance, having an academic record reviewed in preparation for graduation, etc. The more FSAs know about these procedures, or at least where to get information about them, the better they will be able to aid their foreign student clients. They will certainly want to have on hand the institution's catalogue, student handbook, and any publications containing formal rules, procedures, and deadlines.

Personnel

It is not mission statements or procedure manuals that make institutions operate, but the people who work in them. FSAs will want to know the personnel of their institutions on both the formal and informal levels.

Formal. Institutions differ strikingly in the degree to which they stress formality in daily operations. At some institutions, nearly everything is written down and the written words are followed. At others, more is done informally, whether or not much is written down. However much stress is placed on formality within their institutions, FSAs should know the organization chart. Who reports to whom? What procedures are carried out and what decisions are made in which offices?

One aspect of formal organization that rarely appears on educational institutions' organization charts is that of committees. Effective FSAs know what institutional committees have or might take an interest in foreign student affairs, what those committees are formally charged to accomplish, who the members are, and what role the committees actually play in institutional governance. It may turn out, for example, that a particular committee, despite its promising charge and composition, is ineffective in practice, and could not help an FSA bring about changes in institutional policy or procedures.

Informal. FSAs need to know not just the formal institutional structure, but also the individuals who occupy the positions listed on the chart and the nature of the relationships among those individuals. The ideal is to have cordial personal relationships with as many institutional colleagues as possible, since FSAs may have occasion to interact with personnel in all parts of the organization. Appendix D lists institutional personnel an FSA might benefit from knowing. The personal characteristic of sociability, discussed in chapter 3, may be more important here than in any other aspect of an FSA's work.

It is particularly important for FSAs to have constructive working relationships with the people responsible for admitting foreign students, teaching English as a second language, issuing official records and certifications, and handling student accounts. The FSA's clients have significant interactions with all these individuals, so FSAs will inevitably receive questions—and complaints—about them. FSAs cannot serve their clients effectively if their own relationships with these institutional officials are not constructive.

I have repeatedly been struck, in serving as a consultant at various institutions, by the number of instances in which FSAs do not have cordial relationships with their institutional colleagues. Sometimes they have acrimonious ones; more often they simply do not know many of their colleagues. Often the FSAs and their colleagues have, over time, developed what are in their own minds rather clear images of each other and have come to think they know each other's viewpoints and values. They function (inevitably) on the basis of their images or perceptions of each other. When consultants visit and talk with all parties, it becomes clear that the perceptions are mutually inaccurate. (Usually the people are more in agreement with each other than they realize.)

There is considerable irony in these situations. We find people who, in their role as FSAs, are trying to devise ways to encourage constructive interaction between foreign students and their hosts, with the object of breaking down stereotypes and developing mutual understanding and respect among real human beings. At the same time, the FSAs themselves are not interacting constructively with their own institutional colleagues and are building rather than breaking down stereotypes and false assumptions about them.

When FSAs encourage interaction between foreign students and their hosts, with the intention of building constructive relationships based on knowledge and respect, they ought to make sure they are putting their own advice into practice.

Becoming acquainted with institutional colleagues has at least two salutary outcomes, one more obvious than the other. First, FSAs and colleagues who know each other can see each other as individuals rather than as members of groups about which they hold misleading stereotypes. They can therefore treat each other with more respect and compassion.

Second, becoming personally acquainted with each other helps institutional colleagues learn about each other's *situations*. In *Cross-Cultural Encounters* (pages 93-96), Richard W. Brislin offers some pertinent ideas about the role of situations in human conduct. These ideas would be relevant in many parts of this *Handbook* and are summarized here.

Brislin says that people normally look for some motivation behind other people's behavior. Generally, they attribute the behavior either to some *trait* of the other person as an individual or to the *situation* in which the individual is operating. He says that situations explain more about people's behavior than is generally realized. In cases where we are familiar with other people's situations we tend, rightly, to attribute much of what they do to the situations they are in rather than to their individual traits. If we are not familiar with their situations, we are likely to commit what is called the "fundamental attribution error," ascribing their behavior to their traits rather than to their situations.

Brislin is writing about intercultural situations. He makes the point that people in cross-cultural encounters are unlikely to be familiar with each other's situations and so are prone to make the fundamental attribution error. That error will also be made among institutional colleagues who have not come to know each other's individual characteristics *and* situations.

It can also be helpful to view interoffice relationships in an organization as a species of intercultural relationship. Different offices may well be based on and promote significantly different values and ways of treating people. For example, an admissions office or a bursar's office may be more rule-oriented than an FSA's office (at least than an FSA's office with a good-guy orientation). Without a good understanding of the cultural differences involved in their particular situation, an FSA might too readily conclude that individuals who work in those offices are irredeemably "rigid" or "closed-minded." Meanwhile, people in the admissions and bursar offices might view the FSA as "soft" or "fuzzy-minded." On both sides, some understanding of the other side's situation, including its office culture, can diminish the strength and impact of these negative assessments.

FSAs who know their colleagues' situations have a number of advantages. They can understand their colleagues' behavior better, they can more easily empathize and thus build influence with them, and they can serve their foreign student clients better by providing a more accurate explanation of the behavior of particular faculty and staff members.

Those aspects of their colleagues' situations that FSAs might want to learn about, in addition to their office culture, include their job descriptions, work loads, the political situations within their offices, the values and operating methods of their supervisors, and personal issues they may be confronting. FSAs' colleagues' behavior is shaped by these and no doubt other aspects of their situations, apart from any of their personal traits.

I do not mean to suggest that FSAs, if they would but make the effort, will always have harmonious relationships with institutional colleagues. They probably will not. Value conflicts and personality clashes seem inevitable. The suggestion here is to strive to maintain at least a minimal level of civility, politeness, and openness even in the face of the strongest of conflicts. Displays of temper, vindictive actions, gossiping, and principled refusals to interact may provide momentary pleasure, but in the longer term rarely have the beneficial results that patience and politeness can bring. A key skill in working effectively in an organization is that of getting along with people one dislikes.

A final suggestion concerning the informal aspect of knowing one's institution: take the trouble to know and be respectful of secretaries. It is as common to hear that advice being offered as it is to see it being ignored. Secretaries are essential to an organization's operation. Secretaries in educational institutions sometimes offer students important information, social support, and advice. They can often help FSAs get needed information or remedy students' problems. Being in good stead with secretaries can enhance an FSA's influence.

Organizational behavior

Most of the literature in the field of organizational behavior (or organizational development, as it is sometimes called) is based on business rather than educational institutions. Because business organizations are significantly different from educational organizations, much of the literature is not directly relevant to colleges and universities. Businesses, unlike educational institutions, have an identifiable, measurable output or product, so it is relatively easy for them to assess the quality of their operation and to identify more and less productive uses of available resources.

Also business organizations generally rely on a single approach to decision making, based in some way on their hierarchical structure. Educational institutions present a mix of decision-making styles, including the collegial approach that presumably characterizes faculty decision making and the more top-down approaches found in administrative units.

In his study *The Academic Life*, Burton R. Clark illuminates differences in decision-making style that he says are associated with different types of educational institutions. Community colleges, he says, are much more likely to exhibit authoritarian decision making than are research universities. FSAs can place their own institutions into the wider context of American postsecondary education by studying Clark's work.[1]

Even with these differences, all organizations present certain commonalities. In their lighthearted but insightful book on business organizations, *Dinosaur Brains,* Albert J. Bernstein and Sydney Craft Rozen offer what they call their "corporate laws of gravity."

1. There ain't no justice.[2]

2. Nothing ever happens the way it's supposed to.

3. People will not do what they should do.[3]

---

[1] In a short critique of academic administration, economist Thomas Sowell wrote (in the February 14, 1994 issue of *Forbes Magazine*, 14), "Stanford University President Gerhard Casper put his finger on the central organizational problem of American colleges and universities in general when he said: 'Power comes from the bottom up. The most important decisions are those concerning admissions, curriculum, and faculty appointments, and these are areas where the university president has almost no power.'" Sowell goes on: "Power not only comes from the bottom up in academia, it comes from people with tenure, who pay no price for being wrong. Even if professors' decisions ruin the institution, no one can fire them for that.... No other institutions—religious or secular, economic or social, despotic or democratic—have so many people able to make decisions without being held accountable for the consequences."

[2] In elaborating on this point, Bernstein and Rozen say, "Opportunities go not to the most qualified but to the people who promote themselves the best and are in the right place at the right time" (224). This point is particularly important to the many FSAs of the good-guy type, who tend to wait for their obvious good work to be recognized and rewarded. According to Bernstein and Rozen, that waiting will be in vain. Bernstein's and Rozen's second joint book, *Neanderthals at Work* (mentioned in chapter 4), elaborates on the dynamics of being recognized and rewarded and of getting what one wants in an organization.

[3] "Most people will leave most things until the last minute," the authors observe (225).

4. People will consider their own feelings and best interests before they consider yours.[4]

5. Wherever there are people, there will be politics.

6. There will never be a time of smooth sailing.[5]

7. The federal government was not created to make your job easier or more efficient.

8. All the information will never be in (224-226).

Wise FSAs will keep these laws in mind, and consider how they apply to their own behavior and their own organizations.

COMMUNITY

Whether or not they are actively involved in host-family organizations or other community programs of the kinds discussed in chapter 7, FSAs ought to know a number of people in the community and be familiar with certain community organizations. These include civic officials, civic leaders, official procedures, media representatives, helping agencies, service organizations, religious leaders, businesspeople, and what I call generous, helpful individuals.

Civic officials

FSAs will want, at a minimum, to know appropriate government officials and law-enforcement officers. In a small town this might mean the mayor and the chief of police; in a large city it might mean city council members and the head of the nearest police station. Ideally, these civic officials will know who the FSA is, what general responsibilities the FSA has, and what situations can usefully be brought to the FSA's attention.

---

[4] "Never assume malicious intent when ignorance is sufficient to explain." And "If you tell somebody at work something in confidence and it's of any importance, it will get out" (225).

[5] In my work as a consultant at educational institutions, I have seen countless instances where this "law" was being overlooked. Almost invariably in contemporary American colleges and universities there are key positions that are about to become vacant, or have just become vacant, or are filled on an acting basis, or have an incumbent who, it is usually said, "just came on board" and is not yet "up to speed." Each of these situations provides an excuse for waiting until things "settle down" or "get cleared up." By the time the position is filled by someone who has had time to "learn the ropes," another key position is in flux. So there is never a time of smooth sailing. Those who wait for one are always waiting, and key issues remain unaddressed.

Civic leaders

FSAs can sometimes get help of assorted kinds if they are acquainted with the community's influential citizens. Those citizens might aid in circumstances that require emergency assistance, sustained fund raising, favorable public relations, or just a word from an influential person.

Official procedures

To be ready to deal with emergencies that their clients sometimes confront, FSAs have to know (1) what happens when a client is arrested (release on bail, visiting someone in jail), (2) what happens in the courts when a client is charged with a crime (arraignments, hearings, appointment of a public defender), and (3) the procedures for involuntary commitment to a mental institution of a client suffering from a serious psychological disturbance.

Media representatives

International educational exchange, like so much else in contemporary U.S. society, can be dramatically helped or harmed by the media. If they know local media representatives, FSAs can sometimes cast a positive light on an aspect of educational exchange, or at least help provide a balanced view of a situation in which only the negative side is gaining attention.

Local journalists might appreciate ideas for feature stories about interesting individuals from abroad or background information that can help them understand—and explain to the public—aspects of an institution's foreign student program.

Helping agencies

Foreign students sometimes get into situations where they could benefit from the services of the community's helping agencies. Such agencies offer help in a variety of areas, including legal aid, financial counseling, protection of abused spouses, family counseling, alcoholism treatment, education for gifted children, and opportunities for voluntary service.

Service organizations

Service organizations such as Rotary, Kiwanis, and Lions Clubs sometimes have international interests—raising funds, sponsoring trips or other educational or social programs, or helping recruit host families. FSAs enlarge their ability to serve their students if they know the service organizations in their communities. Directories of community organizations are often available from chambers of commerce or public libraries.

Religious leaders

Churches and other religious organizations in American communities often provide social services and cultural, social, and educational activities from which foreign students and scholars can benefit. Churches are often mainstays of host-family programs. FSAs ought to be acquainted with religious leaders, particularly those with a cosmopolitan bent. Campus ministers are often such people.

On the other hand, FSAs must be wary of religious and quasi-religious organizations whose intent is less to serve others than to gain adherents to their doctrines and contributions to their coffers.

Businesspeople

The sentiment may be fading, but I think FSAs are prone to be skeptical of people in the private sector.[6] But businesspeople are the proverbial backbone of many communities, and FSAs ought to make their acquaintance. Businesspeople might turn out to have their own reasons for actively supporting foreign student programs or activities.[7] FSAs are well advised to investigate that possibility.

Generous, helpful individuals

In most communities there are people willing to help others who need it. They might provide temporary housing, transportation for

---

[6] Witness the difficulty representatives of proprietary ESL, study abroad, and other educational enterprises have encountered in trying to find a place in NAFSA. They may be accepted as members, but remain underrepresented in leadership positions.

[7] My own office situation is a good example. One bank in my community sponsors the 100-page handbook we give to all new foreign students and scholars. It also supports monthly luncheon gatherings of nationality organization leaders and provides refreshments and prizes for lucky draws during our orientation program. Another bank sponsors an annual picnic for new students. Several restaurants donate prepared food for a free lunch new students get on the first day of the orientation program. In short, the coincidence of interests between my office and several businesses in the community has resulted in a marked improvement in the quality of our services to students.

excursions, help in locating apartments, English conversation practice, used furniture, or whatever. In many communities these individuals have created relatively formal organizations whose objectives include providing such services to people from abroad and promoting culture learning as well. FSAs will want to know as many of these people as possible, work closely with the organizations they may have established, and be certain they receive appropriate recognition for their efforts and contributions.

PROFESSIONAL COLLEAGUES

Sometimes foreign student advisers at other institutions are an FSA's best source of information, advice, and moral support. (Some FSAs work at institutions where "no one else understands.") At a minimum, an FSA ought to know (1) the FSA in the same INS district who is best informed about immigration regulations,[8] (2) an FSA anywhere who is well informed about immigration regulations, and (3) at least one experienced FSA at an institution of the same general size and type as one's own.

Meeting fellow FSAs most commonly takes place at NAFSA conferences and workshops. Going to visit them in their offices is another approach. In the absence of these possibilities, a relationship can be developed over the phone or by means of electronic mail. FSAs in general are well known for their willingness to assist colleagues at other institutions.

Foreign admissions officers, teachers of English as a second language, and others involved in educational exchange can also provide FSAs with information and support.

EXTERNAL AGENCIES

The term "external agencies" refers here to two different kinds of organizations. The first is U.S. government agencies whose activities affect foreign students. The principal one is the Immigration and Naturalization Service, about which more is said later in this chapter. Other federal agencies whose work touches on the interests of at least some FSAs are the Visa Office of the Department of State, the Internal Revenue Service, the Office of Exchange Visitor

---

[8] In many cases this will be the NAFSA regional GRAC representative, that is, the person assigned by NAFSA's Government Regulations Advisory Committee to be the region's link with GRAC at the national level.

Programs[9] of the U.S. Information Agency, the Social Security Administration, the U.S. Agency for International Development, and the Manpower Administration branch of the Department of Labor.

The second kind of organization is that which sponsors or at least oversees foreign students in the United States. This includes both nonprofit educational agencies (such as the Academy for Educational Development, the African-American Institute, the American-Mideast Educational and Training Service, the Institute of International Education, the Latin American Scholarship Program of American Universities, and Partners for International Education and Training[10]) and certain foreign governments whose representatives at embassies, consulates, or special offices in the United States administer scholarship and/or service offices for students. Examples (at this writing) include Kuwait, Malaysia, Saudi Arabia, and Singapore. Not all FSAs have occasion to deal with all these agencies. All FSAs deal with the INS, of course, but their need to be familiar with the other agencies depends on where their foreign students come from, what sponsorship arrangements they have, and what immigration status they hold.

FSAs can serve their students better, and thus increase their own influence, if they are familiar with the following aspects of those external agencies with which they have occasion to interact:

1. the agency's mission

2. its procedures affecting students at the FSA's institution

3. the personnel responsible for those procedures

With respect to the personnel of external agencies, the FSA ought to know not just the formal structure but also the informal centers of responsibility and lines of communication, and not just the individuals but also their situations. (Compare with the discussion above about knowing personnel at one's own institution.) One cannot hope to fathom the workings of the INS or the IIE without knowing the situations of the people who work there.

---

[9] At the time of this writing, this is the name of the USIA office charged with managing the Exchange-Visitor Program. That office has had a variety of names over the years.

[10] Acronyms are unavoidable in the international educational exchange field, and each of the organizations named here is at least as well known by its acronym as by its full name. Their acronyms, respectively: AED, AAI, AMIDEAST, IIE, LASPAU, and PIET, also often called "Partners."

There are many ways of learning about external agencies. Some publish descriptive brochures or annual reports that give an official view. Some send representatives to NAFSA conferences, or will do so if invited. Some send representatives to visit campuses. Telephone conversations with staff members can be revealing, conversations with ex-staff members even more so. FSAs at other institutions can often provide useful information. Foreign students themselves sometimes know how their embassies, consulates, or sponsoring agencies operate. Sometimes they think they know and they do not (because they have believed a rumor, overgeneralized from a particular experience, or misunderstood the lessons in a friend's experience).

Most FSAs use all these means of learning about the external agencies with which they deal.

CLIENTS' BACKGROUNDS

FSAs and their foreign student clients benefit in several ways when FSAs have some knowledge of the students' educational and cultural backgrounds. First, the FSAs can better understand the new students' situations and the particular adjustments and accommodations they will have to make.

Second, FSAs can more effectively explain things to new students if they are able to use examples and comparisons that relate to the students' own experiences. FSAs add to their influence with students when the students can see that FSAs know something about their respective educational systems and cultural backgrounds.

Third, FSAs can more effectively serve as intermediaries between foreign students and scholars, on the one hand, and institutional faculty and staff, on the other, if they are familiar with the students' and scholars' backgrounds.

At institutions with a small number of students from other countries, FSAs might be able to learn not just about the students' general educational and cultural upbringing, but about each student's particular experiences and aspirations.

Let us look in a little detail at the categories of information FSAs will want to have about their students' educational and cultural pasts.

Educational backgrounds

Most of what FSAs ought to know about the educational systems in their clients' countries is classified under the headings of sociology of education and comparative education. FSAs who do admissions work will need to verse themselves in these areas. Here is a set of questions FSAs could ask about each educational system they wish to understand:

1. What is the official ideal concerning education for the country's citizens? (Until recently, at least, the official ideal in the United States has been that as many people as possible should get as much formal education as possible. Other official ideals might be less expansive, limiting higher education to a smaller portion of the population, based perhaps on academic ability or some demographic characteristic.)

2. What is the national government's role in education? (More specifically, what is the government's role in setting curriculum? Standards? Is the government using the educational system to accomplish any special social or political goal, such as imposing a national language or encouraging diverse ethnic identities?)

3. From what social strata and geographic areas do most students come?

4. What entrance and leaving examinations are required at each level? What portion of those who attempt the examinations pass them?

5. What curricula do college-bound pupils normally follow?

6. What changes and controversies (there usually are some) are currently engaging educators' attention?[11]

7. What methods of education (lecture, laboratory, problem solving, etc.) predominate?

8. What is the predominant conception of the nature of education? (In the United States, the predominant conception, particularly at the postsecondary level and beyond, is that of a continuously expanding body of knowledge being accumulated and reexamined by scholars and by students as well. A contrasting conception, to be found in much of

---

[11] One indicator of the degree to which "international education" has become a mainstream concern in the United States since the first edition of this book was published is the fact that the *Chronicle of Higher Education* now has a regular "international" section, and routinely reports on NAFSA's annual conferences and IIE's reports on foreign student enrollments. FSAs can read the *Chronicle*'s international section for information about issues confronting educational systems in various countries.

the Middle East, is that of a fixed body of knowledge and wisdom being transmitted from teachers to students.)

9. What intellectual skills (for example, memorization, analysis, synthesis) does the system reward?

10. How is students' academic work evaluated?

Some knowledge of the responses to each of these questions will make FSAs reasonably well informed about the educational systems of their students' countries.

Whatever their educational backgrounds, most foreign students in the United States find certain aspects of the American system of higher education novel. The aspects to which they are most likely to have to make some adjustments are the following:

1. having to select from among a number of possible courses rather than following a prescribed curriculum, and being expected to make those selections themselves rather than having them made by a teacher or adviser

2. being assigned an academic adviser rather than simply reading about courses that must be taken

3. specializing later rather than earlier in the undergraduate program and thus having to take courses outside their areas of interest in order to obtain a "liberal education"

4. having to take objective-type tests (such as true-false and multiple-choice) rather than, or in addition to, essay examinations

5. dealing with a sometimes complex system for registering for classes each term, coupled with a complex system, complete with deadlines and extra fees, for making changes in registration

6. encountering teachers, especially at the graduate level, who prefer to be treated far more informally than is normal or even acceptable in other systems

7. having relatively frequent assignments and examinations or quizzes rather than being left to work more independently and at a leisurely pace

8. encountering classmates, especially at the freshman and sophomore levels, who seem ill prepared for postsecondary work and not very highly motivated to succeed at it

9. encountering classmates whose classroom behavior is so informal as to seem utterly disrespectful

10. being expected to raise questions and participate in class discussion rather than sitting quietly and accepting the teacher's word on all matters

11. encountering competitiveness among students, especially in graduate and professional classes

12. having to analyze and synthesize the material to which they are exposed, especially at the graduate level

13. being expected to use the library extensively

14. needing to learn to use computers in conjunction with several normal student undertakings, including writing papers for classes, doing calculations for classes or laboratories, registering for classes, locating books in the library, and doing bibliographic searches

15. having a great deal of importance attached to grades

16. having to do what they might consider menial tasks in laboratory courses

17. being liable to punishment for activities regarded as cheating or plagiarism

FSAs need to know about these characteristics of American postsecondary education so they can understand students' reactions to them and help the students adjust to the demands made upon them.[12]

Cultural backgrounds

The topic of foreign students' cultural backgrounds is exceedingly complex. Anthropologists, who have the longest record of scientific interest in culture and cultural differences, have not reached an agreement as to how the topic is best approached. Nor have social psychologists, some of whom have more recently become interested in the phenomena of culture, culture contact, and adjustment to new cultures. We will elaborate on some of these issues later in this chapter, under "intercultural communication." Meanwhile, here is a list of questions FSAs might want to ask about their students' cultural

---

[12] Gregory A. Barnes's *The American University: A World Guide* offers a highly readable overview of the American higher education system as it compares to higher education systems elsewhere. Especially interesting are his case studies of typical American college students, with information about their high school backgrounds, their attitudes toward education, and the ways they spend their time.

backgrounds. These questions relate to situations that involve students, faculty and staff, and bureaucracies.

1. How are differences in status (for example, student-teacher) handled?

2. What is the prevalent conception of the locus of control over people's lives? That is, are the things that happen to people usually viewed as products of their own decisions and behavior, of the workings of political or social forces, of fate, or of some other factor?

3. What are the predominant friendship patterns, with respect to length of relationship and extent of mutual obligation?

4. What are the most common forms of verbal interaction in everyday relations with respect to the following: discussion topics that are considered appropriate in various situations, volume of voice, length of each separate contribution to a conversation, style of interaction (debate, argument, ritual exchange), and nonverbal accompaniments to speech? How direct and explicit are people expected to be when they speak with each other? Who is deemed mainly responsible for assuring that effective interpersonal communication takes place—the speaker or the listener?

5. Where (if anywhere) do people go for help with personal problems?

6. What assumptions shape male-female relationships?

7. What kinds of evidence—scientific tests, personal observations, the word of the Prophet, etc.—are considered persuasive?

The answers to these and related questions will help an FSA begin to know another culture.

Sources of information about the educational and cultural backgrounds of foreign students

Some people spend their entire professional lives studying selected aspects of the culture and educational system of just one or perhaps a few other countries. FSAs clearly cannot do that. They must content themselves with general familiarity with their students' backgrounds. Publications, conferences, professional colleagues, and foreign students and scholars themselves can provide them much useful information.

Publications. Books and articles about business practices in specific other countries have become numerous in the past decade, but ones devoted to culture and students are still unusual. Two that do focus on students and their cultural backgrounds are Orin Parker's *Cultural Clues to the Middle Eastern Student* and my own *Students from the Arab World and Iran*. My article "Counseling Malay Students"[13] also furnishes information about both the cultural and educational backgrounds of a certain group of students. Both NAFSA and AACRAO (American Association of Collegiate Registrars and Admissions Officers) have publications concerning the educational systems of various countries. A list of these and related publications is available from NAFSA in the form of an "ADSEC Bibliography."

Of course, many publications not mainly about students or education contain culture-specific information that is useful to FSAs. Social science studies, personal accounts, and fiction all provide avenues to learning about foreign students' cultural backgrounds. Many such publications are mentioned elsewhere in this book.

Conferences. NAFSA conferences often include presentations about students from particular countries. These presentations are most often given by teachers of English as a second language and focus on classroom behavior. The information they contain can be helpful to FSAs. Unfortunately, these presentations do not often find their way into print. But audiotapes of most conference sessions are available for purchase soon after the sessions end.

Professional colleagues. It is the job of foreign admissions specialists to know or have ready access to information about foreign educational systems. FSAs can borrow these materials from the admissions personnel on their campuses. Many faculty members are knowledgeable about at least some aspects of other countries, because of their academic interests and/or because they were born or have lived abroad. Certainly they can be called upon to help FSAs learn about foreign students' backgrounds. Both NAFSA and AACRAO have their acknowledged experts on specific foreign countries, and these individuals are normally pleased to respond to inquiries.

Foreign students and scholars. Foreign students and scholars can teach FSAs much that they would benefit from knowing about other countries. The two sets of questions presented earlier in this section, when addressed to foreign students or scholars, will generate

---

[13] In *Building the Professional Dimension of Educational Exchange,* edited by Joy Reid. This book contains several essays useful for FSAs.

many interesting ideas. (The questions on the cultural background list are most likely to be understood and answered appropriately if they are prefaced by the phrase, "Compared to what you have seen in the United States,...")

I like to organize sessions in which a panel of students (selected for dispassion and articulateness in English) from a particular country or world area addresses a set of questions before an audience of faculty and staff who have occasion to interact with students from that country or area. The questions, presented in Appendix E, concern the educational system and cultural background of their country or area as compared to that of the United States. Holding a session of this kind serves a number of beneficial purposes. It helps FSAs and other institutional personnel gain useful information; it promotes constructive relationships and attitudes between foreign students and the faculty and staff who attend the session; it contributes to the realization that foreign students can make valuable contributions to the institution; and it gives the foreign students the pleasurable experience of being in the role of expert, an experience for which the FSA is seen to be responsible. All of these beneficial outcomes strengthen the FSAs' influence among students, staff, and faculty.

Of course, FSAs can learn from foreign students and scholars without organizing formal sessions. Talking informally with them and asking about their experiences and observations in the United States can lead to insightful comments about the culture in which they grew up.

The issues facing foreign students

Foreigners anywhere face certain issues or problems.[14] Of course, the nature and severity of those problems vary. The variations seem

---

[14] Dennison Nash's *A Community in Limbo* is a provocative anthropological study of the American community in a city in Spain. It is based on interviews and documents. Nash offers a typology of adjustment styles: bohemian, creative, and philistine. Among the variables he thinks affect the foreigners' reactions are their social status; organizational affiliations; past experience in other cultures (especially whether or not they have experience in a less rationally oriented culture); gender; personality type (organization person versus individualist); amount of support from home organizations; relations with other Americans in the community; and relations with hosts. One can think in comparable terms about foreign students in the United States and come up with some interesting ideas.

to depend on the individual characteristics and the cultural background of the people involved, and on the situations in which the foreigners find themselves. Social scientists have been seeking a definitive list of the personality characteristics that make for competence or success in intercultural relationships.[15] Milton J. Bennett's list of personal qualities associated with intercultural competence, offered in his essay "Intercultural Communication" (134), includes tolerance of ambiguity, respect for difference, curiosity, cognitive complexity ("the kind of intelligence that allows for multiple and often contradictory frames of reference"), and humor and humility. L. Robert Kohls, in *Survival Kit for Overseas Living*, says the most important characteristics are sense of humor, the ability to fail, and a low goal/task orientation. In a study aimed at determining valid predictors of success in intercultural interactions, D. P. S. Bhawuk and Richard W. Brislin found that the best predictor was willingness to eat ethnic foods!

Ingemar Torbiörn, in an essay "Dynamics of Cross-cultural Adaptation," discusses the idea of "culture barriers" in intercultural interactions and offers some analysis of those barriers. One of his points is that the height of culture barriers is different among different pairs of countries and that people with higher barriers to cross are likely to have more trouble in the new culture. For example, there is considerable evidence that African and Asian students in the United States have more serious adjustment difficulties than do students from Europe and Oceania.[16]

Because there is so much variation in the nature and severity of problems foreign students in the United States encounter, one must be cautious in generalizing about them. But FSAs need to have some broad perspectives on these problems. Here are a few generalizations which FSAs can refine by measuring them against the characteristics and experiences of the foreign students at their own institutions. The students' English proficiency, field and level of study, cultural and religious background, and general level of sophistication all influence the nature of their reactions to their new setting. So does the presence or absence, on the campus or in the community, of other people from their homeland.

---

[15] And of course they have struggled to define "competence" and "success."

[16] For example, see the study *Needs of Foreign Students from Developing Nations at U.S. Colleges and Universities* by Motoko Y. Lee, Makhtar Abd-Ella, and Linda A. Burks.

Most foreign students can be expected to face a number of transitory problems, such as adjusting to new food, climate, and types of housing. These are aspects of what Craig Storti, in his excellent book *The Art of Crossing Cultures*, calls "country shock," which has to do with the novel *physical* aspects of the new setting. Culture shock, by contrast, has to do with the novel *ways people act*. More about that later.

Some new students may sorely miss family and friends and are unlikely to have friends in the new setting, a fact that seems to bother some students more than others.

Some new foreign students suffer from "status shock" when they come to the United States. Those who have been out of school and have been employed and those who come from one of the many countries where postsecondary students are accorded considerable respect, are often disturbed to find that in the United States the status of college and university students, even of graduate students, is relatively low.

Whether or not they suffer from status shock, most new foreign students will experience the discomfort of being treated as stereotypes rather than as individuals. The natives will treat them as "foreign students" or perhaps "Orientals" (or Latins, or Arabs, etc.) rather than as individuals. This experience is often perceived as demeaning.

Most new foreign students, whatever their English proficiency level, need some time to adjust to local English. American regional accents, contemporary colloquialisms and slang, and the local pace of speaking will be new. Some students make these adjustments within a few days; others require weeks or months. It is not at all unusual for new students to be surprised, discouraged, and even depressed when they discover that they cannot readily understand the local people and that the local people have trouble understanding them.

Beyond these usually transitory problems are some more enduring sources of stress, many of them coming under the rubric of "culture shock." The cultural characteristics of Americans that seem to bother most students for the longest period of time are the radical individualism that pervades American society and the relative egalitarianism and informality with which people treat each other. While it seems nearly impossible for many Americans to comprehend, imbued as they are with reverence for freedom, independence, individual rights, and choice, most people in the world are not trained to "look out for Number One" in the way that Americans are. Nor are they taught to minimize the attention paid to differences in social status.[17] Foreign students have told me that even after three or four years in the United States, they still cannot bring themselves to address faculty members by their first names.

Persistent financial shortages afflict many students. They may have planned poorly, perhaps underestimating the quantity of money necessary to live in the United States and/or overestimating the ease with which they could acquire money once they arrived here. Sometimes they have what could be enough money to meet their essential expenses, but they spend it on items not necessary to maintain life or meet obligatory expenses. And sometimes events beyond their control reduce their income and/or increase their expenses.

Prejudice, or at least condescension, from the natives bothers most foreign students throughout their stay in the United States, as was discussed earlier. So do the Americans' low level of knowledge about and interest in other countries and the paucity of sophisticated international reporting in the U.S. media.

Finally, unwelcome events in their own countries can cause continuing problems for foreign students. Events which endanger lives or property, damage their families' financial situation, or diminish their prospects for rewarding employment at home all cause students from abroad to become preoccupied.

This is not to say that foreign students are continuously plagued by problems. That would be misleading. It is not at all unusual to encounter foreign students who view their assorted problems as interesting challenges and who cheerfully learn from the new situations they encounter.

APPLIED LINGUISTICS AND CONTRASTIVE RHETORIC

Knowing something about applied linguistics, and especially about the specialized topic of teaching English as a second language (TESL), helps FSAs understand the language problem many of their clients face. FSAs ought to be familiar with the problems confronting both

---

[17] These ideas are elaborated upon somewhat later in this chapter and in two essential books for FSAs: my own *American Ways: A Guide for Foreigners in the United States* and Edward C. Stewart's and Milton J. Bennett's *American Cultural Patterns: A Cross-Cultural Perspective*.

English learners and TESL teachers. It is important to understand the TOEFL (Test of English as a Foreign Language)—what it seeks to measure, how it is structured, what its scores mean, and what its limitations are. FSAs have frequent occasion to explain the significance of TOEFL scores to faculty members. An Educational Testing Service publication called *TOEFL Test and Score Manual* gives a comprehensive description of the TOEFL.

Some institutions use scores from two other English proficiency examinations, the ALIGU (from the American Language Institute of Georgetown University) and the Michigan Test (from the University of Michigan's Language Institute). Many institutions, at least larger ones, devise their own English proficiency tests to supplement the TOEFL.

Skimming TESL texts at various levels of proficiency, sitting in on ESL classes, and talking with TESL teachers are probably the best ways for FSAs to learn about relevant aspects of applied linguistics. It is especially instructive to hear TESL teachers discuss the English-learning problems of speakers of particular other languages.

In the TESL field, teaching English is not just teaching vocabulary, grammar, and pronunciation, but also a matter of teaching about the cultural context in which English is used. Thus, more and more ESL texts take as their subject matter life, and even student life, in the United States. Two examples: Carol M. Archer's *Living with Strangers in the U.S.A.* and Deena R. Levine's and Mara Adelman's *Beyond Language*.

The relatively new interdisciplinary specialization of contrastive rhetoric grows from scholarly analysis of the relationship between culture and the way members of a given culture use language. Contrastive rhetorical studies can give FSAs insights into their clients' cultural backgrounds and also into the difficulties they face in mastering English, particularly academic English. For example, Fan Shen, a foreign student writing in *College Composition and Communication* about his experience in learning English composition at an American university, said

> the rules of English composition encapsulate values that are absent in, or sometimes contradictory to, the values of other societies (in my case, China). Therefore, learning the rules of English composition is, to a certain extent, learning the values of Anglo-American society. In writing classes in the United States I found that I had to reprogram my mind, to redefine some of the basic concepts and values that I had about myself, about society, and about the universe,

values that had been imprinted and reinforced in my mind by my cultural background, and that had been part of me all my life.

Rule number one in English composition is: Be yourself. (More than one composition instructor has told me, "Just write what *you* think") (460).

Summarizing twenty-five years of work in the field of "Contrastive Rhetoric: Text Analysis and Writing Pedagogies," Ilona Leki concluded that "contrastive rhetoric studies help us to remember that the idea of 'being yourself,' or writing elegantly, or communicating clearly and convincingly has no reality outside a particular cultural and rhetorical context and that our discourse community is only one of many" (139).

Being myself, Fan Shen said, "meant not to be my Chinese self" in which "'I' is always subordinated to 'We'…. It meant that I had to create an English self and be *that* self" (460-461).

FSAs have much to learn from insights of this kind.

CURRENT AFFAIRS

Foreign students and scholars are sometimes dramatically affected by political and economic events occurring in their own countries or others. The Iranian crisis, the Gulf War, and the Chinese student rebellion are examples. FSAs need at least some understanding of the political systems and contemporary issues in their students' countries and regions. It helps to know:

1. What is the basic political system?

2. What is the basic economic system?

3. What internal issues does the country currently face?

4. What intergroup (ethnic, religious, linguistic) differences exist and how salient are they? (These differences may carry over into the relationships among students from a particular country when they come to the United States.)

5. How likely is the country to experience a major disruption (for example, a civil war, radical change of government, drastic currency devaluation, armed international conflict)?

To have some context for understanding these questions and their answers, FSAs might want to read one or two introductory texts in political science, international politics, and international economics. They will find it helpful to stay informed about developments in their students' countries or at least to bring themselves up to date quickly should some drastic event occur. Many FSAs consider the *Christian Science Monitor* to be a particularly good source of information about international affairs. The *New York Times*, Cable News Network, and National Public Radio are other readily available sources.

In some previous sections of this chapter I suggested getting information from students and scholars themselves about their countries. But I urge caution in discussing politics with foreign students. I believe that many foreign students harbor doubts about foreign student advisers' intentions and allegiances. They seem to believe or suspect that FSAs are somehow in the intelligence-gathering business. This impression gets strong support when an FSA begins to ask questions about the domestic politics of a student's country, especially if the questions might lead to a revelation of the student's own political opinions or affiliations. Other FSAs have different views; for my part, I rarely introduce political questions into a conversation with a foreign student or scholar I do not know reasonably well, and I try to avoid questioning that might be construed as an effort to get a student to divulge personal political views. Discussions about general political or social issues, as opposed to ones about a student's own opinions, are acceptable. Many students are quite well informed about political issues and enjoy talking about them, and it is a compliment to them when an FSA manifests some knowledge of the political and social issues that are salient in their countries.

It is not just international politics about which FSAs ought to be informed, but national and state politics as well. Congressional actions affecting immigration law and appropriations for international education concern foreign students and therefore FSAs. Beyond that, foreign students might ask FSAs to explain contemporary domestic political and social issues to them. An uninformed FSA cannot do that and cannot gain influence in the students' eyes.

FSAs in state-supported institutions will want to keep abreast of proposed state government measures that would affect foreign students. In the past, various state legislatures have considered—and sometimes adopted—measures concerning special, higher tuition rates for foreign students, restrictions on their enrollment, and the English-language proficiency of foreign-born instructors.

INTERCULTURAL COMMUNICATION

Intercultural communication is at the heart of an FSA's work. All of the following FSA activities involve intercultural communication:

preparing written information for foreign students and scholars; advising, counseling, and all other daily interactions with students and scholars from abroad; serving as an intermediary or cultural interpreter between foreign students and others; designing and conducting educational programs intended to improve intercultural relationships; and working with foreign student and community organizations. One can even argue that interoffice relationships in an educational institution are in a sense intercultural interactions, given the interoffice differences in assumptions, values, and habits. Certainly relationships between educational institutions and the U.S. Immigration and Naturalization Service can be viewed as intercultural relationships.

FSAs will want to learn as much as they can about intercultural communication, which is discussed here under three headings: comparing cultures, understanding the dynamics of intercultural interactions, and prescribing conduct for improved intercultural relations. After discussing each of those topics I offer a recommended basic bibliography.

Comparing cultures

We can easily see that, in general, Nigerians do not behave the same way as Japanese. Their cultural backgrounds make a difference. But how can these differences be conceptualized and described? What are the differences (and similarities) between Nigerians and Japanese or between other combinations of cultural groups? How can we discuss these differences when we are talking with foreign students, or trying to help staff members in the registrar's office understand some of the behavior they see in students from other countries? Scholars have not agreed on any single approach to this question. A large and growing number of publications from social scientists, social psychologists, travel writers, essayists, and novelists are addressing the issues that cultural differences present, and are trying to help readers understand how cultures differ. How is one to make sense of all this?

Drawing mainly on unpublished work of L. Robert Kohls,[18] I have put together a scheme that has proven useful with many audiences interested in cultural differences:

---

[18] Other contributors to this formulation are Dean C. Barnlund (for the segment about communicative style) and William B. Gudykunst and Stella Ting-Toomey (for the portion concerning dimensions of verbal communication style).

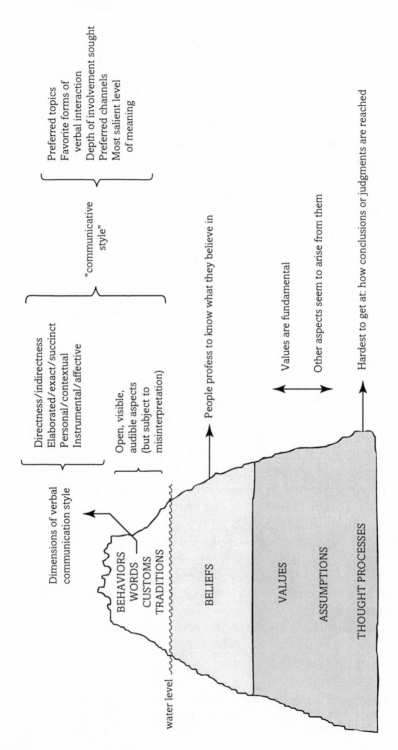

Preferred topics
Favorite forms of
verbal interaction
Depth of involvement sought
Preferred channels
Most salient level
of meaning

"communicative
style"

Directness/indirectness
Elaborated/exact/succinct
Personal/contextual
Instrumental/affective

Open, visible,
audible aspects
(but subject to
misinterpretation)

People profess to know what they believe in

Values are fundamental

Other aspects seem to arise from them

Hardest to get at: how conclusions or judgments are reached

Dimensions of verbal
communication style

BEHAVIORS
WORDS
CUSTOMS
TRADITIONS

BELIEFS

VALUES

ASSUMPTIONS

THOUGHT PROCESSES

water level

Acknowledgments: Dean C. Barnlund, William B. Gudykunst, L. Robert Kohls, and Stella Ting-Toomey

Kohls calls this his "iceberg model" for comparing cultures, because it forces one to give attention to the fact that many manifestations of cultural conditioning are invisible. Aspects of human behavior that are above the waterline—behaviors, words, customs, and traditions (which are patterns of actions associated with particular situations)—are visible or audible. Beliefs are placed at the waterline on the iceberg to suggest that, although they cannot be directly seen, they are relatively accessible to awareness. Moving farther below the waterline, to values, assumptions, and then thought processes, takes us into areas of human functioning that are harder and harder to "see." They must be inferred from actual behavior.

Many publications address aspects of human behavior that are above the waterline. Travel, memoir, and fiction writers commonly recount intercultural experiences they have witnessed or that could be witnessed. Social scientists are more likely to use above-the-waterline behaviors as examples that support their inferences about values, assumptions, and thought processes.[19] Whatever type of publication about cultural differences they read, FSAs can fit what they learn into the iceberg, which serves as a framework for making sense of ideas from many sources. For an example of the use of this framework, see the chapter of my *Learning across Cultures* titled "Cultural Differences on Campus."

The publications mentioned in the section on basic bibliography illuminate various parts of the iceberg. Appendix F, taken from the University of Iowa's *Handbook for Foreign Students and Scholars*, discusses "The Communicative Style of Americans" in a way that is

---

[19] Anthropologist Edward T. Hall's *The Silent Language,* first published in 1959, was a relatively early and still widely used effort to illuminate portions of human conduct that are below the waterline. Two later books of his, *The Hidden Dimension* (hidden below the waterline, one might say) and *The Dance of Life,* continued his exploration of the values, assumptions, and thought processes that underlie visible human behavior. Two other anthropologists, Florence Kluckhohn and Fred Strodtbeck, developed a model for comparing cultural assumptions and values, a model that underlies the ideas in two widely used publications, John C. Condon's and Fathi Yousef's *An Introduction to Intercultural Communication* and Edward C. Stewart's and Milton J. Bennett's *American Cultural Patterns: A Cross-Cultural Perspective.* A more recent look beneath the waterline comes from Geert Hofstede, whose ideas are most accessible to FSAs in *Cultures and Organizations: Software of the Mind.* Yet another model for comparing cultures, this one aimed mainly at the business sector, is in *Transcultural Leadership,* by George F. Simons, Carmen Vazquez, and Philip R. Harris.

intended to be helpful to foreign students and scholars. It is included in this book to illustrate how knowledge about cultural differences can be employed to help foreign students and scholars understand their experiences in another country. It also illustrates how aspects of human behavior at one place on the iceberg—actions, for example—are interrelated with aspects on other places, for example, assumptions and thought processes. Consider, for instance, a typical action among Americans: making a studied effort to speak calmly when annoyed. Assumptions about the potential destructiveness of displays of anger and by thought patterns dominated by what Americans consider facts and logic underlie that behavior.

Understanding the dynamics of intercultural interaction

Intercultural communication, strictly speaking, deals not just with descriptions of cultural differences, but with what occurs in *interactions* between people with differing cultural backgrounds. FSAs and their clients interact every day with people from other cultures. FSAs need to understand the dynamics of those interactions so they can (1) behave as constructively as possible in dealings with their clients, (2) help their clients understand and learn from their intercultural experiences, and (3) help their own compatriots understand and deal constructively with the cultural differences they encounter.

Concepts that are treated in the literature about intercultural interactions include stereotypes, ethnocentrism, culture shock, cultural adjustment, and culture learning. The readings suggested below discuss these and related topics. Two publications that explicitly address the dynamics of intercultural interactions are Richard W. Brislin, et al., *Intercultural Interactions: A Practical Guide* and Raymonde Carroll's *Cultural Misunderstandings.*

Prescribing conduct for improved intercultural relations

Implicitly or explicitly, most of the writings cited below offer suggestions or recommendations for interacting constructively with people from other cultures. Since this is the raison d'être for FSAs, they need to know about and be able to apply the guidelines scholars and practitioners have developed. A brief text on this point is William B. Gudykunst's *Bridging Differences: Effective Intergroup Communication.* George F. Simons's engaging workbook, *Working Together: How to Become More Effective in a Multicultural Organization,* is suitable for many audiences, including FSAs, their clients, and their colleagues.

Recommended basic bibliography

When the first edition of this *Handbook* was published, only a few books addressed intercultural communications and related topics in ways truly helpful to FSAs. That situation has changed dramatically. Even a conscientious FSA now finds it difficult if not impossible to keep up with the helpful literature that is being published. Compiling a recommended basic bibliography on intercultural communication for FSAs thus involves some difficult choices. Here are mine.

Two recent compendiums are addressed to educational exchange practitioners. Both have extensive bibliographies. The first is *Learning across Cultures.* The other is R. Michael Paige's *Education for the Intercultural Experience.* FSAs should be thoroughly familiar with both of these books.

Two books offer insights into mainstream American culture as it is experienced by people from other countries. These are my *American Ways: A Guide for Foreigners in the United States* and Edward C. Stewart's and Milton J. Bennett's *American Cultural Patterns: A Cross-Cultural Perspective.*

A popular textbook in intercultural communication is *Communicating with Strangers,* by William B. Gudykunst and Young Yun Kim. A newer text, *Understanding Culture's Influence on Behavior,* has come from the prolific Richard W. Brislin.

The most widely used classroom reader in this area is probably Larry A. Samovar's and Richard E. Porter's *Intercultural Communication: A Reader,* now in its seventh edition. A shorter reader, with a narrower focus, is Jaime Wurzel's excellent collection, *Toward Multiculturalism.*

Finally, I would recommend Geert Hofstede's highly readable and stimulating *Cultures and Organizations: Software of the Mind,* which draws on his path-breaking studies of multinational corporations and presents thoughts on countless topics of interest to foreign student advisers.

This list includes only nonfiction works, mainly written by social scientists. A list that included useful fiction, memoirs, and accounts of travel would be far too long to include here.

To stay abreast of publications in the intercultural communication area, FSAs will want to be on the mailing list to receive catalogues and flyers from Intercultural Press and Sage Publications. See Appendix C for their addresses.

Perspective

Whether or not they explicitly study intercultural communication and consciously apply their learning to their work with foreign students and scholars, most FSAs operate on the belief that their work will result in improved relationships among representatives of different cultures, which should lead in some way to a better world.

This belief will not easily be realized. University of Chicago psychologist Mihaly Csikszentmihalyi writes that "[E]very human group not only believes itself to be at the center of the universe, but also that it has unique virtues that make it somehow superior to every other group. Every culture instills a similar prejudice in its members" (70).

Csikszentmihalyi's argument is based on the theory of evolution, which, he says, affects not just genetic but also cultural and social traits. "Just as genes use the body as a vehicle for their own reproduction, a culture also tends to use individuals as vehicles for its own survival and growth. In order to ensure this end, it must convince us of its superiority" (71).

Csikszentmihalyi takes the view that human survival is going to require, among other things, people realizing "how partial a view of reality even the most sophisticated culture affords" (75) and opening their minds to the validity of other descriptions of reality. International educational exchange is one way in which people can come to see the validity of those other descriptions. As intermediaries between and among cultures, FSAs are in an excellent position to help people overcome what Csikszentmihalyi calls the "veil of culture" (72).

Edward T. Hall, in *Beyond Culture,* makes a similar argument.

INTERNATIONAL EDUCATION

Whatever one takes the term "international education" to mean, it certainly encompasses international educational exchange or the flow of students and scholars among countries. As used by various people, it also encompasses the scholarly work done under the rubric of area studies and technical assistance undertaken in other countries. Some would argue that it also includes foreign-language instruction.[20] However one defines the term, the general field of in-

---

[20] Stephen Arum and Jack Van de Water have sought to settle the issue of the meaning of the term "international education" in their article "The Need for a Definition of International Education in U.S. Universities."

ternational education includes a large and growing number of organizations, both in the United States and abroad. The one most familiar to FSAs is of course NAFSA: Association of International Educators. Other organizations relatively familiar to FSAs have been mentioned or will be mentioned elsewhere in this book. Many of the organizations that deal with student exchanges, not just at the postsecondary level but at other levels as well, have formed an umbrella organization recently renamed the Alliance for International Educational and Cultural Exchange.

Other American organizations that at least in some people's minds are encompassed by international education are the various area studies associations (for example, the Middle Eastern Studies Association) and various foreign language associations.

NAFSA itself has become increasingly internationalized, with ever growing numbers of people from abroad using its publications and attending its conferences. NAFSA representatives routinely attend conferences of the relatively new European Association for International Education (EAIE), whose members bring their own set of acronyms (such as ERASMUS and TEMPUS) into discussions with their professional colleagues.

These organizations' names and acronyms are bewildering. Nonetheless, FSAs will want to know, at least in general terms, of their existence and the role each plays. One way to stay abreast is to get each revision of the list of "unavoidable acronyms" routinely distributed at NAFSA conferences.

Immigration Regulations

Working with immigration forms is usually considered the minimal, essential function of foreign student advising. Virtually all FSAs carry their institution's responsibility for signing immigration forms. Some FSAs do little else. This section of the *Handbook* does not attempt to provide details about immigration law, regulations, or procedures. Information on those matters is available elsewhere, as we will see. The purpose of this section is to provide general guidelines about the immigration-related work of foreign student advisers. We will consider the difficulties of doing that work, FSA responsibilities concerning immigration, and sources of information about immigration law and procedure.

Difficulties

Several factors make it difficult for FSAs to be competent in the area of immigration advising. First, the immigration law itself is extraordinarily complicated. So is the manner of its implementation, which involves several different federal agencies. Faced with pages and pages of legal language, many people despair of understanding.

Second, the regulations sometimes make no sense. They may be written unclearly; they may be written clearly, but have no rational relationship to what actually takes place in an institution of higher education. Or they may be deliberately vague, leaving FSAs to exercise their discretion.

Third, there are frequent changes in the law, the regulations, the interpretation of the regulations, and/or the personnel responsible for implementing the law. Keeping abreast of those changes is a never-ending challenge.

Fourth, the immigration law gives considerable discretion to INS officers, even those at a rather low level. This means that the law and regulations are interpreted and applied differently by different people. Thus what is good immigration advice in one jurisdiction may be bad advice in another.

Fifth, it seems all too easy to get misinformation about immigration matters. Many people believe they understand aspects of immigration procedures that they in fact misunderstand (usually because they have overgeneralized from some personal experience), and their misunderstandings are accepted by others.[21]

Finally, the FSA's own personality plays a role in the manner in which immigration regulations are treated. The aura of authority that surrounds immigration-related work seems to evoke in some personalities a tendency to dominate or control others. (This idea was discussed in chapter 4.) On the other hand, some FSAs are simply not inclined to study and think about rules and regulations. It is crucial for FSAs, whatever their personal inclinations, to have a clear

---

[21] I operate by two rules of thumb in this area. One is, "People never understand their own immigration situation." The other is, "Whatever your friend told you about your immigration situation is wrong." Once in a while these rules are broken, but I have found it far safer to assume their truth and then allow myself to be proven wrong. Thus, for example, I insist on seeing the immigration documents of anyone who wants me to answer an immigration question on the basis of which they are going to take some action. I want to base my advice on my own understanding of the situation, not someone else's.

understanding of what their immigration-related responsibilities are and are not.

Responsibilities

Federal regulations specify what is required of the "designated school officials" who sign forms related to F-1 status and of the "responsible officers" who sign forms related to J-1 status. In general, the regulations require authorized school officials to follow certain guidelines in issuing immigration forms, to maintain records of specified information, and to make certain reports to the INS (about F-1 students) and to the USIA (about J-1 exchange visitors). The regulations contain no specific requirements for school officials who work with other immigration statuses, such as H-1B and permanent residence.

FSAs need to realize that the INS, not the foreign student adviser or the educational institution, is responsible for enforcing the immigration law. FSAs do not, in fact, carry badges. The FSA's job is to help foreign students and exchange visitors comply with the law and regulations, not to help federal authorities carry out their enforcement responsibilities. NAFSA's authoritative *Adviser's Manual of Federal Regulations Affecting Foreign Students and Scholars* points out that interpretations of the foreign-student regulations vary and that advisers who provide the INS with more information than is required of them face litigation for doing so. The *Manual* suggests certain procedures and guidelines "as being in compliance with a reasonable interpretation of INS regulations regarding release of information" (3-10):

1. Schools should not release information of any kind other than directory information about students to INS, except upon receipt of a written request for specific information. Oral requests should be honored only when a student is in custody, or under unusual conditions in which an immediate response would clearly be in a student's interests. Non-specific requests for information should not be honored.

2. School officials should release information pursuant to regulations only to INS and only about students to whom they have issued Forms I-20A-B or I-20M-N, and not about any other aliens who may be enrolled, unless those other aliens have given a written release of the information or the institution's legal counsel advises release of the information.

3. School officials should release information to INS only about the specific items listed in the regulations....

4. School officials should release information only from school records and not from the personal knowledge school officials might have about such matters as students' employment, marital status, lifestyles and personal conduct....

5. School officials should make a careful search of the records to ensure an accurate response.

The *Manual* goes on to discuss some ethical and educational considerations that make it incumbent upon FSAs, if they want to develop or retain influence among foreign students, to follow these guidelines with respect to giving information to the INS.

The NAFSA Code of Ethics admonishes NAFSA members who advise foreign students and scholars to:

- fully inform students, at appropriate times, of the types of information the institution is required to furnish to government agencies, and furnish those agencies with only that information required by law and regulation,

- decline to reveal confidential information about foreign students and scholars even if requests for such information come from law-enforcement agencies or organizations appearing to have thoroughly benevolent motives, and

- refrain from invoking immigration regulations in order to intimidate students or scholars in matters not related to their immigration status.

FSAs who hope to build and retain influence with their foreign students and scholars must be familiar with these guidelines and ethical standards and follow them scrupulously.

At least in part as a result of NAFSA initiatives, the INS in the mid-1980s began to deregulate foreign students. Foreign students now have far fewer occasions to need INS permission than they formerly did.[22] Some FSAs had difficulty accommodating the increased latitude these new regulations gave them and continued to seek official guidance that the INS did not want to give. It was in this context that my colleague Margaret Brooke and I wrote the article, "F-1 Student Regulations and the Role of the Designated School

---

[22] Before deregulation, F-1 students were required to apply to the INS annually for an extension of their permission to stay in the United States. Transferring schools required INS permission, as did undertaking practical training in any form.

Official," which many FSAs have reported they found helpful, and which is reproduced in Appendix G.

A few years after the INS published regulations deregulating F-1 students, the USIA published J-1 regulations seemingly intended to have the opposite effect. The March 19, 1993 regulations were far longer than the regulations they replaced. They established twelve categories of exchange visitors in place of the previous five and imposed new requirements concerning reciprocity, orientation, health insurance, and other matters. At the time of this writing, the effects of these controversial regulations remain unsettled and unclear.

So far we have been talking mainly about FSA responsibilities relative to the INS and other federal agencies. Now let us turn our attention to the matter of FSA responsibilities vis-à-vis foreign students and scholars.

An FSA's main immigration-related responsibility regarding foreign students and scholars is *not to give any incorrect immigration advice*. The consequences of giving incorrect immigration advice are potentially so serious for the student or scholar that FSAs must be very cautious. FSAs should be aware of the limits on their understanding of immigration law and procedure and be ready to defer answering questions until a correct—or at least a defensible—answer can be given. Or they may want to refer some questions elsewhere. They also need to make sure that staff members in their offices are equally cautious about giving immigration advice.

To do their jobs properly, FSAs must know the purpose of all immigration forms their clients may have occasion to use, when each form can properly be issued, and how it is supposed to be filled out.

Knowing the proper use of forms entails knowing the pertinent aspects of immigration law, regulations, and procedures. The extent of the knowledge an FSA will want on these topics depends on the type of institution involved. An FSA at a smaller institution where only F-1 students enroll will need far less knowledge about immigration regulations than will an FSA at a large institution which has an exchange-visitor program (and therefore has students and/or scholars in J-1 status), students in assorted nonimmigrant categories, and occasion to hire aliens for staff or faculty positions.

At a minimum, FSAs must know the following immigration-related matters:

1. what the Immigration and Nationality Act, as amended, says about nonimmigrants in general, about F-1 students, and about any other category of nonimmigrants the FSA's

institution attracts

2. what the *Code of Federal Regulations* says about F-1 student initial entry, temporary departure, permission to remain in the United States, changes in level of study, transfer from one institution to another, and employment; and about the regulations concerning these topics for F-2 dependents and for any other nonimmigrant categories encountered at the institution

3. what the *Code of Federal Regulations* says about school and DSO reporting requirements

4. the role of the INS and the Department of State in implementing the Act and the regulations

5. the relationship between the Act and the federal regulations

6. the procedure by which the regulations are changed

7. procedures for obtaining a student and other relevant types of nonimmigrant visas

8. the regulations concerning change of nonimmigrant status and reinstatement to student status

9. the general structure of the INS, including its headquarters, regional offices, regional service centers, district offices, subdistrict offices, and remote processing posts

10. INS personnel at the district office and regional service center responsible for the FSA's geographic area

11. the law, regulations, forms, and procedures concerning adjustment of status (for FSAs who have a role in hiring foreign faculty and staff, and/or who wish to be able to answer questions on this topic for nonimmigrant clients)

12. sources of information about immigration matters

Sources of information about immigration law and procedure

FSAs must have the NAFSA *Adviser's Manual of Federal Regulations Affecting Foreign Students and Scholars,* a readable, well-organized compendium of law, regulations, interpretations, and procedures.[23] Equally indispensable is NAFSA's periodic *Government Affairs Bulle-*

---

[23] The *Manual* is also available on computer disk.

tin, which appears more frequently than the *Manual* and carries interpretive information as well as the text of new proposals and regulations.

The fastest way to get information about new immigration developments is Inter-L, which the NAFSA office uses to disseminate information about current developments and sometimes the actual text of new regulations.

FSAs should have their own copy of the Immigration and Nationality Act, as amended, and of the *Code of Federal Regulations* volumes that contain the regulations for the nonimmigrant categories with which they deal,[24] or at least a copy of the *Federal Register* text of the most recent regulations. An FSA without a copy of the regulations is like a physician without a stethoscope or a mechanic without a wrench. Interpretive materials are essential, but do not substitute for the regulations as officially published in the *Federal Register.* FSAs sometimes must be able to read the regulations to see for themselves what they actually say—and do not say.[25]

FSAs with immigration-related responsibilities beyond the F and J categories probably ought to subscribe to the weekly *Interpreter Releases*, which is compiled by attorneys who specialize in immigration law. Much of the material in *IR* is not relevant to an FSA's concerns, but it remains an essential source of information, informed commentary, and occasional good humor. See Appendix C for the address of *IR's* publisher, Federal Publications.

Nonprint sources of information about immigration law and procedure include more experienced FSAs (preferably ones in the same INS jurisdiction), NAFSA's regional GRAC representatives, and some members of the immigration bar.

One might suppose that the INS itself would be the best source of authoritative immigration information for FSAs, but that is often not the case. The Service has not given high priority to answering the public's questions. Furthermore, most INS employees, if they do have

---

[24] The F-1 regulations are in Title 8; the Department of State regulations, where the topic of visa issuance is addressed, are in Title 22.

[25] FSAs should keep in mind that the regulations are *not* what government officials say they are when speaking at conferences or talking on the telephone, or what the prefatory materials published in the *Federal Register* say they are, or what the NAFSA *Manual* says they are (except where it is quoting directly), or what anyone on Inter-L says they are. "The regulations," one venerable FSA used to say, "are the regulations."

information that might be helpful in a particular case, are under such heavy pressure from backlogged work that they cannot easily give close attention to inquiries from FSAs or other members of the public. The INS's system for getting new information and instructions to adjudicators in the district offices and regional service centers is less than perfect, so that FSAs are sometimes better informed about recent developments than INS adjudicators are. FSAs can usually get more thoughtful assistance from other, more experienced FSAs than they can from INS officers. In fact, many INS officers, faced with a question from an FSA, will refer the FSA to another, more experienced foreign student adviser.

It should be mentioned that the instructions printed on INS forms are generally clear and comprehensive. One must be certain, though, that the instructions on any form are based on current regulations. Sometimes the forms in circulation have not been revised to accommodate recent regulatory changes.

Students and others often inquire about retaining an attorney for handling immigration cases. When considering referral of an immigration case to an attorney, it is well to remember that immigration law is a special subject that most attorneys, even some who call themselves immigration specialists, know little or nothing about. Membership in the American Immigration Lawyers Association probably reflects an interest in immigration law, but requires no demonstration of knowledge about it. Thus selecting an immigration attorney is best done with great care. Foreign students and scholars are well advised to interview more than one attorney before selecting one.[26] FSAs cannot properly recommend certain attorneys in preference to others.

---

[26] Some questions to ask of prospective attorneys for an immigration case: How long have you been practicing immigration law? How many cases such as this one have you handled? With what rate of success? What, in your experience, are the most important issues in a case such as this one? Whom do you know personally at the district INS office? What sources of information about immigration law do you routinely read?

6

Skills

Just as good FSAs need to have knowledge of diverse subjects, so do they need an array of skills. Books, audio- and videotapes, formal and informal instruction, guided practice, and careful observation of others (whether they provide good examples or bad) are all means of enhancing one's skills. Generally, putting skills to use and then getting others' evaluations of one's performance is the most effective means of developing them.

FSAs need skills in five areas: communication, administration, education and training, counseling, and self-management. This categorization is arbitrary, as is the subdivision of some of the categories into more specific topics. In this chapter we will identify skills FSAs can benefit from having and offer suggestions for developing them. In chapter 7, we will discuss putting one's knowledge and skills into operation.

COMMUNICATING

"He just can't communicate" is a complaint we have all heard. What people seem to mean when they say someone can't communicate is that the person usually cannot clearly convey thoughts, ideas, or feelings to others. People who "just can't communicate" probably cannot succeed as foreign student advisers because so much of what FSAs do involves making things clear to others. The challenge is all the greater for FSAs because they are called upon to make so many different things clear to so many different others.

The term "communication" can be applied to virtually everything people do vis-à-vis other people. Here, we will discuss interpersonal communication, writing, advocacy, public speaking, and networking. In any of these applications, as I see it, making things clear to others requires first having them clear in one's own mind. Unless one begins with a clear notion of the thoughts, ideas, or feelings one wants to convey to others, the complaint that "he (or she) just can't communicate" is likely to be heard.

Another component of successful communicating is attention to one's audience. Since FSAs are called upon to communicate with such a wide variety of people, they must make a special effort to find ways of sending clear messages.

David K. Berlo discusses these and other aspects of communication in *The Process of Communication*.

Interpersonal communication

Much of an FSA's work is done in face-to-face interactions with other people who have widely varying backgrounds and who may well have had experiences almost unimaginable to the FSA. They may speak English with a limited vocabulary, a strong accent, and/or a poor command of grammar. They may employ a rhetorical style that, by the FSA's standards, wanders and personalizes, seeming never to get to the point. In these circumstances, making oneself understood and understanding others requires constant effort and attention. FSAs need skills in:

1. making clear what they have understood others to say (usually by paraphrasing or summarizing),

2. finding out whether others have understood what they themselves intended to say,

3. being more or less continuously aware of what is taking place in the conversation (called "the process" in social science jargon),

4. adjusting the manner of presentation (relative to level of English used, the use of written and oral messages, choice of examples, extent of self-revelation, rate and volume of speech, nonverbal behavior, etc.) to suit the particular audience,

5. listening—perhaps the most important interpersonal communication skill of all.

Some of these skills have been mentioned already, in the section in chapter 2 on self-awareness. It was suggested there that people who want to become more effective in interpersonal communication may need to take a course or participate in an organized program to improve their communication skills. Reading alone is rarely sufficient, because other people's reactions to one's behavior are needed, though I recommend Robert Bolton's *People Skills* to all FSAs.

Writing

As administrators, FSAs are often called upon to write. At a minimum they have to answer their mail. They normally prepare written information on assorted topics, such as prearrival information for newly admitted foreign applicants, instructions for routine immigration procedures, and newsletters or other messages to students. They also have the usual interoffice memos, and they commonly write reports and proposals for their superiors. Some FSAs also write articles for publication.

FSAs can be more efficient and more effective in their jobs and far more influential among institutional and professional colleagues if they write clearly. The administrator who writes the minutes of a meeting, the report on a study, the position paper on a proposed new policy, or the proposal for a project is often the one best situated to influence the outcome. Skill in writing pays many dividends; the inability to write well, especially to an audience of academics, is punished by deprivation of attention, respect—and influence.

William Zinsser's *On Writing Well* is a good general overview of the craft of writing. Jefferson D. Bates's *Writing with Precision* gives practical advice to people who want to learn to write better. In *Revising Prose,* Richard A. Lanham describes procedures for improving something one has already written.[1] Courses in expository writing can help; so can a colleague who writes well and is willing to act as an editorial mentor.

Many of the deficiencies in the type of writing FSAs do can be avoided by following these few guidelines:

1. Before starting, organize your ideas. Clear writing is based on clear thinking. A useful approach to stimulating and organizing ideas before starting to write is what is often called "mindmapping." See Gabriele Lusser Rico's *Writing the Natural Way.*

2. In a piece of any length, explain to the reader how the piece is organized. "The purpose of this letter is to...," "The first topic is..., which leads to consideration of...," "In conclusion...."

3. Avoid jargon, slang, and fad words. The field of education is notorious for its jargon and use of "new" terms. Recent

---

[1] One very simple suggestion: Read aloud what you have written. Most awkward constructions leap to attention if read aloud.

examples are "proactive," "prioritize," and "empower." Make it a rule to use such words carefully, if at all.

4. Avoid using the passive voice (for example, saying "It was suggested by Professor Winston that…" instead of the more lively and direct "Professor Winston suggested…"). Using the passive voice is one way in which some people manifest a need to make their writing seem formal or official. It results in stiff and unnatural wording that no one enjoys reading. (In academia, people often use the passive voice in order to obscure responsibility for some decision: "It was decided that…").

5. Make sure that indefinite pronouns (*this, these, those*) have clear antecedents.

6. Use no extra words. Make every word contribute to the message being conveyed.

7. Reread a completed piece of writing from the viewpoint of a new foreign student who has an intermediate command of English. Would such a student understand it? If not, modify the writing until you think she or he will. Then other types of readers are likely to understand it too.

Another extraordinarily useful skill to complement writing is *dictating*. Most people write six to ten words per minute, and type thirty to fifty words per minute. They can speak, though, more than a hundred words per minute. Obviously, dictating can save time, especially on longer writing projects. For a brief, readable guide to the basics of dictating, see Jefferson D. Bates's *Dictating Effectively*, which addresses not just the mechanics of dictating, but some of the mental blocks that discourage many people from trying dictation.

Advocacy

As financial support diminishes and as other interests compete for money, time, attention, and even legitimacy, FSAs and others in international education often engage in "advocacy," which is a particular form of communicating, focused on efforts to influence governmental and institutional policy.

An example of effective advocacy was on display via electronic mail when, in the early 1990s, Chinese students and scholars were mobilizing support for proposed legislation that would allow certain PRC nationals to remain in the United States if they were already in the country at the time of the Tiananmen Square incident. E-mail messages on the *China News Digest* kept people informed of the status of the legislation and the advocacy effort, encouraged them to get involved, and made specific suggestions for action. Here are some guidelines for effective advocacy, based on the Chinese students' successful effort:

- Have a clear idea of the decision you want made, whether it is wording for a particular piece of legislation or regulation, the adoption of a proposed law or rule, or whatever.

- Know who is empowered to make the decision you want, whether it is legislators, administrators, members of the board of trustees, or some other individual or group. Know the ideological and political situation of those people and, if possible, their personal interests. Know the staff members who work closely with them.

- Know who has influence over the decision makers. Is it the public? Voters only? Experts in the subject-matter area? Influential public figures? The decision-makers' staff members? Those in the decision-makers' social and political circles? The people back home?

- Know the points at issue, including the arguments in support of your point of view and the arguments against it.

- Prepare a persuasive message, whether it is to be delivered in person or (more often) in writing. Include enough background information to enable the decision maker to understand the issue and your view of it. If the decision maker is a politician, include a local angle. Emphasize the interests you share with the decision maker, and counter the arguments you expect your opponents to make. Make your message clear and concise. Specify exactly what you are seeking. Encourage and cajole like-minded others to express their views.

- In the end, express appreciation for those who lent their support, whatever the outcome.[2]

The Chinese did all these things. They were supporting a proposed piece of legislation. They identified the legislators in a position to influence the outcome of the voting, and conveyed those legislators' names, addresses, telephone numbers, and telefax numbers to Chinese students and scholars throughout the country. They furnished the same information about the legislators' staff members. They told their supporters what issues were at stake and offered talking points supporters could address in letters and telephone calls. They urged the students and scholars to get the active support of their faculty members and others of their acquaintance who had the right to vote in the United States.

Ultimately they were successful and made a point of thanking, as publicly as possible, the legislators and others who supported them.

For issues in international educational exchange, NAFSA plays the role the Chinese students' and scholars' national organization played during the post-Tienanmen period. NAFSA alerts members to issues on which an expression of their viewpoints would be helpful, identifies the decision makers with their addresses and other contact numbers, and presents arguments and sample letters.

FSAs need not wait until a particular issue arises before engaging

---

[2] In a brochure called *Advocacy and the International Educator,* Norman Peterson offers his own list of "Ten Key Principles for Effective Work with Policy-Makers." For many years Peterson was the best-known Washington spokesperson for educational exchange. His ten key principles:

1. View things from the policymaker's perspective.
2. Define and move toward common ground.
3. Build your coalition.
4. Never lie.
5. Nurture your sense of timing.
6. Work to build long-term relationships.
7. Cultivate the art of the fifteen-minute meeting and the one-page briefing paper.
8. Do your homework.
9. Involve policymakers in your activities.
10. Some animals are more equal than others. (Peterson's point here is that some policymakers are better positioned than others to exert influence on particular matters, and some international educators are in turn better positioned than others to influence those policymakers.)

For some elaboration of these and related ideas, see Peterson's article "Pulling Public Policy Levers for International Education."

in advocacy. They can at any time identify people in a position to influence laws and regulations about educational exchange and become acquainted with those people in advance, so they already know them when the time comes to seek support.

Public speaking

FSAs can avoid public speaking, but if they do so they forsake opportunities to develop influence among students, institutional and professional colleagues, and members of the community. (Of course, if they speak in public and perform poorly, they likewise fail to gain influence.)

Most people are not skilled public speakers. They start without a clear idea of what they want to convey, or fail to organize their material well, or neglect to make their presentations interesting. Many people convince themselves that they can't speak in public, as though the ability were genetically based. It is not, of course. People can improve their skill in public speaking.

A useful, lively book for public speakers is Ron Hoff's *I Can See You Naked*. Audiotapes such as "Powerful Presentation Skills" (from CareerTrack) do likewise. But books and tapes are not enough. As Hoff makes clear, one needs to practice and to get critiques of one's performance. Audio- or videotaping one's own performance and critiquing it can also help. Classes in public speaking are relatively easy to find. Toastmaster clubs offer good printed materials and a supportive atmosphere for practicing public speaking and receiving feedback.[3]

Would-be public speakers must pay particular attention to their audience. How much does the audience know about the topic?[4] How can ideas best be conveyed to them—through speaking alone or with visual aids as well? Is a theoretical or practical approach better? What sort of illustrations are likely to hold interest? Will the audience consider humor appropriate? Self-revelation?

---

[3] Foreign students and scholars who are serious about improving their English can be encouraged to join Toastmasters International. It can do wonders for students' vocabulary, pronunciation, rhetoric, and self-confidence.

[4] FSAs need to be particularly cautious about using the jargon they so frequently employ among themselves. Most people have no idea what an I-20 or an IAP-66 is, for example, or what an F-1 visa might be, and many don't know the difference between an embassy and a consulate. They are certainly unfamiliar with the INS, the USIA, the DOL, the DOS, and NAFSA.

After they have prepared a presentation, would-be public speakers ought to ask themselves if they would like to be in the audience when it was delivered. Would it hold their attention? Would they learn something from it or be entertained by it? Simple courtesy requires that a speaker not bore an audience by failing to prepare an interesting presentation.

In *Intercultural Communication Training: An Introduction,* Richard W. Brislin and Tomoko Yoshida encourage aspiring trainers to take courses not just in public speaking, but in debate as well. Doing so can help prepare them to deal with the disagreements, confrontations, and emotional reactions they will encounter during training programs.

Networking

Another special kind of communication, what has come to be called "networking," pertains to the establishment of cordial relationships with a group of people one does not see every day, but whose positions render them potentially helpful. These people might work in other offices in the institution, in the community, or even in other educational organizations. I include networking here because I have been struck by the degree to which the presence or absence of a network affects an FSA's influence. Some FSAs operate in relative solitude or even isolation, remaining unknown as individuals to others in their institutions. Others have large networks. They know a number of institutional colleagues personally and sometimes interact with them on matters unrelated to work.

FSAs with a good network have more influence. After all, people in organizations—even those with power—can in reality accomplish little alone. Things that happen in organizations do so because a group of people work harmoniously toward some end they consider worthy, and those who get things done are those whom others know and respect.

To enhance their influence, FSAs should build a network among the faculty, staff, and community members who potentially have something to contribute to the foreign-student program. Being sociable is of course a key to networking, but even relatively shy people can take the initiative to get out of the office and get to know people elsewhere. Good networkers are personally acquainted with those who make things happen in the organization. They know not only what responsibilities those individuals have, but something about their work and perhaps even their home life. They make it a point to see others in their network from time to time, or phone them or send an e-mail message. They attend receptions, retirement parties, holiday gatherings, and other social events where they can, as my colleague Tim McMahon says, "schmooze." They clip or photocopy articles for people in their network and send a note of congratulation if someone in the network accomplishes something noteworthy. They offer help when it seems appropriate to do so. When a new person joins the staff of an office whose work touches on theirs, FSAs who attend to their network make a point of meeting them and making them feel welcome. Having a network pays off incalculably when the time comes to deal with some pressing issue.

ADMINISTRATION

FSAs are rarely high-level administrators responsible for long-range planning, formulating large budgets, developing significant new undertakings for the institution, or coordinating large-scale operations. Nevertheless, FSAs can benefit from developing skills in the traditional administrative areas of planning, evaluating, and coordinating. Managing time well and using committees and meetings effectively are other administrative skills FSAs need. Before turning to these topics, however, let us consider two less precise but equally important subjects—working within a bureaucracy and playing politics.

Working within a bureaucracy

Whether they work in small or large institutions, FSAs are in hierarchical structures with certain job descriptions, reporting channels, and routine procedures for getting things done. The advantages and disadvantages of the bureaucratic form of organization have long been debated and no doubt will continue to be. Whatever one's views on this topic, FSAs can be more successful if they learn how to work within the confines of the bureaucracy, changing (or trying to change) the way the bureaucracy works when it seems warranted to do so.

Attitude. Probably the most constructive attitude to take toward one's bureaucracy is one of bemused engagement. That is, be serious, but not too serious. Not being serious enough—doing whatever one feels moved to do, whenever and however one feels moved to do it—will earn one the reputation for being a "loose cannon," that is, an unpredictable person lacking judgment and common sense.

Loose cannons evoke skepticism, if not fear, among their colleagues in the bureaucracy. Even their best ideas will not attract allies. They have no influence.

On the other hand, it is easy to become cynical about bureaucracy. One sees in academia all too many examples of the workings of "the Peter Principle,"[5] which says that people in an organization are promoted until they reach their level of incompetence. In academic bureaucracies, things change with legendary slowness. Responsibility may be so diffuse that one cannot determine who has made, or could make, a particular decision.

Cynicism can also result when management trends from the corporate world find their way into education. Some colleges and universities have taken very seriously—at least for a while—such techniques as zero-based budgeting, quality circles, strategic planning, and total quality management. When it is all over and nothing seems to have changed, the cynics' point of view is reinforced. Cynics hold to the view that "It doesn't matter what I do. Nothing ever changes. Nobody cares." Cynics may have influence, but it will be negative influence.

FSAs are probably best equipped to function effectively if they accept that bureaucracy is a reasonable form of organization, one in which beneficial ends can be accomplished by people who are patient, persistent, and skillful at working within its confines. Things *do* change, if slowly.

People who work in bureaucracies need to fully accept and act upon the idea that it is their supervisor's job to answer their questions and respond to their requests. I have encountered many FSAs who express reluctance to "bother" their superiors with requests they know will be unwelcome. I think that view leads to inaction, ineffectiveness, and festering discontent. A more appropriate view is, "I know that my boss won't want to hear about this, but it's my job to bring it to her attention and her job to do something about it. I wouldn't be doing my job if I didn't raise the issue, and she would not be doing hers if she didn't try to do something about it. If she doesn't like to hear about things like this, that's her problem, not mine." (Review the discussion about problem ownership in chapter 4.)

---

[5] Laurence Peter's and Raymond Hull's *The Peter Principle* is amusing and insightful. So are the two Albert J. Bernstein and Sydney Craft Rozen books mentioned previously, *Dinosaur Brains* and *Neanderthals at Work*.

Timing and approach do need attention, however. Issues can be raised at better and worse times and in better and worse ways.[6] An effective administrator will raise them, though, rather than try to ignore them.

Knowledge. To reiterate: FSAs, and anyone else who wants to work effectively in a bureaucracy, must know the institutional structure—the locus of authority for decision making on any matter that may arise. FSAs need to know who makes decisions on such matters as registration procedures, special fees for students, how the institutional seal can be used, who can best help resolve roommate disputes in the residence halls, and what variations in student billing or fee payment procedures can be allowed. Otherwise, FSAs cannot put their bureaucratic skills into practice and won't be effective.

Skills. The skills required for working in a bureaucracy are far easier to list than to elaborate upon, because the manner of their implementation varies so much from institution to institution and from situation to situation. Most of these skills require making judgments that take many factors into account.

1. Acting within the scope of one's authority, not exceeding it (by making promises one is not in a position to keep, for example, or approving things one is not empowered to approve), or failing to act within one's authority to its fullest extent (by referring clients elsewhere for matters that one is expected to take care of oneself). To assist in making judgments as to whether or not a particular matter is within the scope of one's authority, one can ask, "Am I the proper person to make the decision needed here?"

2. Including superiors in questions that involve policy or ethics (as opposed to the implementation of settled procedures). Ask, "Do we have a routine way of dealing with this or does it raise issues that need attention from people with more authority than I have?"

---

[6] Books on managing your boss and on being effective in organizations commonly suggest that one learn whether one's boss prefers to deal with issues that are presented in person or in writing. More precision than that is possible. I recently talked to an effective bureaucrat from a country where the fine points of interpersonal dealings get more attention than they commonly do among Americans. He said he paid attention not only to whether people preferred to get new ideas in writing or in person, but whether those who preferred the "in person" approach were most receptive when they were in the office, out for a walk, sharing a meal, or riding in a car.

3. Consulting others whose approval or participation would be required to implement a decision, for example, consulting with the housing officer before telling a sponsoring agency that your institution could accommodate twenty new students next term. Ask, "Can I implement this decision myself or would I need someone else's agreement or participation to do so?"

4. Going through channels, that is, referring to the appropriate person, via the proper organizational route, those matters of which one cannot dispose independently. Ask, "From whom does the person whose action is needed on this receive requests (or orders) to take action?" Remember that the organizational route to a person who is above oneself in the hierarchy, or who is in a different chain of command, is normally through one's own superior.

5. Keeping others informed about what you are doing or have done. Ask, "Who would want or need to know about this? Would it be to my advantage (as the FSA) if someone knew about this?" Memos, copies of correspondence, meetings, and reports are conventional ways of keeping others informed within a bureaucracy. FSAs usually find it advantageous to have those above them in the hierarchy (all the way to the top, if possible) informed, at least in general terms, of what they do and what issues they face.

6. Writing down important things—as an aid to memory, as a record of decisions made or advice offered, and as a basis for handling subsequent, similar cases. Ask, "Is it absolutely clear that it would be a waste of effort to have a record about this?" Unless the answer is unambiguously positive, write something down. I have been amazed at the number of instances when I have been inconvenienced, hampered, or perceived as inept for failing to have kept notes about some interaction that seemed trivial at the time it took place.

7. Being persistent and patient. Worthy things can be accomplished in a bureaucracy. Perhaps not today or this week or even this year, but eventually. Persistent and patient effort—combined with influence—can make things happen.

Playing politics

"I don't get into playing politics," many FSAs will say. They might as well go on to say that "I deliberately avoid increasing my influence and effectiveness in my organization," because that is what they are doing if they stay out of campus politics, for campus politics is how things get done.

"Politics," says Paul L. Moore,[7] "refers to the processes that produce policy and direction for an organization. Political behaviors are those behaviors designed to influence or determine institutional policy and direction"(2). Those who opt out of politics opt out of the opportunity to influence institutional policy and direction.

Peter Block's insightful *The Empowered Manager*[8] explains why playing politics has a bad name among good-hearted people. The *old* way of playing the political game, he says, involves

- manipulating situations and, at times, people;
- managing information and plans carefully to our own advantage;
- invoking the names of high-level people when seeking support for our projects;
- becoming calculating in the way we manage relationships;
- paying great attention to what the people above us want from us;
- living with the belief that in order to get ahead, we must be cautious in telling the truth (9).

Block advocates what he calls "authentic tactics" in place of these traditional political behaviors. Among them:

- Say no when you mean no
- Share as much information as possible
- Use language that describes reality
- Avoid repositioning for the sake of acceptance (96)

Some books mentioned in footnote 7 contain specific suggestions for those who realize the importance of campus politics and seek to play it effectively. The nub of the suggestions in these and in many

---

[7] Moore's book, a collection of essays, is called *Managing the Political Dimension of Student Affairs.* Other useful books on the subject of organizational politics include Christopher Matthews's *Hardball: How Politics Is Played—Told by One Who Knows the Game,* Andrew J. DuBrin's *Winning Office Politics,* and Marilyn Moat Kennedy's *Office Politics: Seizing Power, Wielding Clout.*

[8] Although the title of Block's book indicates that it is addressed to managers, it contains ideas and suggestions that anyone in a hierarchical organization could benefit from reading and taking to heart.

of the popular books on organizational leadership seems to be, tell the truth, or be straight with people.[9] For whatever reasons, people in organizations sometimes seem inclined to avoid or obscure the truth. They fail to acknowledge their own contribution to whatever problems they do see, and/or fail to tell other people the truth about what they see. An excellent way to gain influence in an organization, over the long run, is to tell the truth as one sees it. In doing so, one must consistently acknowledge that others might see things differently.

Planning

In one of the encounters that form the basis of his book *Cross-Cultural Dialogues: 74 Brief Encounters with Cultural Difference*, Craig Storti recounts an interchange between an American businessperson named Bev and an Arab employee named Latifah. In the interchange, Bev suggests that a better job of analyzing fuel price trends might have made a previous month's projections more accurate. "Something tells me we should have seen that coming," Bev says of the fuel price increase that adversely affected profits. "How do you mean?" Latifah responds.

Storti's analysis of this encounter deserves to be quoted at length:

> Bev [the American] believes the world is essentially a predictable place, that it operates according to certain laws and patterns, and that those laws and patterns, once pinned down and figured out, will always hold true. If something unexpected happens, it's not because the world is capricious and arbitrary, but because one didn't read the signs well enough. In other words, there's a reason or an explanation for why things happen the way they do, and one can know those reasons if one but takes the trouble.
>
> Latifah, who is an Arab, believes there's a reason too, a very definite pattern or plan in the way events unfold, but she does not feel that people can know it. They're welcome to try, of course, and may even figure out a few minor patterns here and there, but there is much that will ultimately remain unknowable. This is not to say that we shouldn't plan for the future or try to take matters into our own hands, only that we shouldn't become too fond of our plans or too sure of our hands (109).

---

[9] My colleague Tim McMahon, a zealous reader of literature on leadership, pointed this out to me.

The world of international educators has been buffeted by major, unanticipated developments in the last two decades. The rise and fall of OPEC, the Iranian revolution, the collapse of the Soviet empire and the opening of Eastern Europe, and the Tiananmen Square fighting and its aftermath are examples. The fax and electronic mail are bringing about dramatic, largely unpredicted and unpredictable changes in the way international educators work. On individual campuses, too, unexpected changes often take place. A supportive supervisor takes a job elsewhere, or an obstructive dean moves on. Latifah is correct to believe that, no matter how thoughtful and deliberate we are, we cannot develop foolproof plans.

But Storti is no doubt also right to suggest that there can be value in planning, as long as the result is not taken too seriously.

Why plan? Having a plan gives an FSA something to work toward, some basis for establishing priorities. The activity of planning forces one to think systematically about what and how well one is doing, about what the future might bring, and about what one is truly trying to achieve. However busy they may be with "putting out fires," FSAs do have spare moments at the office and in the shower when they could be thinking about or working toward some longer-term objective. Without such an objective in mind, however, those spare moments are likely to be spent thinking about the day's fires.

How to plan. Keeping in mind Storti's caution about becoming too fond of our plans, FSAs can employ strategic planning to help themselves think systematically about the present and the future. In *Strategic Planning for Public and Nonprofit Organizations*, John D. Bryson offers a framework I have found helpful. His procedure has eight steps:

1. *Initiating and agreeing on a strategic planning process.* The procedure will not work without widespread common understanding of what it entails and widespread agreement to take part.

2. *Clarifying organizational mandates.* Determine what responsibilities you are *required* to undertake, for example, signing certificates of eligibility for F-1 and perhaps J-1 status.

3. *Clarifying organizational mission and values.* What, generally, is your office trying to achieve? In responding to that question, carry out a *stakeholder analysis*. Stakeholders are those who have a valid reason to be concerned with what you do and how you do it. Who are your stakeholders? How well do they think you are doing what they think you should be doing?

4. *Assessing the external environment.* What are the opportunities your office faces? The threats?

5. *Assessing the internal environment.* What are your office's strengths? Its weaknesses?

6. *Identifying the strategic issues your organization faces.* Given the above, what issues do you face now, and what issues can you anticipate?

7. *Formulating strategies to manage the issues.* What can you do to get where you want to go from where you are now, given the factors delineated so far in the process?

8. *Establishing an effective organizational vision for the future.* These vision statements, Bryson says, typically include "the organization's mission, its basic strategies, its performance criteria, some important decision rules, and the ethical standards expected of all employees" (61).

Strategic planning, its adherents continually stress, is a *process.* One must regularly go back and look at the eight steps and accommodate changes that have occurred in the meantime.

If such a strategic planning approach seems too elaborate, an FSA can do something simpler. Ask some foreign students and some institutional colleagues to assess what you do and to give their suggestions for improvement. Ask them, and yourself, what problems recur. Can better written instructions or staff training help? What procedures take too long or are boring to carry out? Can you think of ways to improve them? What situations represent potential for learning but are not being exploited? Are there programs you could develop to capitalize on these missed opportunities? What external conditions that you can foresee (for example, budgetary changes, increases in enrollment of students from Country X, changes in the health-insurance industry) indicate the need for changes in your policies and procedures, and/or point to areas about which you need to learn more? What would *you* rather be doing more of and less of?

Considering these questions will give you ideas for the future. Rank them, taking into account such factors as urgency, the importance of pleasing those who offered suggestions, practical matters such as the availability of time and space, and your personal preferences. This gives you a set of objectives, in order of priority. It is not irrevocable, but it can help guide your efforts and use of time for the present.

Following through on the plan. It is not enough to go through a planning process such as either of those suggested above. One must implement them. List the steps that are needed to accomplish the top two or three objectives. Schedule time each week to take those steps. Schedule time each month to review progress toward realizing the plan. At least once yearly, schedule a longer time to assess what has been done, what new conditions need to be taken into account, and how the plan should be adjusted.

An alternative, or perhaps a supplementary, way of thinking about dealing with future developments. The usefulness of planning is limited by the fact that unplanned developments occur. So, while making plans to the degree that doing so seems reasonable and feasible, FSAs might think about *developing the attitudes, knowledge, and skills that will presumably help them respond constructively to whatever does come to pass.* With this idea in mind, my staff composed a list of "guiding ideals" that we thought would equip us for facing the uncertain future:

1. Show unconditional positive regard to clients and colleagues:

    patience

    kindness

    respect

    tolerance

    evidence that you understand their situations

    respect for confidentiality

2. Make sure the information given is accurate

3. Work efficiently

4. Maintain constructive relationships with colleagues

5. Be responsive to clients' needs

6. Produce high-quality written materials (correspondence, handouts, publications)

7. Show sound, ethical judgment

8. Always be involved in some professional development activity

9. Always be learning from and about intercultural interactions

10. Always strive to do better

Evaluating

Evaluation can be more or less elaborate. George Renwick, in his *Evaluation Handbook*, offers ideas about the systematic evaluation of cross-cultural projects, and those ideas are often generalizable to other kinds of undertakings. Sometimes a few informal questions addressed to students or institutional colleagues (for example, "Does this problem come up as often as it used to?") will provide the evaluation needed to decide whether a particular problem or subject-matter area needs additional attention. Sometimes mere reflection is enough. The point is that evaluating what one is doing is an inseparable part of doing a good job, but does not have to be a complex enterprise.

In some institutions, periodic evaluations are part of normal administrative procedure. FSAs might be given guidelines for evaluating their own offices or be subject to reviews conducted by others within the institution. These procedures often entail a formal self-study, which affords the opportunity not just to assess what and how well one is doing, but to have other people in the institution become more familiar with your operation.

Coordinating

In the literature about management and administration, the term "coordination" usually refers to the activity of assuring that the various people or organizational units under one's supervision are working harmoniously together toward common aims. Some FSAs are in a position to be concerned with coordination of this type, but most are not (except insofar as they themselves are the objects of someone else's coordinating). Most FSAs are concerned with coordination of another and probably more difficult kind. They must try to assure that the people and offices in their institution are working harmoniously together toward developing and maintaining a sound foreign-student program. This is difficult because, among other factors, FSAs generally have no power over the people whose work they are trying to coordinate.

How can FSAs proceed when they are faced with the task of coordinating the work of people who are not responsible to them? First, they need to accept two important assumptions:

1. FSAs cannot hope to develop high-quality foreign student programs on their own. There is too much to do, and too many other people have roles in what needs to be done. The FSA, again, is an intermediary, a catalyst, and an informal leader.

2. Coordinating takes time, patience, perseverance, and attention to detail. The temptation to do things oneself because it is simpler must be resisted.

Operating on the basis of these assumptions and employing the suggestions offered throughout this book, FSAs can set out to coordinate their own efforts with those of their colleagues.

Time management

"He just can't meet deadlines."

"She's always running behind."

"He doesn't follow through."

People described in these ways are going to lack influence in the organization. (They may have power, but not influence. Others must wait for them if they have power. Those without power can be ignored.) FSAs, who lack power but seek influence, will follow through on their commitments. They will not keep other people waiting, either for the meeting to get started or the proposal to be written. People with influence know how to manage their time.

Books and tapes on time management are readily available, and, in many localities, so are seminars or short courses.[10] Books which I think are especially useful include Alan Lakein's classic *How to Get Control of Your Time and Your Life,* Alec R. Mackenzie's *The Time Trap,* Edwin C. Bliss's *Getting Things Done* (also available on an audiotape from CareerTrack), and James T. McKay's *The Management of Time.* For some important ideas on the psychological and philo-

---

[10] Many colleges and universities have professional development units that offer short courses for faculty and staff. Time management is a topic such courses commonly address. Professional development firms such as CareerTrack and Nightingale Conant offer one-day seminars on time management and other management and self-improvement topics, conducted by trainers who travel from city to city. These firms also sell audio- and videotapes of their seminars. Their addresses are in Appendix C.

sophical context of time management, see Covey's *The Seven Habits of Highly Effective People.* The third of his seven habits is "put first things first."[11]

I recommend buying two or three of these relatively inexpensive paperback books or audiotapes about time management and reading or listening to one every nine months or so, and then reviewing them periodically. This approach helps in developing and maintaining good time-use habits. The maintenance part is important, because people tend to regress into sloppy practices.

Most people readily find reasons for not committing themselves to improving their time-management habits. The principal explanation FSAs offer for not modifying their time-use habits is that they cannot adopt any practice that would limit their availability to foreign students. They know that time-management experts all recommend scheduling times that are kept free from interruptions. "I can't do that," many FSAs say. "A student may need to see me."

FSAs who cannot overcome the assumption that they must be accessible to students at virtually any time will always be firefighters. Reading for professional development purposes, writing reports and proposals, planning a new orientation program, and evaluating a cross-cultural training session are activities that require some concerted attention, free from interruptions. It took me two years as an FSA to realize that. Then I began setting aside one day or two half days per week when I had no appointments, took no telephone calls, and locked my office door. I told the secretary to interrupt me only in case of fire or poisonous gas. "If there's a *real emergency*," I said, "dial 911."

No disaster ensued. No student ever died or got deported for having to wait one day to talk to me. Meanwhile, I accomplished a great deal, and my mental health improved dramatically.

---

[11] See also Covey, Merrill, and Merrill, *First Things First,* which contains an interesting critique of the various schools of time management. It makes the point that it doesn't matter how efficiently you climb the ladder if the ladder is leaning against the wrong wall (20). In other words, attention to effective time management is subordinate to the establishment of proper goals. The authors give several warnings against overzealous use of time-management techniques, arguing that many crucial functions of administrative leadership, such as establishing constructive working relationships with colleagues, cannot be done efficiently.

Making productive use of committees

Committees, like bureaucracies, have advantages and disadvantages. Wise FSAs will recognize the advantages of committees, seek their establishment when appropriate, get themselves placed on pertinent ones (at least in an ex officio capacity), and develop the skills needed to profit from committee work.

Committees, especially those mainly concerned with foreign students and/or scholars, can perform several functions that are valuable for foreign student advisers. The functions include:

1. providing a forum for disseminating information about specific issues or problems related to foreign students or about the institution's foreign student program

2. providing a source of ideas, reactions, and suggestions from disinterested colleagues

3. lending legitimacy to acts that might otherwise be attributed to the FSA personally (such as decisions about financial aid or admission)

4. involving in the foreign student program institutional colleagues who might otherwise have no occasion to develop an interest in or informed opinions about students and scholars from abroad

5. providing a basis for constructive, informal relationships with institutional colleagues

To realize these benefits, most FSAs will favor the existence of a faculty-staff (and student, if that is in the institution's tradition) committee to serve in an advisory capacity to the foreign student office or as a forum for discussing foreign student matters. These committees seem to work best when their membership includes representatives of the various offices that work regularly with foreign students, and some additional, disinterested staff or faculty members as well. Membership on these committees is best limited to some fixed term. Otherwise there is the risk of stagnation or the development of unhealthy vested interests.

Once such a committee exists, FSAs should develop skill in assuring that it functions well. This skill has the following components:

1. providing members with the background information needed to understand the committee's role and any issues the committee confronts

2. working informally with the committee's chair to assure that each meeting is well planned and that the chair has the information and sense of direction needed to conduct a good meeting

3. working informally with any committee members who appear to need additional information in order to understand some issue the committee is dealing with or who need some encouragement to take a more constructive role in the committee's work

A final point about committees: The FSA cannot guarantee that advisory committees will function well or accomplish their intended objectives. Certain mixes of people do not jell, and clashes of personality, viewpoint, or style can disrupt a committee's operation. Members cannot be compelled to be interested in the committee's work, so some may remain silent or fail to attend meetings. Or the chair, even though an admirable and capable person otherwise, may not be skillful at conducting meetings. That skill is our next topic, and the final one of this section on administration.

Making productive use of meetings

As administrators, FSAs spend considerable time in meetings. That can be dreary in the extreme, because many people are not skilled in leading meetings in a way that makes them interesting, productive, and enjoyable. Nor is everyone skilled in participating constructively in meetings that other people lead. Meetings have a bad reputation in academia, especially among faculty. People come to meetings reluctantly, fully expecting their time to be wasted. They expect meandering, seemingly purposeless discussion, much of it a reiteration of sentiments they have heard the same people express many times before. They do not expect clear conclusions to be reached or any action to be taken.

Conducting meetings takes skill, and so does constructive participation in them. FSAs can make their own lives more interesting and at the same time increase their influence if they can run meetings well and help other people's meetings be efficient and fruitful.

Learning to make productive use of meetings can begin with reading or tapes, but, as with other skills, requires actual practice followed by evaluation from others who see the performance. Some institutions offer meeting-leadership workshops or short courses. In the absence of such formal opportunities for developing the skill, an interested group of colleagues can put together its own short course,

using readings, tapes, or films about conducting meetings, and holding practice meetings in which the participants critique each others'
performance.

In *Leader Effectiveness Training*, a book I think could benefit any
FSA, Thomas Gordon offers several useful suggestions for people
who are responsible for conducting meetings. My favorite books
about running meetings are Michael Doyle's and David Straus's *How
to Make Meetings Work* and Thomas A. Kayser's *Mining Group Gold*.[12]

Common flaws in conducting meetings include the failure to have
in mind or make clear to the group what the meeting's purpose is;
the absence of priorities among the various items before the group;
bringing up (or allowing to be brought up) matters that are not appropriate for the particular group; failure to keep discussion relevant
to the topic under consideration; and failure to make a clear decision about each item that is considered. People who conduct meetings ought to see it as their responsibility to make them as interesting and fruitful as possible. That is not always easy, because some
topics are boring to nearly everyone and some participants staunchly
engage in counterproductive behavior. Meeting leaders can partially
compensate for these difficulties by exhibiting enthusiasm and a
sense of purpose. In addition, they can try to follow these guidelines:

1. Accept responsibility for leading. Do not let a fear of seeming authoritarian or undemocratic interfere with fulfilling
   the group's need for leadership. Leading a meeting does
   not mean making decisions in the group's name. The group
   can still make decisions; the leader is responsible for conducting a process that helps the group reach the best possible decisions.

2. Make sure the topics on the agenda are appropriate for the
   particular group attending the meeting. The topics should

---

[12] Doyle and Straus stress, among many other things, the importance of having a
group's mutual agreement, at any given time, as to what issue is under discussion,
and as to the manner in which the issue is going to be addressed and decided
upon. They offer a long and helpful chapter called "Solving Problems in Groups:
The Tools." Kayser posits three phases of a meeting, each with its own tasks for
facilitators: "start-up" (hold short warm-up; initiate an open, collaborative climate);
"move-out" (maintain an open, collaborative climate; manage confusion; manage
differences; manage disruptive behavior; conclude along the way); and "wrap-up"
(tie up loose ends at session's close; check session's outcomes against desired
outcomes). He presents suggestions for carrying out each of these tasks.

be relevant to the interests of all or nearly all group members and within their area of competence and authority.

3. Know what is to be accomplished at the meeting.

4. Have an agenda, one that is either prepared and distributed in advance or developed at the outset of the meeting. (Members are best given an opportunity to modify an agenda that was prepared in advance so that the agenda is not seen as one imposed by the leader.) A good agenda will have separate sections for *information* and *decision* items, since these two categories require different mind-sets and approaches. Writing decision items in the form of questions can help focus thought and discussion. (For example, an item that says, "Should our arrangements for picking up new students at the airport be changed?" will focus discussion more than will an item that says, "Airport pickups.")

5. Follow the agenda. Cut off conversation not aimed at treating the item under consideration, recognizing that complex topics or topics being addressed for the first time may require lengthy, exploratory conversation that seems to wander.[13] If new and important topics come up, add them to the agenda or to a posted list of "matters arising" or "loose ends," so participants are assured they will not be forgotten.

6. Reach a clear decision on each agenda item. This may mean that a particular person is assigned to carry out a particular task by a certain date. Or it may mean that the

---

[13] Be mindful, during the meeting, of the distinction between "dialogue" and "discussion," because these differing approaches to conversation are likely to be appropriate at different stages of consideration of a topic. In his extremely provocative book *The Fifth Discipline*, Peter Senge talks about this distinction, and urges organizational leaders to cultivate dialogue as a means of reaching better decisions. *Discussion*, says Senge, typically involves a sort of competitive exposition of individuals' points of view. The purpose of a discussion is normally "to win," he says. But "the purpose of a *dialogue* is to go beyond any one individual's understanding.... In dialogue, a group explores complex difficult issues from many points of view. Individuals suspend their assumptions but they communicate their assumptions freely. The result is a free exploration that brings to the surface the full depth of people's experience and thought, and yet can move beyond their individual views." (241) Dialogue can help a group reach a better decision than any individual could make.

item is referred elsewhere, dropped from further consideration, or placed on the agenda for a subsequent meeting. (To conclude consideration of an item by saying, "Well, let's all think about this and we'll discuss it later" is not likely to produce a positive result, a favorable reaction to the leader, or enthusiasm for attending the next meeting.)

Thomas Gordon (1977, 136-138) lists the responsibilities of people who are attending meetings led by others:

Before the meeting, (1) reread the minutes of the previous meeting, (2) arrange to avoid being called out of the meeting, (3) plan to get to the meeting on time, (4) have your agenda items in mind, (5) have background information for your agenda items ready, (6) study the agenda if it is available in advance, and (7) inform and prepare your alternate if you cannot attend.

I would add to this list: If any background material has been distributed ahead of time, read it before the meeting.

Gordon goes on:

At the meeting, (1) submit your agenda items clearly and without elaboration, (2) state opinions and feelings honestly and clearly, (3) stay on the agenda item under consideration and help others to do likewise, (4) ask for clarification when you need it, (5) participate actively, (6) make contributions that will help the meeting move along, such as asking questions, summarizing, and clarifying others' statements, (7) encourage silent members to participate, (8) listen to others, (9) think creatively about solutions, (10) avoid disruptive communications such as sarcasm...and asides, (11) keep notes on what you agree to do after the meeting, and (12) keep saying to yourself, "What, right now, would help this group move ahead...? How can I help...?"

These suggestions about leading and participating in meetings can be effectively put to use by those who have some of the characteristics and skills discussed in this *Handbook*, particularly self-awareness and the ability to communicate well in interpersonal situations. It also helps meeting leaders and participants to have some sense of the manner in which groups typically function (called "group process" in the jargon of social psychology). Various schema for observing and analyzing group process are available (see, for example, those by John E. Jones and Philip G. Hanson). These schema draw attention to such matters as competition for leadership, the ways leaders and members can contribute to a group's functioning (by summarizing, for example, or clarifying a point), and ways in which leaders and members can interfere with a group's work (for example, by digressing, not paying attention, conducting side conversations, or making personal attacks on other members). People who are aware of these and other aspects of group process can almost always exert a beneficial influence on meetings because they can see the problems in the process and take steps to allay them.

Effective group leaders teach the group to be aware of group process and to behave constructively in meetings. One device that can help achieve these ends is called "Taking a Meeting's Pulse," reproduced in Appendix H.

EDUCATION AND TRAINING

Facing mounds of paperwork and a string of student clients, FSAs sometimes have to stop and think to realize that they are not—or need not be—just firefighters and paper-pushers. They have an educating and training role. They acquire knowledge and skills in intercultural relations that are unusual, important, and potentially helpful not just to foreign students and scholars, but also to American students, institutional personnel, and people in the community.

FSAs function as educators and trainers in many of their activities with foreign students and scholars, including orientation programs, workshops on cultural adjustment and intercultural relations, predeparture workshops, counseling (the subject of our next section), and the daily interactions in which they are trying to help students understand their situations or better manage their affairs while living in another society.

FSAs might also organize and conduct orientation and other programs for community volunteers and for institutional staff who work with foreign students. Most FSAs have occasion to train personnel in their own offices.

To educate and train others well, FSAs must develop a number of skills, some of which have already been discussed in other contexts:

1. *Clarifying objectives.* Education and training programs, if they are well conceived, begin with a clear notion of what it is that is to be conveyed and *to whom.* A careful consideration of the particular audience's situation, needs, interests, aptitudes, and proclivities is crucial.

2. *Selecting and combining appropriate approaches.* Lectures, tapes, films, exercises, written information, role plays, case

studies, and critical incidents are useful education and training methods. Selecting methods that are appropriate for a particular purpose and audience and combining them in a sequence that has some logic and that holds participants' attention requires skill and judgment.

3. *Conducting training exercises.* FSAs can provide guided practice for the program participants. To do that they need skill in conducting training exercises and discussions. This entails knowing the purpose of the activity, giving unambiguous instructions, answering questions clearly, encouraging reticent participants, dealing constructively with participants who might be combative or emotional, drawing pertinent points from any discussion, and curtailing digressions. To conduct training exercises and the ensuing discussions, FSAs need a wealth of knowledge about intercultural communication—about the role of culture in human behavior, the dimensions along which cultures vary, their own culture as it compares with others, and the dynamics of intercultural interaction.

4. *Public speaking.* Even trainers who rely heavily on experiential training techniques and avoid giving lectures have to be able to speak with confidence in front of a group.

5. *Writing.* Written materials are more effective, of course, if they are well organized and clearly written.

6. *Evaluating.* People who organize educational and training activities want to know how well they have done and how they might do better next time. This knowledge can come in part from evaluations of their programs.

Once again we will offer here the names of some useful publications, but not before reemphasizing the point that skill development requires *practice.* FSAs who hope to build education and, especially, training skills, can sometimes find appropriate programs at their own or nearby institutions. They can observe the design and conduct of programs in which they themselves are participants. Also, they can often arrange to assist a more experienced program director, paying close attention to what that director does and how effective he or she is.

NAFSA conferences, both regional and national, afford opportunities for watching experienced trainers in action and for learning about training methods. SIETAR and the Intercultural Communication Institute (addresses in Appendix C) offer short courses in cross-cultural training.

To gain perspective on the issues underlying cross-cultural education and training, FSAs ought to read two essays by R. Michael Paige in his volume *Education for the Intercultural Experience,* "On the Nature of Intercultural Experiences and Intercultural Education" and "Trainer Competencies for International and Intercultural Programs." (In fact, FSAs who engage in education and training activities ought to read the entire book.)

Margaret Pusch's chapter "Cross-Cultural Training," in *Learning across Cultures,* gives lucid, step-by-step instructions for designing and conducting a training program, offers suggestions for evaluating the program, and culminates in an extensive list of references, training materials, and sources of training materials. A more extensive treatment is found in Richard W. Brislin's and Tomoko Yoshida's *Intercultural Communication Training: An Introduction.* That book conveys considerable information about cultural differences along with its ideas about training. The portion about needs assessment is particularly thoughtful.

L. Robert Kohls and John M. Knight's *Developing Intercultural Awareness* provides training modules that novice trainers and others can use.

It is not only in formal programs or sessions that FSAs serve as educators and trainers. They do so in their work as counselors as well.

COUNSELING

Counseling is a particularly troublesome area for many who work with foreign students. FSAs are not usually trained counselors and frequently work at institutions where there are either no trained counselors or where the counselors' training has not prepared them to work with non-American (or even nonwhite American) clients.

Interest in cross-cultural counseling is increasingly common, yet the quantity of ideas and practical material on the subject is relatively limited, especially from the point of view of an FSA. While entire graduate degree programs are built on learning to counsel middle-class, white clients, cross-cultural counseling is often dispatched in a single course, or a single book or chapter. Also, cross-cultural counseling, in the context of the usual American counselor training program, usually refers to counseling relationships that involve a Caucasian and a non-Caucasian American, not someone from another country. Counselors who work effectively with students from other countries have usually taught themselves how to do so.

Nothing in this discussion of counseling is intended to suggest that foreign students frequently approach FSAs in search of counseling. They rarely do. Most foreign students come from societies where, if the concept of counseling exists at all, it is deemed suitable only for gravely disturbed people—other people than oneself. Foreign students usually take their problems elsewhere on the campus or in the community, if they do not simply try coping with them on their own. FSAs are more likely to become involved in counseling by chance, as when an unexpectedly strong reaction crops up in the midst of an otherwise routine interaction with a student or when students with problems are referred to the FSA by colleagues, other students, neighbors, host families, or law-enforcement officials. Troubled students sometimes visit the FSA and ask routine questions, seemingly hoping their distress will be noticed and then discussed. FSAs and their clerical staffs ought to watch for students whose attitude or demeanor bespeaks a problem more serious than the one being voiced. Some signs of psychological disturbance are mentioned later.

However they come to an FSA's attention, there will be foreign students who need counseling. Let us look at some perspectives on counseling foreign students, then at some of the assumptions that underlie typical American approaches to counseling. Following that we turn to the skills counselors need. Finally I'll offer a few comments about my own approach to counseling and suggestions on ways to learn counseling skills.

Perspectives

Counseling is an art, not a science. Training might help some people become more effective as counselors, but it does not always do so. Many untrained people are effective at helping others with their personal problems. Stephen H. Rhinesmith, writing for host families of foreign students, put it well:

> The chief thing to remember is that the best way to approach a counseling session is to feel natural and relaxed. Counseling should be something you enjoy and take up easily. You should do it because you have a real concern about people and you care about them in a way that enables you to empathize with them.

FSAs to whom Rhinesmith's second sentence does not apply are probably in the wrong line of work. Those to whom it does apply can learn more and thereby enlarge their ability to be helpful.

Counseling is part of a rapidly changing field. Developments in neuroscience and psychopharmacology are enlarging the number of behavioral maladies treatable with medication.[14] Meanwhile, "talk therapists" (that is, counselors and psychologists who rely on talking with clients rather than on medication) are continuously reassessing traditional approaches to treatment and exploring new ones. While talk therapy treatments are inevitably culturally based and likely to need modification when employed with people from other cultural backgrounds, treatment with medications that restore psychological balance seem effective without regard to a patient's cultural upbringing.

A misleading by-product of the talk-therapy tradition is the popular notion that counseling is largely a matter of the counselor's saying just the right thing at just the right time. A correlative notion is that something dire will ensue if the counselor says the wrong thing. I do not know its source, but I believe this dictum is apt: "Clients won't remember the words you said, but they will remember the way you made them feel."

Two other misleading ideas are that foreign students are psychologically fragile and that their cultural backgrounds are somehow sacred. These assumptions together can lead to a coddling of foreign students and an unwillingness to confront them when their own attitudes and behaviors are causing them problems. I have seen too many foreign students persevere through too much difficulty for me to be able to view them, in general, as unusually delicate or vulnerable.

Furthermore, some culturally based behaviors do not transplant well to other environments and need to be changed if the client is to be able to realize valued objectives such as completing a course of study or establishing satisfying social relationships. Thus, cross-cultural counselors may have to confront clients whose culturally based

[14] FSAs are well advised to read Nancy C. Andreasen's *The Broken Brain*, a helpful discussion of developments in neuroscience and of the best approaches to treating assorted behavioral disorders. The book is rather old, given the speed with which neuroscience is developing, but it still offers a good framework for understanding what maladies are likely to be amenable to counseling.

behavior is causing problems. One example: the passivity of many Asian females is likely to deprive them of both social and academic opportunities. They are likely to need to learn to be more assertive in order to obtain the help they need in a course or to get a scholarship or graduate assistantship.

Assumptions underlying counseling

Awareness of the culturally based assumptions FSAs and their clients bring into their interactions is crucial in counseling. In *A Handbook for Developing Multicultural Awareness*, Paul B. Pedersen lists ten culturally biased assumptions in Western approaches to counseling:

1. We all share a single measure of "normal" behavior.
2. "Individuals" are the basic building block of society.
3. Problems are defined by a framework limited by academic discipline boundaries.
4. Others will understand our abstractions (such as good, bad, fair, and humane) in the same way as we intend.
5. Independence is desirable and dependence is undesirable.
6. Clients are helped more by formal counseling than by their natural support systems.
7. Everyone depends on linear thinking to understand the world around them, where each cause has an effect and each effect is tied to a cause.
8. Counselors need to change individuals to fit the system and not the system to fit the individual.
9. History is not too relevant for a proper understanding of contemporary events.
10. We already know all of our assumptions (39-43).

Some additional culturally biased assumptions of which FSAs and others counseling foreign students ought to be aware were set forth in David Horner's and Kay Vandersluis's chapter on cross-cultural counseling in the first edition of *Learning across Cultures:*

1. Personal growth and change are valuable and desirable.
2. Individuals have control over their own life circumstances.
3. Personal problems are often soluble, through greater understanding of their origins and/or through remedial action undertaken by the individual.

4. Professional people can help others solve their problems. People (including counselors) can be genuinely interested in the welfare of strangers. People (including counselors) can be dealt with as occupants of roles (rather than as whole persons).

5. Open discussion of one's problems can be beneficial.

6. People are (more or less) equal.

7. Males and females are (more or less) equal (37-38).

As Pedersen points out, one can imagine logical contrasts to, if not opposites of, these assumptions. Experienced FSAs can recall countless instances in which it became clear, during the course of advising or counseling a particular student, that one or more of these assumptions was not shared.

FSAs cannot hope to know the assumptions and values, communicative styles, and patterns of thought that predominate in all the cultures their clients represent. A small step in that direction can be taken, though, with the help of Paul B. Pedersen's and Allen Ivey's *Culture-Centered Counseling and Interviewing Skills,* which posits four synthetic cultures and gives detailed suggestions for interviewing and counseling representatives of each.

What counselors *can* do, if they cannot know the assumptions and values of all cultures, is be keenly aware of the impact of culture on themselves and others, and know what some common cultural variations are and how to accommodate them. For example, consider the case of the synthetic "Alpha Culture" that Pedersen and Ivey create. Alpha is a "high power distance[15] culture, meaning that Alphas accept the idea that power is unequally distributed in the society and that society is hierarchically divided in a sensible, acceptable way. "In questioning the Alpha client," Pedersen and Ivey say,

> it will be important to keep in mind the importance of respect, the vertical ordering of authority in which the client has found a place, the importance of wisdom and insight, the willingness to obey orders and to please authority figures. It is also useful to remember that when Alphas ask for help they are showing their trust in you.

---

[15] Like an increasing number of people who write about aspects of intercultural communication, Pedersen and Ivey use Geert Hofstede's "dimensions" for comparing cultures. See *Cultures and Organizations* for Hofstede's presentation of his work.

Alphas will be formal and will expect you to be formal also. Alphas will tend to blame themselves as a form of politeness and to avoid conflict (138-139).

The Alpha outlook and resulting behaviors do not come naturally to most middle-class Caucasian Americans, so keeping it in mind and responding within its terms is a constant challenge. Learning and practicing ideas from Pedersen and Ivey's book can help.

Skills

Effective counseling begins with *listening* to the client. Sometimes the client's disturbed condition presents obstacles to the counselor's listening. Clients may cry, shout, or speak at great length and with great intensity. Or they may show evidence of disturbed thinking, as did a student who one day ran shirtless into my office, panting and sweating. He had evidently run most of the way across the campus. "They're trying to shoot me!" he shouted, over and over. "Please, dear God, don't let them shoot me!"

FSAs have to maintain their equanimity in the face of strong emotions and bizarre behavior. A box of tissues and an emergency telephone number should be immediately at hand. Beyond that, they must be skilled at "active listening." Margaret Coffey in her book on cross-cultural counseling lists (in italics) some aspects of active listening[16]:

Stop talking. Obviously, one can listen more attentively if one is not talking. Many Americans find it difficult to stop talking when confronted by a person with a problem. They want to calm the person down, give reassurance and advice, and somehow get the problem solved quickly. (They assume it can be solved.)

Put the speaker at ease. An attentive posture, paraphrasing and summarizing the client's comments, and mirroring the client's volume and rate of speech can serve to put the client at ease. Some typical American approaches to putting people at their ease can be counterproductive. These include frequent smiling, casual informality, and blithe statements of encouragement.

React appropriately. If you understand what is being said, let the client know that you do, perhaps by nodding and maintaining your

---

[16] Robert Bolton's very helpful *People Skills,* mentioned earlier, goes into detail on many of these points.

attentive posture. If you do not understand what the client is saying, ask for clarification, thereby showing interest and respect.

Concentrate.

Don't give up too soon. Let the client find a way to make ideas and feelings clear. Help by offering summaries and paraphrases and by asking open-ended questions.

Avoid making assumptions. People really are different from each other. Stereotypes really can be misleading. Inferring too much from the way a client looks, says, or seems to feel, and projecting one's own viewpoints onto the client may result in misapprehensions about the situation or the client's view of it. Unfortunately, it is easy to bring one's own assumptions actively to bear when one is trying to understand someone else's situation.

Ask questions. Continuously seek clarification, as well as verification that you have understood.

Listening to the client (and that includes watching the client, and sometimes taking into account information about the client that has come from other sources) readies you to employ the next skill entailed in intercultural counseling, namely, *assessing the nature and severity of the problem.* In an article called "Assisting ESL Students in Need of Counseling," Coffey offers a list of "signs and symptoms of a distressed student"[17]:

1. Dramatic decline in academic performance, reflected perhaps in marked declines in classroom attendance, classroom participation, or performance on assignments or tests

2. Exhibition of highly unusual behavior:

   a. Demonstrations of extreme emotion (for example, open crying, open and loud expressions of anger, severely blunted affect [zombie-like behavior], apparent lack of awareness of current location, date, time, etc.)

   b. Exhibition of bizarre behavior (for example, visual or auditory hallucinations, delusions [persistent beliefs which contradict reality], agitated behavior [disruptive actions; fighting])

   c. Physical appearance...dramatically different from the norm for that individual (for example, presence of physi-

---

[17] The segment of Coffey's article included here is based on a presentation by Frank DeSalvo, the director of Counseling and Psychological Services at the University of Kansas.

cal injury such as cuts or bruises; severe body odor; markedly underweight or dramatically losing weight; markedly overweight or dramatically gaining weight; seasonally discrepant attire [heavy coats in the summer, shorts in the winter, etc.])

3. Manifestation of disturbed thinking or perception

   a. Implies or states that others are watching or listening in his/her private space

   b. Implies or states that someone is "out to get me"

   c. Implies or states that suicide is a viable solution to [his or her] current situation

   d. Appears groggy, incoherent; processes information slowly or inaccurately

What is an FSA to make of behaviors such as these? For an FSA's purposes, we might divide foreign student behavioral or emotional problems into two categories, those that are related to culture adjustment and those that are not. The latter might be divided into two further categories, dysfunctional behavior and disturbed behavior. Careful observing, listening, and questioning on the FSA's part usually make it possible to place the problem in one of these categories.

If the problem falls within the area of culture adjustment, which includes normal student problems related to growing up and being college age, then an FSA might be as able as anyone to aid the student. In "Counseling Student Sojourners: Revisiting the U-Curve of Adjustment," Kay Thomas and Teresa Harrell provide a framework that can help FSAs relate many foreign student problems to issues foreign students face in the process of accommodating to the academic and social demands of a U.S. educational institution. Furthermore, they offer suggestions as to how FSAs can approach such issues. We will look shortly at the skill of giving helpful reactions.

Outside the area of cultural adjustment, students' problems might fall into the category of dysfunctional or disturbed behavior. Dysfunctional behavior might be more or less normal, but it prevents students from getting what they want or deserve. Excessive (in the competitive American context) passivity is one example. Other examples are inappropriate study habits, faulty money-management habits, and destructive ways of expressing anger. Some FSAs can help foreign students modify these dysfunctional behaviors. Others should refer them to qualified counselors.

Some students' problems fall into the category of disturbed behavior, as did that of the shirtless student who ran into my office. He was obviously suffering from a paranoid episode and needed to see a psychiatrist, who could administer medication.[18]

The skill that comes into play after assessing the nature and severity of a problem is *giving helpful reactions*. That unfortunately vague term is used here to encompass the wide variety of responses a counselor might offer a client once the problem has been made clear and assessed. Reactions might include any or several of the following (which appear in no particular order of importance or appropriateness):

1. questioning to get a more comprehensive understanding of the client's problem, situation, history, behavior, opinions, feelings, or tentative solutions

2. offering support or understanding

3. providing information the client seems to need

4. challenging the client's assumptions, information, or analysis of the situation

5. telling something relevant about one's own experience or viewpoint (called "self-revelation" or "self-disclosure" in counselor parlance)

6. suggesting a course of action or alternative courses of action

7. helping the client devise possible courses of action and choose from among them

8. suggesting or teaching an alternative way of viewing the situation

---

[18] In a recent workshop for FSAs, I presented a case study involving a student obviously suffering from the symptoms of manic depression (or bipolar disorder, as it has come to be called). It became clear to me that workshop participants who lacked personal experience with truly disturbed individuals had no concept of the nature and effects of serious psychological disorder. They suggested various ways of "establishing rapport" with the disturbed student and of logically pointing out the flaws in his reasoning. Participants who had previously dealt with disturbed individuals simply shook their heads. They knew quite well that a person in a manic episode is not accessible to rapport or logic. I left the workshop wondering if there were some way in which FSAs in training could routinely be exposed to some seriously psychologically ill people, so they could develop a realistic understanding of the limits of talk therapy.

9. commenting on the apparent reasonableness of the client's behavior or feelings

10. formulating a contract in which the client agrees to undertake some modification of behavior

11. remaining silent or otherwise encouraging the client to continue talking

12. asking the client what next steps might be desirable

13. identifying, with the client, some other person whose assistance might be desirable

14. instructing the client to proceed in a specified way

15. listening

16. referring the client to a person or agency presumably better qualified to help

What makes counseling an art rather than a science is the fact that no formulas can be offered for choosing from among these various responses. A would-be counselor must hope to develop a sense for what is—or seems to have the best chance of being—helpful to the particular client at the particular time. At the very least, the counselor has to be able to judge when a response has not been helpful and to have something else to offer.

It is worth mentioning that the sixteen types of response listed above are those familiar to Western counselors and therapists. Other approaches can be found elsewhere. Consider, for example, two approaches found in Japan—the Naikan method and Morita therapy, both of which are briefly described in Takie S. Lebra's book, *Japanese Patterns of Behavior.* Under the Naikan method, a client spends several days or even a week or more in complete isolation from other people and stimuli. The object is intense and prolonged introspection. Morita therapy begins with a period of absolute bed rest, again in isolation from outside stimuli. Then comes a period of physical work.

Both the Naikan and Morita approaches have as their ultimate aim reinforcing the client's sense of interdependence with and obligation to other people. Western approaches are not likely to have that goal.

The last of the helpful reactions listed above, *making referrals*, is a skill in itself. FSAs commonly have the experience of realizing that a particular client would be better served by another person and then finding that the client is reluctant to see that other person.

The first aspect of making a referral is, of course, knowing where on your campus or in your community the client could get better assistance than you are able to offer. It is good to know not just the names of other offices (student health, counseling center, women's center, etc.), but their locations, their intake procedures, and the names of key people there. With this information, you can more confidently explain what your client could do in pursuing help.

The second aspect of making a referral is providing the client enough support so that the act of going to the alternative helper is not excessively threatening. This may entail just giving a telephone number, but it may involve giving more information, including the location of the service, its hours, and the name of a person to see. Making a referral might involve telephoning the other office yourself and making an appointment for the client. Perhaps you can arrange for a client's friend to accompany the client. Or you might go with the client to the other office yourself, as I did in the case of the shirtless young man who ran into my office.

My approach

In addition to having the skills and awareness discussed above, it is helpful for counselors to adopt a conceptual framework for analyzing a client's problem and deciding how to proceed with the counseling. Students of counseling are exposed to an array of schools of thought about counseling. Psychoanalysis, reality therapy, transactional analysis, gestalt therapy, nondirective or client-centered therapy, and Adlerian psychology are examples. *Handbook* readers who are familiar with the various contemporary American approaches to counseling will have recognized the influence of Albert Ellis on these pages. Ellis is a psychologist who labels himself the father of what he calls Rational Emotive Therapy, or RET. Ellis's ideas stem from the Greek philosopher Epictetus, whom Ellis frequently quotes as having said, "Men are disturbed not by things but by the views which they take of them." The basic belief is that people's feelings stem not so much from what happens to them as from their *ideas* about what happens to them. Ellis argues that most people retain many irrational ideas which, when applied to what happens to them, cause them to upset themselves. To get rid of the upset and into a more constructive frame of mind, one must attempt to discern and eradicate the irrational ideas. Ideas, after all, can be changed. Not easily, but they can be.

Ellis claims great efficiency for RET. My own experience using RET with students, colleagues, and myself bears out this claim. With RET, one quickly gets at the client's irrational ideas, shows how they are contributing to the problem, and helps the client learn to dispute them and replace them with rational ideas. In the process, the client usually learns the RET approach well enough to be able to apply it without a counselor's help.

RET commends itself to use with foreign students on at least three grounds. First, it is highly directive. In general, foreign students seem less responsive to the nondirective methods many American counselors prefer. They want teaching and direction. RET offers it.

Second, RET seems to be less based on the individual-as-the-center-of-the-universe assumption characteristic of most U.S. approaches to counseling. While it rests on the way a particular individual thinks about things, it recognizes consideration of others as a legitimate criterion in decision making.

And third, RET is particularly effective with educated people, who are likely to be accustomed to thinking about things and, in one style or another, talking them over.

I would not want to suggest that all FSAs adopt the RET approach. But I would urge them to investigate it. Ellis's and Harper's *New Guide to Rational Living* is the most widely read general explication of RET. A more recent overview is in *How to Stubbornly Refuse to Make Yourself Miserable about Anything*. I think Ellis's *Humanistic Psychotherapy* is more helpful to people who would use RET in counseling. His *Growth through Reason* contains transcripts of RET counseling sessions, while *Reason and Emotion in Psychotherapy* is a thorough discussion of the theoretical basis of RET. The last chapter, which offers a number of reasons why Ellis believes human beings are predisposed to emotional disturbance, is particularly interesting.

Most of Ellis's own writing is addressed to a lay audience. Three of his associates—Susan Whalen, Raymond DiGiuseppi, and Richard Wessler—have written *A Practitioner's Guide to Rational Emotive Therapy*, an almost jargon-free book that would help anyone employ RET.

Ellis and/or associates have produced an array of books on specific problems that many people, including foreign students and scholars (and FSAs!) confront, such as procrastination, depression, anger, poor financial management, and difficulties in romantic relationships. Information about these publications is available from the

Institute for Rational Living (founded by Ellis), the address of which is given in Appendix C. Later in this chapter, the RET approach is applied to cases of angry foreign student advisers.

Learning counseling skills

Reading can provide a foundation for learning to be a counselor, but counseling is a skill, so reading is not adequate to teach it. For published overviews, see Kay Thomas's and my article on "Counseling Foreign Students," Kay Thomas's and Teresa Harrell's article on "Counseling Student Sojourners," and Paul B. Pedersen's special issue of the *Counseling Psychologist*. All of these overviews include bibliographies.

Several books can be helpful, including *People Skills* (Bolton), *A Handbook for Developing Multicultural Awareness* (Pedersen), *Parent Effectiveness Training* and *Leader Effectiveness Training* (Gordon), *Counseling the Culturally Different* (Sue and Sue), *Microcounseling* (Ivey and Authier), and some of the Ellis books mentioned just above.

"Microcounseling" refers to the crucial "attending skills" (as Ivey calls them) and "influencing skills" that make up the counselor's side of the counselor-client interaction. Ivey markets videotapes that are intended to help people develop attending and influencing skills. For information about those tapes, contact the counselor education department at a nearby university or write Microtraining Associates, Inc. (see Appendix C).

Through the Institute for Rational Living, Ellis markets books, tapes, and other learning aids, as well as seminars and courses on RET.

A number of colleges and universities offer counselor training courses or programs, sometimes with courses condensed for the summer. Such courses offer excellent opportunities for would-be counselors to get feedback and coaching concerning their performance.

Community crisis centers may provide training for people who volunteer to serve a certain number of hours.

Finally, short-term, intensive training programs on cross-cultural counseling are sometimes available through professional or nonprofit organizations. One such organization is the Summer Institute for Intercultural Communication, operated by the Intercultural Communication Institute (see Appendix C). Counseling departments at major universities will have information about other such opportunities.

SELF-MANAGEMENT

Foreign student advisers, to be effective on the job and to achieve influence on their campuses, must be healthy enough to go to work; attentive enough to learn quickly from what they read and what they see going on around them; organized enough to be able to make good on their commitments; even-minded, self-aware, and rested enough to make sound judgments; and decisive enough to lay a matter to rest without great delay and move on to the next. All this might seem obvious, but one can easily find FSAs who would not be able to use such terms to describe themselves. Rather, they would describe themselves as "burned out," "stressed out," "stretched too thin," or "overcommitted." One can easily find FSAs who, in short, are often too tired to think straight. Their lives are out of balance.

Elsewhere in this book we have discussed outlooks and skills that can help an FSA keep from being overwhelmed. For a more comprehensive look at managing not just the professional but also the personal aspects of one's life, see Stephen R. Covey's *The Seven Habits of Highly Effective People*.[19] Look also at the works of Tony Buzan, who has popularized some of the results of research on the workings of the human brain. Buzan argues that most people do not know the basics of the brain's operation. If their "brain literacy" scores were higher, he says, people would be more effective at learning, remembering, and thinking creatively.

One skill associated with the "brain work" of Tony Buzan (in *Use Both Sides of Your Brain*) and others is *mindmapping*, a pencil-and-paper technique that draws on both of the brain's hemispheres for such tasks as analyzing, planning, writing, decision making, and formulating presentations. Joyce Wycoff's book, *Mindmapping*, provides suggestions and guidelines. Mindmapping can clear your mind of clutter and help you prepare agendas, outline reports and presentations, take notes on meetings or talks, organize your "to do" pile, organize your thoughts about a new project, and devise creative solutions to problems you confront. I use mindmaps every day; I used dozens of them in the course of preparing this book.

The suggestions made so far in this section might apply to anyone in any line of work, not just to foreign student advisers. But

---

[19] Covey recommends systematic attention to four aspects of one's life: the physical, mental, social/emotional, and spiritual.

FSAs face unique frustrations, and they have to cope constructively with them. In a lively presentation called "The FSAs Must Be Crazy," Robert Ericksen and Dogan Cuceloglu listed ten common difficult advising situations:

1. *"They'll believe anything."* The student has shared information with the adviser which the adviser assumes to be accurate and complete. Later the adviser learns that the information is false or incomplete. The adviser feels manipulated and angry.

2. *"Poor me."* The student presents herself as a victim of life/circumstances and seems not to take any responsibility for having created a problem or for resolution of the problem. The adviser feels uncomfortable and angry.

3. *"Rules don't apply to me."* Ignorance or direct violation of university or immigration rules are casually dismissed by the student. The student assumes that the adviser will also disregard the regulations. The adviser feels used and angry.

4. *"It's your job."* When the student does not get the answer he is seeking, he responds with, "But...it's your job to help me." The adviser feels angry.

5. *"I won't take that from a woman."* The student (usually a male) appears to disregard information or advice offered by a female FSA. The adviser may learn that the student sought similar advice from a male colleague and the advice was well received. The adviser feels devalued and angry.

6. *"I'll only remember what's good for me."* The student appears to have a selective memory for regulations that work in her favor while ignoring others. Adviser feels used and angry.

7. *"I don't take no for an answer."* The student will not accept the adviser's response, offering a litany of excuses and "yes, but..." responses. The adviser rephrases the response in many ways, always getting the same student response. Adviser feels frustrated and not listened to.

8. *Shopping for a yes.* The adviser becomes aware of a student who has visited a number of school officials with the same inquiry. The student may be successful in getting the assistance originally denied by the adviser. The adviser feels betrayed and angry.

9. *"My friends told me."* The student reports that her friends have been given different information at other campuses or elsewhere on campus. The adviser feels devalued and frustrated.

10. *"My time's more important than yours."* The student expects immediate service in the office and does not make an appointment. The question that needs "just one minute" is often very complex. The adviser feels very uncomfortable and used.

We might say that these situations push the adviser's button. The adviser's negative emotional reaction leads to polarization in the adviser-student relationship, Ericksen and Cuceloglu say, seriously reducing the possibility that anyone will learn anything from the encounter. The adviser wants to be true to certain important principles and values, according to these two authors, and of course wants to feel comfortable with him- or herself. The typical American values that the students have violated in the incidents above include honesty (as the Americans conceive of it), self-reliance, personal responsibility, equality, and fairness.

Meanwhile, the student is focused on the relationship with the adviser, not on the principles or rules, which the student deems less important. Up until the time of this conflict, the signals from the FSA have said, "I'm your friend." The student, who presumably does not share the values the FSA sees as crucial in the situation, seeks help from that friend.

FSAs must have skill in defusing such situations, not only to do their jobs well, but to maintain their emotional health. Ericksen and Cuceloglu suggest four strategies. The first is to focus on yourself and your own reactions, realizing what value conflicts are at issue and how you are responding to this challenge to your values.

The second strategy is to explore, along with the client and with the client's permission, your respective conceptions of the situation. Ericksen (in personal correspondence) offers the example of

the student who is attempting to register well after all published deadlines, [in which case] the adviser would share the Americans' expectations for careful planning, self-initiative, etc., and the unspoken but often deeply felt reactions to the student's request. "Well, doesn't he think he's special?"...Then the adviser would encourage the student to respond to this and to share the assumptions/values which motivated him or her to handle the situation in the way he or she did.

The third strategy proposed is to explore via confrontation, telling the student

> that I am going to respond with a direct [statement of my feelings] in the hope that he will be better able to understand why I and others may seem so reluctant to help. "This really makes me angry. I work hard every day to be fair and helpful to all students. I go through a lot of work and effort to prepare our newsletter and other information materials so that students are aware of deadlines. Now you come here after four weeks of class, trying to register, and it seems you expect me to stop all my other work in order to solve a problem you created by your own lack of responsibility."

The adviser listens to the student's response and uses the discussion as an opportunity for both parties to better understand the other's viewpoints.

The fourth strategy is to discuss the case with professional colleagues, who might be able to help you regain a constructive perspective.

Noticing how often the adviser's reactions to these situations include anger, I would add another suggestion, derived from Albert Ellis's Rational Emotive Therapy. When you are experiencing anger or any other negative, destructive emotional reaction, Ellis says over and over, "look for the 'should.'" That is, look at your own internal dialogue, at what you are telling yourself, and you will nearly always find a "should." In the cases above, the adviser is very probably saying to herself things like this: "The student *should* be completely honest with me," or "the student *should* assume responsibility for this situation," or "the student *should* show more respect for me."

Any of this self-talk that includes a "should" conveys an irrational idea, in the RET framework. The "should" is based on wishful thinking (or "magical thinking," Ellis sometimes says), not on evidence about how the universe operates.

Once you find the "should," Ellis advises, *dispute it*, and do so vigorously. "Who says the student should be respectful toward me, just because I'd like it?" you can ask yourself. "Who am I to suppose that I should be treated with respect at all times?"

Then find a rational idea to substitute for the irrational one that is fueling your anger: "It *would be nice* if the student showed me respect, but I realize there is no reason to suppose the student sees it the same way." Accepting the rational idea in place of the irrational one deflates the anger and clears the way for more sensible thoughts and actions.

This is easier said than done, but it can be done. Imbibing the wisdom of Ellis's *Anger: How to Live with and Without It* can help.

The line between skills and practices is not always clear. Now we will look at an array of practices that can help an FSA be effective and influential.

7

Practices

This chapter seeks to provide detailed suggestions for dealing with several aspects of an FSA's work: aiding foreign students, serving foreign scholars, promoting culture learning, administering an office, cultivating influence, making wise decisions, and, finally, pursuing professional development.

AIDING FOREIGN STUDENTS

At a minimum, FSAs are expected to assist foreign students in overcoming obstacles that may hinder pursuit of their academic objectives. Typical FSA activities are discussed here under the headings of admissions, orientation, housing, financial matters, health care and health insurance, advising and counseling, handling emergencies, immigration advising, general problem solving, liaison activities, working with student organizations, programming, community relationships, and relations with foreign alumni. In all of these areas it is important to remember that people from different backgrounds and in different institutional situations are likely to have different ideas of what constitutes help. A foreign student seeking an FSA's assistance may expect the FSA to provide information,[1] list alternatives, recommend a certain course of action, offer emotional support, personally carry out some task on the student's behalf, and/or intercede for the student with some other individual. Sometimes FSAs need to ask a student, "What is it that you would like me to do in this case?" The FSA may or may not be able to accede to the student's

---

[1] Raymonde Carroll (in *Cultural Misunderstandings*) points out an interesting cultural difference with respect to the matter of providing information to other people. She says that Americans think they have done a good job if they furnish extensive written information, leaving any choices to the information seeker. But French people, she says, generally prefer to get information personally from a trusted individual, who may well make whatever decisions are required.

wish, but at least both will have a clear understanding of each other's expectations and limitations.

Admissions

FSAs have a keen interest in foreign admissions, because (1) the institution's policies on foreign admissions do much to shape the overall foreign student program, (2) the applicants who are admitted become the FSA's charges, and (3) many matters that come to the FSA are, at least in part, admissions matters. FSAs and foreign admissions officers have common interests in institutional policy regarding foreign students, administrative arrangements for dealing with them, evaluation of academic credentials, transfer of academic credit, financial eligibility of applicants, assessment of English proficiency, orientation of new students, academic advising, the students' academic success, relationships with other institutional offices and personnel who deal with foreign students (for example, the registrar's office and the business office), data collection, relations with academic departments and faculty, relations with sponsoring agencies, relations with foreign alumni, and staff training and development.

FSAs must be intimately familiar with the admissions procedures of their own institutions, whether or not they have direct responsibility for this function. Furthermore, they ought to know something about the fundamental issues of foreign admissions in general. These include credential evaluation, TOEFL scores, and documentation of financial resources. A brochure called "No Two Alike," available from AACRAO (address in Appendix C; ask for the larger of the two versions of the brochure), provides a good overview of a foreign admissions officer's concerns. And, of course, FSAs can learn about foreign admissions through conversations with people who do that work.

It is prudent to have a mechanism whereby the FSA, if not responsible for admissions decisions, is routinely notified of the admission of any foreign applicant. The FSA can routinely be sent a copy of the Certificate of Eligibility and perhaps of the letter of admission as well. It is good for the FSA, for counseling purposes, to have a copy of each student's application form and, particularly, documentation of financial support. As discussed in NAFSA's *Orientation of New Foreign Students,* newly admitted foreign applicants should be sent prearrival information covering a number of topics, such as transportation to the campus, housing, and costs. Whether this information is mailed by the admissions officer or the FSA, the latter will normally have much to say about its contents because it is the FSA who deals with new students and is therefore in the best position to judge what prearrival information might be useful.

FSAs need some way, formal or informal, of letting admissions officers know how the foreign applicants who do arrive are faring. Is this group doing exceptionally well? Or poorly? Are individuals in certain circumstances consistently having academic or financial problems? Admissions officers need information of this type in order to make adjustments in their requirements or procedures.

Clearly then, FSAs and admissions officers have to work closely together if both are to do their own jobs and serve their institution well. Some institutions have a formal arrangement, such as membership on a foreign student affairs committee or regularly scheduled meetings, to assure that FSAs and foreign admissions officers have an adequate forum for sharing information and ideas. Sometimes informal relations suffice.

A harmonious relationship between the FSA and the foreign admissions officer can do much to enhance an institution's foreign student program and at the same time make the professional lives of the two individuals less stressful. Sometimes, though, FSAs and foreign admissions personnel see things differently, have significantly different values, and do not get along well. Sometimes their respective offices have an historically acrimonious relationship, with the FSA viewing the admissions office as excessively rule-and-regulation oriented, and the admissions office viewing the FSA as excessively softhearted and gullible. It is desirable for both to try to understand the other's viewpoints and to develop a relationship based on mutual respect. When the FSA–foreign admissions relationship lacks harmony, calling on the services of a third party to serve as a consultant or mediator may establish a more constructive relationship.

Orientation

Orientation is the one enterprise that brings all of an institution's foreign students into contact with the foreign student office. Thus, it sets the tone for the student-FSA relationship, revealing the FSA's stance, style, and standards. So FSAs will want to pay particular attention to the quality of their orientation efforts.

As NAFSA's *Orientation of New Foreign Students* points out, orientation is best construed as a process that begins with the institution's first mailing to a prospective foreign applicant. FSAs can assure that all prearrival mailings to new foreign students are comprehensive and lucid.

The phrase "foreign student orientation" usually brings to mind the formal program FSAs organize just before the academic term opens, which can, indeed, be a major undertaking. *Orientation of New Foreign Students,* along with its accompanying bibliography, several of the chapters in *Learning across Cultures* and in Paige's *Education for the Intercultural Experience,* provides a substantial base of ideas and information for FSAs who are designing or conducting orientation programs.

In designing the orientation program, FSAs will want to keep the following in mind:

- The new students' capacity to absorb information is likely to be limited by the effects of jet lag, English-language problems, preoccupation with logistical matters such as finding housing and appetizing food, lack of knowledge of the local situation, and/or general anxiety. In these circumstances, program planners will want to ask themselves over and over, "What is this audience in a position to understand?" and "What does this audience really need to know at this time?"

- Many foreign students come from countries where ceremony is more important than it generally is in the United States, countries where high-level officials are expected to be present and to make appropriate welcoming comments. So including a *brief* official welcome is probaby a good idea.

- On the other hand, introducing a large number of institutional personnel whose names and job titles are meaningless to new foreigners is probably a waste of time and effort, if not a display of disrespect for the audience.

- New students' affiliations are more likely to be with their compatriots, their academic departments, or with other foreign students than with the foreign student office.

- Thousands of foreign students survive and even prosper without attending any orientation program.

The orientation program represents not only an opportunity to provide information and support for new students and initiate relationships with them, but also an opportunity to secure the participation and commitment of people on the campus and in the community. "Old" students, nationality organizations, community program participants, and campus and community leaders might all have a place in the program. FSAs must be judicious in including such people, however, making sure they have something useful to contribute and that the style of their contribution is appropriate. I will never forget the experience of listening to an INS official we invited to tell the new students about the F-1 student regulations. He turned out to be as nervous about speaking before the students as the students were about being in the presence of a law-enforcement official. He spoke rapidly, with a regional accent that even native speakers had difficulty comprehending. He mumbled in his mustache and relied heavily on special immigration vocabulary, assuming everyone already knew about I-20s, I-94s, I-538s, AR-11s, and so on. Since that disastrous experience, we have one of our own staff members deliver the presentation about immigration regulations.

It is easy to overestimate the importance of an orientation program. Some believe that if everything that "should" be covered in an orientation program is included, then neither the students nor those they encounter on the campus and in the community will ever have any problems. It is not like that at all, of course. FSAs need to devote significant energy to orientation, be ready to modify their approach if that seems warranted, and then explain from time to time that no orientation program can anticipate and solve all of everyone's problems.

Some FSAs say they "require" new foreign students to attend the orientation program. To me this seems misguided. FSAs in fact have no way of enforcing such a requirement, so stating that simply casts doubt on the FSA's credibility and limits the FSA's influence among the students. FSAs might be tempted to require students to attend their orientation programs because the FSAs put so much effort into planning and organizing them and may develop an unrealistic notion of the programs' importance in students' lives. FSAs are advised to adopt a somewhat more lighthearted attitude, experimenting with various approaches to orientation and trying to find ways to make their programs so enjoyable and attractive that students will want to take part.

Orientation ought not to end with the closing event of the on-arrival orientation program. As Cornelius R. Grove points out in *Orientation Handbook for Youth Exchange Programs*, the most important time to have an orientation program is several weeks *after* the students have arrived. By then students have their own questions, some of them urgent, and they have an experiential base for understanding the answers to the questions.

Different foreign student offices have different approaches to what is called "continuing orientation." Some smaller schools have an orientation class for academic credit. Other alternatives are follow-up orientation programs taking place a few weeks into the academic term, workshops or presentations on practical topics, and individual interviews with recently arrived students.

Housing

From the students' point of view, the most important issue under the heading of housing is simply finding a suitable place to live. New students naturally expect FSAs to render as much help as possible— or more help than is possible. Of course, FSAs will want to be as helpful as they can. This entails (1) providing comprehensive information about the kinds of housing available, the difficulties in finding housing, and the costs; (2) providing information about how to find housing, the nature of leases,[2] and the advantages and disadvantages of the different kinds of housing available; and (3) actual help in the housing search, whether offered personally by the FSA, through the institution's housing office, or by volunteers.

From the FSA's point of view, the topic of housing has additional aspects. These include international housing units, culture learning in residence settings, liaison with campus housing personnel, and, in some communities, off-campus housing issues.

International housing units come in various forms, including international houses and international wings or floors in residence halls. Such arrangements, if well run, can have great educational value. FSAs whose situation allows them to do so will probably want to support the maintenance or establishment of some form of international housing. NAFSA's special-interest group on international houses can provide information and guidelines.

International housing units provide obvious venues for culture-learning programs in residence settings, but such programs can take

---

[2] Many foreign students fail to appreciate the significance of leases, and too readily sign leases that bind them to conditions that soon come to appear unfavorable. The battle is probably a losing one, but FSAs have to stress the importance of reading and understanding leases and of declining to sign them in the absence of thorough comprehension and agreement.

place even without special international housing. FSAs can promote culture learning wherever there are American-foreign roommate arrangements. Providing copies of my *Learning with Your Foreign Roommate* is an easy way to begin. Holding workshops or at least culture-learning sessions with roommate pairs or trios is another constructive step.

For both administrative and program reasons, FSAs must attend to liaison with campus housing personnel, including resident assistants. The latter can be helpful in mounting culture-learning programs and in dealing with problem situations involving particular students. Participating in resident-assistant training is a good way for FSAs to be introduced to the ever changing cast of resident assistants.

If an appreciable number of foreign students at an FSA's school live outside of campus housing, then FSAs must tend to certain off-campus housing issues, including housing standards and discrimination. FSAs will want to be acquainted with the housing inspector and with the personnel and procedures involved in filing antidiscrimination complaints. They might also work with individual landlords or landlord associations to try reducing the likelihood of misunderstandings between them and tenants from abroad.

Financial matters

An FSA's responsibilities with respect to foreign students' finances begin well before the students arrive on the campus. FSAs have to make sure that the information sent to prospective foreign applicants includes complete estimates of the cost of attending. Specify items and the cost of each: tuition, housing, food, health insurance (about which more is said later), books, vacation housing, transportation, incidental expenses, and any other items that can reasonably be anticipated. Allow for inflation, and state that costs can increase. In short, do everything possible to assure that incoming students have an accurate understanding of the amount of money they will need, and state that the institution cannot promise assistance beyond any that might be offered before the student leaves home.

FSAs have to make sure the institution requires documentation from foreign applicants showing the availability of adequate financial support from reliable sources. The documentation should include a statement, signed by the applicant, affirming that funds in the designated amount are or will be available. Applicants dependent on funds coming from countries with strict currency-exchange limitations can legitimately be required to make advance deposits of a full year's expenses, or even more. Many schools have found it wise to adopt such a policy.

When newly arrived or recently arrived students say they do not have enough money, tell them the institution cannot help them. Point to the information the institution supplied about costs and to the student's own signature on the financial verification form. Explain that the institution made every effort to inform the student of the costs of attending and to assure that the student had enough money, and it simply cannot accept responsibility for students who do not heed the information.[3]

Despite the best intentions and all precautions, some students will experience circumstances beyond their control that cause them financial difficulty. For such situations, the institution needs an emergency loan fund, preferably with formal, written guidelines governing eligibility, application procedures, and terms for repayment.

FSAs cannot solve all foreign student financial difficulties. FSAs who have adequately internalized the idea of problem ownership will realize that worthy foreign students are sometimes victims of circumstances that make it necessary for them to interrupt, if not abandon, their academic programs. Not all problems can be solved.

Some countries require documentation from citizens who wish to have dollars remitted abroad. In the case of students, the documentation usually entails certification from the school indicating that the student is registered and stating the costs. FSAs should know which countries have such procedures, and be certain that students can easily get the certifications they need.[4]

---

[3] Still, differences in cultural and social background will become evident in these cases. Many students come from places where providing documents and signatures are "just formalities" and are not taken as seriously as they are in the American system.

[4] Sometimes students will ask for a certification stating that the costs are higher than the institution's official estimates. Only with such a certification can they get the quantity of money they wish to get from home. One way to accommodate such requests is to furnish a document saying that Student X "states that her monthly living expenses" are such-and-such an amount. This in effect attests to what the student says her costs are, not to what the school officially estimates the costs to be.

Some students may legitimately need more money than others, for example, students enrolled in programs that require special supplies, equipment, or supplementary lessons. Such costs can be specified in certification letters.

Some foreign students perform well academically and are interested in scholarships or fellowships that might be available at their schools. Fairness dictates that foreign students be eligible for such opportunities on the same footing as Americans. The citizenship requirements some schools place on governmental financial aid are often not legitimate, and they certainly have a deleterious effect on the morale of foreign students who, after all, pay tuition just as domestic students do.[5]

Students also look to employment as a way of meeting their costs. To be as helpful as possible to those students, FSAs must know the immigration regulations regarding student employment and be able to furnish information, or direct students to information, about finding jobs on campus.

Personal financial management is another area where FSAs can aid foreign students. Orientation can include information about banks (how to open an account, the different types of accounts, how to write a check), credit cards (pointing out their disadvantages as well as their advantages), places to purchase low-cost items, sales tactics and scams of which prudent people need to be wary, and personal budgeting practices. Despite these efforts, some students will get into financial difficulty as a result of unwise spending habits. The FSA can do some financial management counseling or refer students to places where such counseling is available.

The final financial matter mentioned here is tax advising, a vexing topic for many FSAs. The Council of Advisers to Foreign Students and Scholars (CAFSS) of NAFSA (that is, the foreign student advisers' component of NAFSA) has adopted a statement pointing out the hazards of income tax advising, mentioning alternative sources of assistance with income tax matters and urging those FSAs

---

[5] I once did a consultation at a private college that offered scholarships to currently enrolled students who achieved high grades. But only U.S. citizens were eligible for those scholarships. Many foreign students complained to me about that requirement. At my closing meeting with the school's president, he asked me how the foreign students felt toward his school. In general they liked it, I told him, but they felt that the scholarship requirements discriminated against them. He asked why they thought that. It was because the requirements *did* discriminate against them, I explained. They had to compete for admission, pay tuition, and study hard for good grades just as domestic students had to do, but they could not reap the rewards of good performance in the way Americans could. "I hadn't thought about that," the president said. Within a week the policy was changed.

who do tax advising to be certain they are thoroughly equipped for the enterprise.

The CAFSS Team statement recommends that FSAs limit their actions to:

1. Informing their nonimmigrant...students and scholars of their obligation under the tax codes and, possibly, maintaining a supply of forms, instructions, and other relevant IRS publications. FSAs should inform students and scholars that filing an accurate and timely tax return may result in money being refunded due to overpayment of taxes.

2. Encouraging institutional financial officers to become knowledgeable in proper withholding practices regarding nonresidents. This includes directing these officials to NACUBO [National Association of College and University Business Officers] for information, advice, and training in these matters.

3. Working with campus and community support organizations to encourage interested people to become trained VITA [Volunteer Income Tax Assistance] volunteers with particular training in matters of nonresident taxation.

4. Urging low-cost commercial tax preparation services and/or local, independent tax accountants to become knowledgeable in matters of nonresident taxation.

5. Arranging for campus visits from the taxpayer education personnel from nearby IRS offices.

Some FSAs go beyond this, to the point of assisting individual students and scholars in completing their tax return forms.

NAFSA publishes a "Tax GRAC Pack" with basic tax information.

Health care and health insurance

Foreign students typically have difficulty comprehending a health-care system that can leave an individual responsible for paying astronomical medical costs and that relies heavily on a health-insurance industry known for the special vocabulary and obscure language in its official documents.[6] The unbelievable costs of medical

---

[6] For some help in understanding the health-insurance industry and explaining it to people from other countries, see NAFSA's *Risks and Realities: A Guide to Health Insurance for FSAs*. A more general but equally useful NAFSA publication on health matters is *Optimizing Health Care for Foreign Students in the United States*.

care and the crucial role of insurance companies are only two of the factors that make the area of health care and health insurance complex. Others include the possibility of a federal health-care program, the AIDS epidemic, the increasing incidence of tuberculosis (sometimes in drug-resistant forms), the USIA's mandate concerning health insurance for people in J status, and the nagging issue of health insurance for foreign students' dependents. And, of course, there are underlying cultural differences in people's ideas about the causes and treatment of illness (physical and mental) and about the patient's and the healer's role in the treatment process.[7]

FSAs should be ready to deal with several health-care and health-insurance issues. These include institutional policy, orientation, health education, health-insurance administration, liaison with health agencies, and professional development.

Institutional policy. The NAFSA board of directors has recommended that institutions require foreign students to buy health insurance,[8] and FSAs will probably want to support such a requirement on their own campuses if it does not already exist. FSAs must make sure that the interests of foreign students (and scholars, if relevant) are represented in any campuswide discussions of institutional policy related to health insurance.

Some schools require foreign students to have health-insurance coverage for their dependents as well as for themselves. Enforcement usually entails refusal to issue any immigration document to students who cannot demonstrate that they have health-insurance coverage for accompanying family members.

Orientation. Through the orientation program, new foreign students should have the opportunity to learn about the institution's (and, if relevant, the community's) arrangements for meeting student health-care needs, and about any requirements or information relating to health insurance. Health education can begin at orientation with information about health-care topics that are of general concern on the campus (AIDS, sexually transmitted diseases, substance abuse, and tuberculosis, for example) and that are salient in the FSA's part of the country (for example, cold winter weather or

---

[7] See Andrew Weil's *Health and Healing* for an interesting, readable review of alternative approaches to medical care.
[8] See NAFSA Working Paper #49, *Mandatory Insurance for International Students at U.S. Educational Institutions.*

poisonous snakes). Health education is getting increasing attention from campus health services, and FSAs will want to assure that institutional health education efforts do not overlook the special needs and interests of students from other countries.

Health-insurance administration. Foreign students will inevitably have questions about health insurance: What policies are available, which one to buy, whether this or that treatment is covered, whether a particular claim can be processed quickly, and so on. To accommodate these questions, FSAs ought to have brochures available about alternative health-insurance policies (including a policy for short-term visitors from abroad, for the use of students who have friends or relatives paying visits). They need to know at least the basic health-insurance vocabulary (deductibles, copayments, pre-existing conditions, payment limits, exclusions, etc.) and where to refer students with questions the FSA cannot answer.

They should also know the details of any administrative arrangements relating to a health-insurance requirement.

Liaison with health agencies. As has already been implied, FSAs must work cooperatively with student health personnel, both the medical practitioners and the health educators. At institutions where foreign students get much of their health care off campus, FSAs need to liaise with the doctors, clinics, or hospitals where foreign students and their dependents go for care.

Professional development. The academic specialty known as "medical anthropology" provides useful information about comparative medical belief systems and health-care practices. FSAs will want to delve into this topic and try to get health-care professionals on their campuses and in their communities to do likewise. Foreign students bring diverse ideas about the cause and treatment of physical and mental illness and about the proper role of the patient and of the healer. These differences can create obstacles and even animosities when foreign students seek help from American-trained doctors or nurses.

For some basic information about cultural differences concerning health and health care, see NAFSA's "Healthgram on the United States," subtitled "A Guide for International Students and Scholars to Wellness and Health Care." Personnel from the American College Health Association helped write that booklet. Also see the chapter called "Cultural Differences on Campus" in *Learning across Cultures.*

The *NAFSA Newsletter* reports on helpful information available from NAFSA's Health Insurance Advisory Committee.

Advising and counseling

The initial posture. Many texts and courses in counseling place considerable emphasis on the manner of the initial contact between counselor and client and on the process of what is called "establishing rapport." This generally involves being friendly and cheerful and showing genuine interest in the client. I question this prescription as applied to foreign students. Genuine interest needs to be evident, but I believe FSAs are best advised to withhold that characteristic American friendliness and cheeriness until they are certain that it suits the client's frame of mind. I believe an emotionally neutral, businesslike approach to each client is preferable.

I was present once when a graduate assistant working in my office encountered a foreign student who had come in for an appointment. "Hello!" was the graduate assistant's cheerful greeting. "How are you doing? Just fine, I hope."

Had the student not been doing just fine, it would have taken great courage to say so. Such a cheerful and optimistic greeting would keep many students from bringing up an unpleasant, unsettling, or embarrassing subject. A death in the family, problems with an adviser or a roommate or a girlfriend, a poor grade on an exam, a sudden financial emergency, gnawing questions about whether to return home soon or stay on for another degree—these and many other topics that are on the minds of many foreign students are far less likely to be expressed to an FSA (or even a receptionist) who is unremittingly cheerful. A more neutral opening is probably more appropriate and even more respectful.

Giving advice. An FSA, the title implies, is a person who gives advice. But we persistently hear the warning as we grow up, "Never give advice." And, "People don't want your advice, even if they ask for it." And, "There's no point in giving other people advice, because they do what they want to do anyway." Our personal experience generally tends to confirm that giving other people advice is often futile (just as others in our lives can probably confirm that giving *us* advice is futile!).

What, then, is the role of advising in a foreign student adviser's work? Much of the "advising" FSAs do is not really advising in the sense of telling others, or suggesting to them, what they ought to do. Often FSAs are simply explaining or interpreting things to students. What does a particular form letter from the insurance company mean? Why do fellow students seem so reluctant to share their class notes? Explanations and interpretations can be offered without giving advice.

Sometimes FSAs are just supplying information, another activity that can be separated from giving advice. "These are the policies on…." "Here is how that procedure works."

FSAs sometimes help students reflect on an idea or course of action they are considering. Assistance of this sort entails listening, paraphrasing, and helping students make sure they have thought of all the relevant aspects and implications of the issue and have them in a reasonable perspective. For example, an FSA might not advise a student for or against entering into an intercultural marriage, but might try to make sure that the student has thoroughly considered the implications of doing so.

Students sometimes benefit from help in listing alternative courses of action. "I'm about to graduate. What should I do?" This activity often entails giving information ("Here is the procedure for applying for practical training permission"), explaining, and helping students reflect. It might also entail estimating the likely outcome of various possible courses of action. Such estimates can be based on the FSA's knowledge and judgment, but need not be in the form of advice. "In my experience, students who do that usually…." "Whether that will work depends on…."

Students can also benefit from hearing the FSA list the criteria and considerations that ought to be taken into account in making a particular decision. "It depends in part on what kind of person you are," I sometimes tell students. "If you prefer not to take any risks, then you should do this. If you don't mind taking a moderate risk, then you could do that." Or, "I think you need to think about what you want to accomplish in the end. Is it more important to you to finish the degree or to get a job?"

There are few situations in which FSAs actually are called upon to give advice, in the sense of saying, "Here's what you should do." I reserve that phrase for occasions when it seems clear that there is only one prudent course of action open to the student and that failure to follow that course is likely to have serious negative consequences. "You should buy health insurance for your family." "You should send that application form now if you want a response by the end of the term." "You should go to the dinner and get there on time, if you have accepted the invitation." "You shouldn't put false information on an immigration form."

When students press me for advice about what to do in a particular set of circumstances, I will usually not be any more direct than to say, "If I were in this situation, I think I would...," and then explain why I would do it. I try to convey to students the idea that *they* must decide, that the decision is not mine. I furthermore try to convey the sense that it does not matter to me what decision they make. This is the natural—and constructive—outcome of having a clear idea of problem ownership and of being respectful and nonjudgmental toward students. Giving advice is best restricted, in my view, to situations where the FSA clearly knows more than the student or is in a better position than the student to make a judgment and the student clearly wants and is open to following the advice.

Of course, this is a quintessentially American point of view, based on the American reverence for independence and self-reliance. Sometimes it is helpful to explain that idea to students, to put the issue of decision making into a cultural context. Students might be asked how such a decision as the one they are facing would be made at home, to add further to their—and often the FSA's—understanding of the cultural context.

Referring. FSAs are frequently presented with problems or questions that must be referred elsewhere. The registrar has to decide, or the business manager, or the instructor in the course. Or someone in the counseling center is better qualified to deal with the situation. When a student's problem or question needs to be referred elsewhere, the FSA can do a variety of things. The choice depends on several factors, including at least these:

1. The student's English proficiency.

2. The student's apparent psychological readiness to deal with someone other than the presumably sympathetic and patient FSA.

3. The estimated likelihood that the person who must actually deal with the issue will understand it adequately if the student conveys it.

4. The other person's receptivity to foreign students. (Is she kind and reasonable? Is she a bigot?)

Taking all these factors into account, FSAs can do anything from telling the student, "Don't worry, I'll take care of the whole thing" to saying, "Go see the registrar." My own inclination is to encourage students to do as much as they possibly can for themselves. This approach is in line with the "student developer" stance I generally try to assume. When referring students elsewhere, I find it helpful to give them a piece of paper on which I have written the name and office address of the person to be seen. If the question to be asked seems complicated, it is helpful to write down suggested wording. If it is likely that the person who makes the decision will need background information the student cannot supply as readily as the FSA can (for example, about the general problems of getting dollars from Country X), the FSA might phone the other person to explain the background or give the student a note to take along.

Following through. Advising often leaves FSAs with follow-up work to do: write a letter to the embassy; call the business office; get information about the procedure for legally changing one's name; and so on. FSAs gain influence if they follow through on such commitments promptly and capably.

Saying no. As much as they may wish to help foreign students in all possible ways, FSAs will encounter instances in which they must decline a student's request. Some FSAs find it difficult to say no to a student. This may be attributable to the FSA's strong desire to be a nice person, truly dedicated to helping students from abroad. The difficulty in saying no may also stem from not wanting to be the one who bears the bad news, implements the harsh policy, takes the hard line, or brings the dream to an end.

Some student requests, though, would require actions or decisions that are impractical, illegal, unethical, against the institution's policies or rules, against good practice, and/or simply unwise. The wise FSA will firmly deny these requests.

One common example of a request that should be denied is for a letter affirming something that is not true. The student may "absolutely need" a letter saying that he is enrolled full-time when he is not, or that he is studying engineering when he is not, or that he is getting better grades than the record shows. He may need such a letter "just this once. Otherwise the school won't get its money." It is wrong, unprofessional, unethical, and illegal to attest to untrue statements. Disastrous personal and professional consequences can result from knowingly making false statements.

Another fairly common request that should be denied is for a signature on a blank form. The potential for abuse is simply too great to make the risk worthwhile. Requests for personal loans, or for cosigning for loans, are also best denied in all cases.

A less specifiable sort of request that also ought to be declined is one that may aid the student in the short run but will, in the longer run, produce even greater difficulty. Approving short-term loans to a student already hopelessly in debt is an example. Helping an academically inept student change majors is another. When it becomes clear that a student is on a course that will end unhappily, it is better to help the student face up to the difficulty than to prolong it by granting a request that will simply delay the day of reckoning.

Saying no often requires saying the word no itself, sometimes repeatedly or even loudly. When we say no to fellow Americans, we often do so in rather indirect ways. We say such things as, "I really don't think that could be done in a case like this." Or, "That's not what our policy says." Americans may recognize these gentle ways of saying no. Non-Americans may not; indeed, they may interpret them as invitations to negotiate. Many foreign students are more practiced negotiators than Americans, so when negotiation starts, the foreign students often win. Negotiating is much less likely to occur in the first place if the student's request has been answered with a clear, unequivocal no.

Say no with authority. A denial or negative response coming from a person who appears unsure or tentative is much more likely to be overlooked or challenged, especially if the request is for something the student perceives as important. Sometimes it is possible to anticipate the need to say no and to say it before the question is actually asked. "Since you are registered for only eight credit hours, we can't give you a letter saying you are a full-time student." Sometimes it is helpful to move quickly to a discussion of what *can* be done. "But we can give you a letter saying simply that you are a student here."

It is usually appropriate and helpful to explain in full why a negative response is being given. This may entail an explanation of the institution's policy on a given point or of the political factors involved in a decision (for example, why a public institution cannot devote millions of dollars to financial aid for students from other countries). If a rational explanation for the no is not offered, or if the FSA who is saying no does not appear to be acting in a rational way, the student may suppose the FSA is being arbitrary or unfair. The student is then likely to take the question to another person who is perceived to be more fair or more "interested in students." Students deserve a simple, rational explanation for denials of their requests.

Another way to account for a no is to refer to the FSA's role in the situation: "I do not have the authority to issue the kind of statement you want."

If there is an avenue for appealing the FSA's negative decision, the student should be told about it in full. The student should be told who can hear the appeal, in what form (oral or written) the appeal can be made, and what criteria will be applied in deciding the appeal.

Some students may have more difficulty accepting a no from a female FSA, since many students come from places where females are not in positions where they can deny important requests. Female FSAs can confront this openly: "You may not think someone who is a woman can make a decision on a matter like this. But I can. It is the foreign student adviser's job to make decisions about requests like yours, and I am the foreign student adviser here."

In making their requests for actions the FSA deems unwarranted or improper, students will frequently try to get the FSA to feel responsible for solving the problem—to own it, in other words. As has already been said (in chapter 4), FSAs want to avoid accepting ownership of students' problems. If the student has a financial problem, for instance, it is best kept clear that the student has the problem, not the FSA. The FSA will want to help and will do so if possible. It may not be possible, though, to offer anything other than sympathy. The FSA might discuss ways of confronting the problem, such as transferring to a less expensive school, borrowing money from a distant relative, or even leaving school.

Many students believe they can get what they want from an institutional official by mere persistence—asking and asking until the official gives in. (Sometimes their experience on the campus teaches this lesson.) If indeed the answer to a student's request ought to be no, then the FSA ought not to say yes just to avoid seeing the same student yet again about the same request. The FSA might say such things as these: "We have already discussed this. Unless you have some new information for me, there is no point in discussing it again." "If you keep coming back to see me about this same thing, the secretary and I are likely to get annoyed. It probably won't help you if the secretary and I get annoyed." "If you want to pursue this matter further with me, you need to give me your request and your rationale in writing."

None of this is to say that an FSA cannot be sympathetic to students with problems. On the contrary. But FSAs need to be more concerned about their general standing within the institution than about the feelings of an individual student.

Handling serious counseling cases. FSAs, however well prepared they may be as counselors, will not be able to treat all cases of emotional disturbance that might arise among their clients. Suicidal or manic behavior and persistent paranoia are examples of problems most FSAs cannot handle. They are faced with the need to get help from a mental health professional. Unfortunately, such help is often unavailable. Either there are no certified counselors or psychiatrists in the vicinity, or those who are present cannot be assumed to have the awareness needed to work constructively with students from other counties. Financial problems often further complicate these situations.

When these cases arise, FSAs have two principal responsibilities. The first is to do everything possible to keep the students from hurting themselves or others. This is likely to entail referring the student (and maybe taking the student personally) to whatever professional help is available, even if it means traveling some distance and even if the desired awareness of cultural factors seems absent. FSAs themselves sometimes have to sign papers to commit students to mental institutions. In these cases, FSAs probably have to take the view that the students may or may not be helped by the professionals, but they are more likely to be helped by them than by an FSA or someone else without appropriate training. At least they will be prevented from hurting themselves or others.

The second thing FSAs usually want to accomplish in these serious cases is to get the student home, because long-term treatment of emotional disturbances is expensive in the United States and often less effective than it could be at home. Getting the student home is likely to involve contacts with the student's family and, perhaps, with the appropriate embassy or consulate. In these instances—and sometimes in less serious counseling cases as well—FSAs may want to call on the student's friends or compatriots for help of a kind that would not be needed with native students. FSAs and counselors or psychiatrists might need the help of a student's fellow nationals for understanding the student's problem from the perspective of the student's culture, for ideas about the way the case might be handled at home, for communicating with the student in a language other than English, and/or for communicating with the student's family. If the student has no known friends among fellow nationals, then FSAs can work with nationality group leaders to get the necessary help. Sometimes the search for helpful conationals extends to nearby educational institutions.

In my experience with cases of serious psychological problems among foreign students, the expense issue ultimately becomes irrelevant. If the case is serious enough, the student will get some care even if there is no insurance or other provision for payment. The ultimate issue is less often expense than it is laws that, in effect, make it necessary for a person actually to carry out a dangerous or harmful act before the legal machinery for commitment to an institution can be put into motion.

For more elaboration on this topic, see the article by Barbara A. Clark-Oropeza and her colleagues, "Managing the Mental Health Crises of Foreign College Students."

Handling emergencies

FSAs are normally expected to assume an active role in emergency situations that involve foreign students. These may be deaths, serious illnesses or injuries, or arrests. It is not always clear what FSAs ought to do in these cases and, again, different stakeholders may have different expectations in that respect. In general, it seems reasonable for the FSA to do what the afflicted student's family would presumably do or to see that some other responsible person does those things.

In the case of a death, the next of kin and also the student's embassy should be notified. The FSA may be the one who arranges a funeral or the repatriation of the remains. The FSA may be the one to box a student's belongings and send them home and to take care of the affairs of an estate.

In the case of injury, illness, or arrest, it may be prudent to delay or forego notifying the family, depending on the student's wishes and the prospects for the family's taking some constructive action in the situation.

When students are arrested, it is important to make certain that they have qualified legal assistance. FSAs should realize that treaty obligations in many cases require local law-enforcement agencies to notify an alien's embassy of an alien's arrest. Many local law-enforcement agencies routinely notify the INS of the arrest of a noncitizen, if only to verify the individual's immigration status.

FSAs can usually get help in dealing with emergencies that involve foreign students. The student's friends and fellow nationals may be eager to assist. Fellow nationals from a nearby city might become involved if there are none closer by. Host families, student service organizations, insurance agents, hospital personnel, community service organizations, legal aid societies, religious institutions, the Red Cross, domestic violence centers, and embassy or consular officials might also be asked to assist.

FSAs ought to have in each student's file a form on which the student has given the name, address, and telephone number of the next of kin and, when possible, of a relative or acquaintance who is in the United States. When handling an emergency, keep a log of all activities, including dates, people talked to and their telephone numbers, information conveyed, and decisions reached.

Another sort of emergency in which FSAs are likely to become involved is that of a crisis in a student's home country. This may be an individual matter, as when a student's parent is taken seriously ill or dies. Or it may be a nationwide crisis, either natural (such as an earthquake or typhoon) or man-made (such as a breakdown in civil order).

Dealing with home-country crises has two aspects, the psychological and the logistical. Psychologically, students might need anything from a brief reassurance that someone cares to long-term counseling on dealing with grief. Major upheavals such as the Iranian revolution and the Tienanmen Square shootings compelled thousands of foreign students in the United States to reassess their entire life situation and plans, because the students foreclosed the option of going home, at least for the foreseeable future. FSAs talked with many such students directly and also sought to inform faculty and staff members of the effects the events in their countries were having on the students, particularly on their ability to concentrate on their studies.

The logistical aspect of helping students deal with home-country crises can have a wide variety of components such as:

- Arranging to sign outside of office hours an I-20 or IAP-66 for reentry

- Finding someone to care for the apartment (for example, a pet, or food in the refrigerator) of a student who has to leave suddenly

- Helping a student obtain a loan to buy a ticket home

- Disseminating information about the U.S. government, (particularly the INS) response to the situation in a student's country

- Helping students whose financial support has suddenly stopped: getting permission to work, taking a loan, finding ways to cut expenses, seeking supplementary financial aid, raising funds

- Seeking modifications in institutional procedures, so that students might be allowed, for example, to drop courses later than the usual deadline or postpone the due date for payments

- Alerting host families of students who might benefit from special attention

- Seeking to forestall antiforeigner or anti–Country X feelings (often called "backlash") on the part of the local people, should such feelings be stimulated by the overseas development

- Handling media requests for interviews with students from affected countries

- Keeping affected students informed of any institutional measures taken with respect to them

- Helping the public understand the situation of students who are suddenly, and through no fault of their own, confronting major financial and psychological difficulties

Immigration advising

Advising on matters involving the Immigration and Naturalization Service or the U.S. Information Agency deserves special attention because of its importance in the FSA workload and its special significance to students and scholars. The main point to be made about immigration advising, again, is *do not give incorrect immigration advice.*

We have already (in chapter 5) discussed what FSAs will want to know about immigration law and procedures. Here we will offer a few practical suggestions about dealing with students and scholars on immigration matters.

Effective immigration advising is based on the FSA's knowledge of the law, regulations, and procedures. FSAs can do a number of things to become and remain knowledgeable about immigration matters:

- Read, and periodically review, the pertinent parts of the Immigration and Nationality Act, as amended.

- Read and periodically review the pertinent federal regulations.

- When new regulations are published, do not just read them, but compare them with the regulations they supplement or replace. Make lists or charts of the changes.

- Identify a mentor, a seasoned FSA who can help you master the immigration aspects of your work.

- Telephone experienced colleagues with your questions or send them questions via electronic mail.

- Cultivate a relationship with a knowledgeable member of the American Immigration Lawyers Association.

- Know when the information in your copy of the *Adviser's Manual of Federal Regulations Affecting Foreign Students and Scholars* has fallen out of date, and have a system for keeping track of the changes.

- Cultivate a constructive relationship with a knowledgeable INS and USIA representative.

- Attend conferences where immigration matters are going to be addressed and where you can meet people who are knowledgeable about immigration.

- Be aware of those aspects of immigration law and regulations that are widely misunderstood, and be prepared to try to counter those misunderstandings.

- Develop a good relationship with the NAFSA GRAC (Government Regulations Advisory Committee) representative in your NAFSA region, not just because the "GRAC rep" is knowledgeable about immigration regulations, but because that person is the official liaison with the INS Regional Service Center and can deal with RSC on your behalf.

- If there is a law school on your campus or in your community, cultivate a relationship with faculty interested in immigration law.[9]

It is helpful to have written handouts on routine immigration procedures such as practical training, reentering the United States after a temporary absence, and applying for permission to work off campus. NAFSA offers what is known as the GRAC Pack, a collection of generic information sheets FSAs can use as is or modify to suit local and institutional conditions. Having these handouts saves staff time and serves students better by providing needed information in a form they can study as often as needed.

---

[9] My colleague Margaret Brooke, the immigration adviser at the University of Iowa, suggested most of the items on this list.

In responding to particular immigration-related questions, I think it is helpful to keep in mind the "Can I blow my nose on Tuesdays?" test. The scenario behind this test is simple: An undergraduate F-1 student, in his third year as an economics major, comes to see the FSA and asks, "Can I blow my nose on Tuesdays?" The FSA carefully looks through those parts of the Immigration and Nationality Act, the *Code of Federal Regulations*, and the NAFSA *Adviser's Manual* that pertain to F-1 status and then tells the student, "No, I guess not. I can't find anything in my references that says it would be okay."

This is ridiculous, of course, but it reflects the approach some FSAs seem to take when responding to immigration questions. They look for explicit statements about what nonimmigrants in the United States *can* do and, in the absence of such statements, assume that the nonimmigrant *cannot* engage in the proposed activity. A moment's thought tells us that the law and regulations cannot conceivably list everything that is permitted. In general, the law and regulations specify what is not permitted, or at least not permitted without completing certain procedures.

In general, then, if a proposed activity is not prohibited by the law or regulations, then it is permissible.

Students and scholars very often misunderstand their own immigration situations. Before answering their immigration questions, FSAs will want to make certain that their clients' situations are clearly and mutually understood. This may well require having their immigration documents at hand. Only after there is clear, mutual understanding of the situation should consideration of the question begin.

It is prudent to keep notes on immigration advising sessions, recording in the student's file the topic(s) of discussion, the alternatives considered, and the conclusions reached. These notes often prove handy in later sessions.

FSAs should exercise great care in issuing any immigration form. This entails making sure that the appropriate form is being used, that the student or scholar is eligible to receive or use it, that it has been filled out completely and correctly, and that it is being sent to the correct place. Retaining photocopies of completed forms in the student's file can help answer questions or resolve problems that may arise later. Any immigration documents mailed to the INS, the USIA, or elsewhere should be sent by certified mail or by a delivery service that obtains a signed receipt from the addressee.

Although the deregulation of F-1 students has reduced the need for FSAs to interact personally with INS personnel, developing as constructive a relationship as possible with district and regional INS employees can contribute to an FSA's success in immigration-related work. So can a good relationship with the USIA staff who operate the Exchange-Visitor Program. It often helps if FSAs approach their dealings with the INS and the USIA as they approach any other cross-cultural experience. Patience, open-mindedness, and the constant effort to see things as the other person does are helpful in dealing with INS and USIA representatives.

Frustration with the INS, the USIA, and/or the Department of State sometimes leads to the temptation to try pulling strings, usually by requesting help from a local member of Congress or a U.S. senator. Some members of congress (their local staffs, actually) are more effective than others in getting information or action from government agencies. Agency personnel rarely appreciate congressional involvement in a case, because it can disrupt the normal order of things and requires extra time and effort. In the interest of developing a long-term, constructive relationship with federal agency personnel, FSAs must be circumspect about seeking congressional involvement in a case or encouraging others to call the legislator's office.

General problem solving

Foreign students and scholars frequently bring their problems—or perceived problems—to FSAs. Sometimes they want a solution to the problem, and sometimes they wish only to talk it over. Sometimes they are not yet certain whether they want any action taken. The variety of these problems is enormous. There are complaints about neighbors, allegations of racial discrimination, incorrect or overdue bills, misunderstandings with landlords, disagreements with teachers, roommates, or fellow students, reports of stalking female students, allegations of spouse abuse and of what might be called academic abuse on the part of graduate advisers, and so on. Sometimes it is the other party to the problem, not the foreign student, who brings the situation to the FSA's attention.

The first step in responding to these complaints is to listen, reflect, and ask questions until you are certain you have a clear understanding of the complainant's viewpoint.

The second step is to ascertain whether the complainant wants something done about the problem. Often she does not, because she believes nothing can be done or because she fears retribution should it become known that she has gone to someone about the problem.

If the complainant says she wants something done, the next question is *who* ought to do it—the FSA, someone else, or the FSA together with someone else. It may be that the problem needs to be referred elsewhere, for example, to a department head, a dean, an ombudsman, a resident assistant, a counselor, or some formal body set up to deal with a certain category of complaints.

If it emerges that there is a role for you as the FSA in addressing the problem, then there needs to be discussion of what you can and cannot do—what your role might be, and what the limitations on your authority are. Then you and the client can agree on a course or courses of action. If the action would entail your discussing the situation with some other party, then you will want the student's permission to do so.

If the problem the student wants you to help solve involves a dispute with another party, then you will want to talk with the other party or otherwise ascertain *their* viewpoint, which may well differ, even quite radically, from the complainant's viewpoint. In fact, FSAs often find that they can locate no "truth" between or among the divergent perceptions in a dispute.

After hearing from both (or all, if there are more than two) parties, FSAs can decide whether to assume a mediator role or an advocacy role. As mediators, FSAs place themselves between the parties and try to help them find an agreement or a resolution. FSAs work as mediators when they judge that neither side represents the side of goodness and that both have some legitimate or at least understandable demands, wishes, or feelings. Roger Fisher and William Ury's brief *Getting to Yes* offers extraordinarily useful suggestions for negotiating differences. The authors point out the deficiencies of the usual "positional bargaining" approach, in which one party makes an offer and the other accepts, rejects, or makes a counteroffer. In its place they propose "principled negotiation," which places the two parties side by side in a joint effort to solve a mutual problem. FSAs can use the approach described in this book not just in helping clients negotiate differences with others, but in many other aspects of their work.

When they judge that one side clearly represents the side of right, FSAs can serve as advocates for that side, trying to persuade the other side to go along.

In my experience, mediating is the more commonly assumed role.

Helping clients solve miscellaneous problems is one (but by no means the only) activity that brings FSAs into contact with people they dislike. I suggest making it a practice to try to get along constructively with people you dislike. The tone of your interactions may be civil at best, and you may often simply have to agree to disagree, but, in my experience, there are long-run benefits in trying to get along with everyone with whom you must interact. FSAs' lasting animosities limit their ability to serve students.

Fairly often it turns out, after looking into a situation a student has presented, that there is no problem. There has been some misunderstanding which has led to the impression that a problem exists, but once the misunderstanding is cleared up the apparent problem has vanished.

Liaison activities

Liaison activities represent an important part of an FSA's work. Some of the work is done within the institution and some with external organizations. Those two categories will be discussed separately here, but they have much in common. Both call on the same characteristics, knowledge, and skills described earlier, and both are best done with conscious attention to the other person's viewpoint and situation. In both cases, it is well to try to establish good working relationships *before* some problem or issue arises.

Two of the objectives of liaison work are essentially the same with respect to liaison within the institution and liaison with external agencies. These objectives are making things easier for foreign students and scholars and making things easier for FSAs. Liaison work within the institution has the additional objective of helping institutional colleagues gain the knowledge and develop the skills needed for them to work constructively with students from other countries.

Liaison within the institution. In the previous chapter we discussed committees as one means of maintaining communication among people in the institution who work with foreign students. Other means include periodic informal meetings in each others' offices; lunch meetings; periodic meetings with each others' office staffs; joint attendance at social functions; sharing printed information; and formal sessions designed to convey information about students from particular countries, some particular aspect of foreign-student affairs (for example, English-proficiency testing or intercultural communication), or a current international situation that is affecting foreign students and scholars.

Sending formal thank-you letters to helpful colleagues (and copies to their supervisors!) is nearly always a good idea.

It is beneficial as well for foreign student office staff members to be acquainted with their counterparts in other offices. FSAs can arrange for their assistants, secretaries, and/or student employees to meet with their counterparts in those offices with which they routinely interact, so they can share information about the structure and operations of their respective offices. Meetings such as these can produce constructive personal relationships, mutual understanding of viewpoints, and sometimes ideas for improved procedures.

When an institution has other offices with an international focus, such as an international programs office that works with faculty, the FSA will want to maintain liaison with personnel there. While the work of the two offices may not overlap significantly, there will be a common interest in developing institutional and community support for international activities. Cooperative efforts in that area are easier to arrange if a cordial relationship between the offices already exists.

Liaison with external agencies. FSAs work with an array of external agencies, including the INS, other U.S. governmental agencies, foreign governments, and nongovernmental sponsoring agencies.

1. Liaison with the INS. Maintaining a constructive perspective on working with "the Service," as INS personnel often refer to it, is one of the biggest challenges foreign student advisers face, even though the quantity of their direct dealings with the agency has declined as a result of the deregulation of F-1 students. FSAs now have little occasion to interact with district INS offices, since most of the applications in which they have an interest are sent to regional service centers. Despite the fact that the Service has directed each field office to appoint a "student-school officer" to oversee liaison with schools, FSAs, when they get together, have little that is positive to say about the INS. They have trouble getting through to the Service, either by telephone or by mail. (The Service's use of an automated telephone answering system has not endeared it to FSAs.) They are often unable to get clear or consistent answers to their questions, the answers they do get often enough prove to be incorrect, procedures take too long, papers get lost, and/or INS employees may be less patient than the FSA would like.

The fact is that the INS has long been a troubled operation. It has been, as numerous studies have by now shown,[10] badly conceived, badly managed, and undersupported. Huge increases in the flow of people across borders, in routine applications, and in asylum applications have simply overmatched it. New commissioners assume office and announce reorganizations that are intended to increase efficiency and responsiveness and raise morale and standards of performance. Improvements might occur in some areas for a period of time, but those improvements are usually offset by problems in other areas.[11]

Faced with this, FSAs need to adjust their attitudes. First, they must find ways to carry out their immigration-related responsibilities with as little reliance on the INS as possible. Several ways to do that have already been suggested. Then they must work at understanding the situation INS employees face, including the complex and ever changing nature of the law and regulations they are trying to implement; the remarkable demands on their time; the fact that foreign student-related procedures constitute such a minute portion of their work that they have little opportunity to learn the regulations well; their limited opportunities to get training; their faulty record-keeping system; the leadership deficiencies in their organization; and the number of lies they have been told by aliens and their native supporters anxious to get some immigration benefit. People who work in that kind of situation deserve all the patience and understanding FSAs can muster.

When a Service employee does perform in a way an FSA can appreciate, writing a thank-you message, with a copy to the supervisor, is a good idea.

2. Liaison with other U.S. government agencies. Most foreign student advisers have at least some occasion to deal with several fed-

---

[10] For example, see *The Immigration and Naturalization Service: Overwhelmed and Unprepared for the Future,* published by the U.S. House of Representatives, Government Operations Committee, Subcommittee on Information, Justice, Transportation, and Agriculture. See also "Chaos at the Gates," a five-part *New York Times* report that found mismanagement, inefficiency, corruption, and general ineptitude in the INS.

[11] On the occasion of his retirement after thirty-six years of service to INS, ending as Acting Assistant Commissioner for Adjudications, Richard M. "Mike" Miller wrote an essay for *Interpreter Releases* in which he gave his critique of the Service's operations. He cites several examples of reorganizations that solved some problems but at the same time created or exacerbated others.

eral agencies besides the INS. These include the United States Information Agency, the Visa Office and assorted consular posts of the U.S. Department of State, the Internal Revenue Service, the Social Security Administration, the Agency for International Development (AID), and the Department of Labor. These are all large and complicated organizations, and in many of them personnel and telephone numbers change frequently. None has a reputation for being especially responsive; some have a reputation for being thoroughly inept. One has to expect such organizations to need considerable time to respond to any nonroutine questions (and to many routine questions) that FSAs might bring them.

For most FSAs, the major problem in dealing with these organizations is knowing where to direct their questions. FSAs at smaller institutions can often find large-institution colleagues who know whom to call within the large government agencies. The local offices of members of congress are another source of help in getting answers from Washington agencies. Some of these agencies send representatives to NAFSA conferences, where FSAs can meet them, record their names and numbers, and get information about where to direct questions on assorted topics.

FSAs who have frequent occasion to interact with these agencies will probably have to engage in some of the attitude adjustments recommended above, in the section on liaison with the INS. Here are some irrational ideas (to invoke Albert Ellis yet again) FSAs might harbor about these agencies:

- USIA personnel *should* understand what it's like dealing with three hundred foreign scholars at a large university.
- The IRS *should* train its people well enough so they can agree in their answers to questions about taxation and foreign students.
- The Social Security Administration *should* keep up to date on immigration regulations and stop inappropriately denying social security cards to people from other countries.
- AID staff members *should* call back when they say they are going to.
- The Visa Office *should* exercise more control over the arbitrary decisions of visa-issuing (or denying) officers.
- The Department of Labor *should* appreciate the problems of salary differentials among faculty in different fields of study.

The FBI and the CIA sometimes ask FSAs for information about particular foreign students or scholars. Most institutions have written policies restricting the dissemination of information about students, whether to law-enforcement agencies or to other parties. FSAs should confer with their institutions' attorneys before responding to FBI and CIA requests.

3. Liaison with other governments. As is the case in dealing with large U.S. government agencies, the major problem in working with other governments' embassies and consulates is usually knowing whom to ask for particular information.

FSAs usually have to rely on the telephone when dealing with embassies and consulates, because letters often evoke tardy replies or none at all. A clerical person at an embassy or consulate will usually know where a particular question should be addressed. Telephoning person-to-person is often the best way to get through if the embassy or consulate is one where staff members are often away from their desks. It is a good idea to make notes on these telephone conversations, recording the name of the person spoken to, the date, and any agreements reached. A follow-up letter confirming the details of the conversation is a good way of giving the exchange an appropriate degree of formality and helping assure that it is remembered on the other end.

FSAs need to remember that embassy officials, and consulate staff even more so, are at or near the bottom of a chain of command, the top of which is in the capital city of the country in question. They therefore have limited authority to make decisions, especially with regard to unusual issues. Getting an official decision or up-to-date information through an embassy or consulate can require considerable time. Still, some embassies and consulates are more responsive than others.

4. Liaison with nongovernmental sponsoring agencies. In this context, nongovernmental agencies are those which sponsor foreign students in the United States—IIE (Institute of International Education), AAI (African-American Institute), and others mentioned in chapter 5. In dealing with them, the FSA is usually an intermediary between an agency staff member and its students at the FSA's institution.

From the viewpoint of sponsoring agencies, FSAs are the people on the scene, the ones on whom the agencies must rely for complete, current information on the students' situations.

Agency personnel appreciate FSAs who (a) take the time to become familiar with their students, (b) show respect for the students, (c) notify the agency if any special problem develops with a sponsored student, (d) recognize the agency's right to information about students it supports, (e) have good rapport with the faculty, (f) refer students' questions about agency procedures to the agency if there is doubt about the correct answer, (g) realize that the agency itself is but an intermediary between the student and the funding organization and is thus not in a position to make independent decisions about a sponsored student's academic career, and (h) refrain from criticizing the agency in a student's presence.

When sponsored students get into differences of opinion with their agencies, FSAs had best stand aside and let the students and the agencies interact directly with each other. Being in the middle as a channel for messages is rarely efficient or helpful.

FSAs have many occasions on which to explain a sponsoring agency's role and operations to students, since students often misunderstand what the agencies do. In particular, students often suppose that decisions about such important matters as extensions of programs or changes in field of study are made by the agencies, when in fact they are made by the home-country organizations on whose behalf the agencies are working.

FSAs will want to remember that personnel turnover at the lower levels of some sponsoring agencies (the title is usually "program officer") is relatively high. Program officers often have large caseloads and limited experience in working directly with students on a specific campus. Keeping these factors in mind can help FSAs appreciate the situation of program officers and explain it to students.

Working with student organizations

Working with foreign student organizations is a continuing source of frustration for many FSAs. Whether the organizations are based on nationality (for example, the Indian Student Club), on region (European Student Union), or are cosmopolitan (International Student Association), FSAs are unlikely to obtain benefits they consider equal to the efforts they expend. The most important reason for this seems to be that the FSA's expectations of these groups tend to be unrealistic. FSAs often begin with ill-founded assumptions about the ease with which these organizations can be formed, what the groups can accomplish, and their own ability to influence them. Let us look at each of these points.

FSAs seem inclined to make one or more of the following questionable assumptions relative to foreign student organizations on their campuses:

1. That the foreign students see themselves as an identity group, with enough common characteristics and interests to make it reasonable to form an organization.

The category "foreign students" is usually more prominent in the minds of the Americans than in the minds of the foreign students themselves. To the latter, differences in language, politics, religion, ethnic background, social class, gender, age, shade of skin color, and field of study are likely to be important and to hinder the development of organizations.

2. That those students who agree that an organization is a good idea also agree on what the organization's goals should be (that is, on the extent to which the organization should seek educational, political, and/or social objectives).

In fact, any group of foreign students is likely to include people with diverse ideas about what the goals of a foreign student organization ought to be. Bitter disputes over these differences are not rare.

3. That a group of students can readily agree on such matters as goals, form of organization, leadership selection, decision-making procedures, and division of labor. Appendix B analyzes many of the problems that arise in these areas. The problems stem from culturally based differences in such matters as communicative style, ways of thinking, and the treatment of differences in social status and/or gender.

These common FSA assumptions appear to be questionable at best and are often clearly without foundation.

What can foreign student groups accomplish if they are formed? Many FSAs think the groups should: (1) develop smoothly running organizations, with easy transitions from one year to the next; (2) provide for members' social needs; (3) help newly arriving students get settled and oriented; (4) integrate American students into the organization for mutual enrichment; (5) organize cultural programs from which Americans will learn something about the countries the students represent; (6) represent the foreign students, or segments of them, to the institution's administration; and (7) either avoid political activities altogether or at least restrict them to unobtrusive expressions of opinion the local population can be expected to consider reasonable.

Some of these objectives are incompatible with others. For example, the foreign and the American students might have differing ideas about what constitutes an enjoyable social or recreational activity. On my campus, as an instance, large numbers of foreign students spend Friday evenings at the Field House, where they play badminton, table tennis, or other sports. Meanwhile, the American undergraduates are downtown at the bars.

Some of the objectives FSAs have in mind for foreign student organizations, particularly those involving extensive cultural programs, fairs, performances, and the like, require too much time and energy from a group of people whose main purpose in being at the school is to achieve academic success.

And some objectives overlook the generic problems of student organizations, especially the lack of consistency in leadership and uneven motivation to participate.

American-born FSAs are likely to have in mind an American-based ideal for a student organization,

> one that plans and executes a reasonable number of activities or events that are carefully planned, well-publicized, well-executed, well-attended, and then evaluated. The good organization has an appropriate number of well-run meetings, meaning that there is an agenda for the meeting, discussion—always temperate—is conducted according to Robert's Rules of Order, decisions are made by voting ("the majority rules"), and minutes are kept and distributed promptly afterwards. A well-run meeting begins at the scheduled starting time and is not "too long" (67).

These and related ideas about student activities are discussed in the chapter "Cultural Differences on Campus," in *Learning across Cultures*.

FSAs also frequently suppose they will have more influence on foreign student groups than they are in fact able to exercise. When foreign students do form vital organizations, it usually means, almost by definition, that the members have a purpose or small set of agreed-upon purposes. Often that purpose is the propagation of a particular political viewpoint; many times it is to provide relaxed social occasions for a particular language group. Additional or alternative purposes promoted by the FSA are not easily incorporated.

Despite all the obstacles enumerated here, some foreign student organizations persevere and even thrive. The leadership abilities of particular students are often responsible for an organization's success. It also seems that some nationality groups are more inclined to cooperate in the context of an organization than others, depending on their culturally based ideas about the importance of cooperation and community.

In working with student organizations, FSAs ought first to examine their assumptions and make sure their expectations are reasonable. Taking a longer view, they can, with patience and perseverance, seek ways in which to help foreign students—and perhaps some domestic students as well—learn useful lessons from forming (or trying to form) organizations on their own.

Here are some things FSAs can do to support foreign student organizations:

1. provide information about the institution's regulations and procedures for forming official student organizations, and aid the students in complying with those procedures

2. identify prospective student leaders and meet with them to give encouragement and support

3. provide information about means by which a nationality group or international club can identify prospective members, raise funds, communicate with members, publicize activities that are open to the public, and better achieve its goals

4. make clear what assistance the FSA or others in the institution can provide in the form of money, administrative support, meeting space, audiovisual or other equipment, publicity, leadership training, and so on

5. help students see the lessons that arise from their organizational experiences, even if those experiences do not always have the outcome the students themselves or the FSA would like

Important lessons can be learned from efforts to get groups of people to work together cooperatively toward common ends. The efficiency and productivity many foreign students admire in the United States are products of a fairly widespread ability to cooperate in the framework of various organizations. Experience with student organizations can induce students to examine their own and their compatriots' ideas and feelings about joint efforts with others.

Programming

FSAs are often considered responsible for mounting various programs that involve foreign students in some way. International fairs and festivals, nationality nights, meals from different countries, tours, and assorted social activities are common examples. Such programs are traditional on many campuses and may routinely attract large audiences.

For guidance on the logistical aspects of program planning, FSAs can refer to Margaret J. Barr's and Lou Ann Keating's *Establishing Effective Programs* or similar publications, which are probably available from colleagues in the student activities area. They give thorough guidelines on such matters as figuring out the objectives of an event, reserving space, arranging for equipment, getting publicity, holding rehearsals, and so on. A list of "Programming Considerations" appears in Appendix I.

As long as FSAs have the time and ability to do what programming they want, and as long as the programs are more or less successful, no serious questions about the FSA's programming role are likely to arise. But if the FSA has more and more competing demands and finds it ever more difficult to invest time in programming, or if the programs that are done are not deemed successful, questions arise. Those questions concern the goals of foreign student programming, its audience, and the FSA's role in the activity. A few comments on each of these topics appear here; a more extended treatment is in C. Wayne Young's thoughtful article in Appendix J.

Goals of programming. While most programs have multiple goals, one or another is likely to be paramount. The main goal of a foreign student-related program might be educational or social. The program might be intended to train participants or to provide beneficial publicity for foreign students, the FSA's office, and/or the institution.

Of course, a program's goal is the first thing to consider in deciding what kind of program to develop. An educational program might include an expert in some discipline or a film.[12] A social program will probably entail music and refreshments. And so on. When planning programs, or assessing past ones, FSAs need to determine just what they are trying to accomplish.

Serious cross-cultural trainers and educators suggest that program planning should take into account the intended audience's level

---

[12] Ellen Summerfield's *Crossing Cultures through Film* discusses and gives suggestions for using more than seventy different films for cross-cultural educational purposes.

of interest, knowledge, and sophistication, with program components then calculated to move participants from one stage or level to another. (See Richard W. Brislin's and Tomoko Yoshida's discussion of Milton J. Bennett's ethnorelativism model, in their book *Intercultural Communication Training*.) Serious trainers and educators question the value of relying entirely on "exposure" programs such as nationality nights and international fairs. Some programs, they say, need to offer deeper and longer-term experiences.

Audiences for foreign student programs. Foreign student programs might have one or more of several audiences, including foreign students themselves, their families, American students, faculty and staff at the institution, or the general public. FSAs will want to assess which potential audiences are most likely to benefit from their programs and devote their limited attention to programs aimed at them.

The FSA role in programming. Perhaps the most difficult issue in programming is determining what role the FSA ought to play. At some institutions, FSAs or their staff members assume an active role. They determine what programs are going to be carried out, reserve the rooms, send the invitations, set up the tables, and so on.

Other FSAs leave these matters entirely to other people, perhaps to student groups or to institutional colleagues whose responsibilities include student programs. (The latter can include not just student activities staff, but personnel in residence halls, the women's center, the career or placement center, the counseling service, health education, campus ministries, and community programs.) Between these extremes are those FSAs who lend support or advice or cooperate in assorted ways with other offices, but refrain from direct involvement in programming.

There is obviously no correct answer to the question about the FSA's proper role in programming. In general, it is probably advisable to rely on others as much as possible: on students so that they will have the challenging experience of planning and implementing an organized activity, or on colleagues so that they can become increasingly involved with students from other countries. More is to be learned that way, and the FSA's attention can be directed to matters with which other people are less able to help.

Community relationships

FSAs have educational and political reasons for cultivating relationships with members of the community. For educational reasons, FSAs have to maximize the number of opportunities for constructive interaction between foreign students and people in the community. Host-family programs, elementary and secondary school programs, home visits, and foreign student participation in community service and recreational programs are means whereby students and community members can learn from each other.

Politically, FSAs have an interest in developing a constituency knowledgeable about and supportive of international educational activities. Community programs contribute to that and can work to combat the antiforeign sentiments and actions of the kind that have culminated in violence in some U.S. communities.

Developing community programs requires patience and perseverance, because the programs normally depend on the efforts of volunteers. Interested, capable volunteers must be identified, given gentle direction, and supported in as many ways as possible. Some would-be volunteers have motives FSAs cannot approve of, such as religious or political proselytizing or an unhealthy need to compensate for some perceived deficiency in their personal lives. Handling such situations requires attentiveness and tact.

Stephen H. Rhinesmith's *Bring Home the World* is an excellent guide to managing volunteer community programs. NAFSA offers a *Handbook for Community Organizations Working with Foreign Students* and several smaller publications concerning aspects of community programs.

Relations with foreign alumni

Some people argue that an institution's foreign student program is incomplete unless it includes an organized effort to develop and maintain constructive ties with foreign alumni. Alumni abroad can seek out qualified students for an institution, screen applicants, help orient applicants who have been admitted, and assist an institution's faculty members who might be traveling in their countries. They can find opportunities for collaborative research projects and help organize student exchanges. They sometimes prove to be key contacts in setting up institutional linkages or technical assistance programs.

Foreign alumni sometimes find each other to be welcome sources of social and professional support. They often appreciate being kept appraised of developments at their alma maters, just as many American alumni do. In some cases, foreign alumni, like U.S. alumni, have made financial contributions to their old schools.

FSAs who want to develop programs or services involving foreign alumni usually need to work with their alumni offices to determine what services or publications can be provided to alumni abroad and what contributions can reasonably be expected from them. Common impediments to developing a comprehensive foreign alumni program are the difficulty of maintaining an accurate address list, the high cost of international postage, the relatively low place foreign alumni usually hold in institutional priorities (and in the priorities of most alumni offices), and the amount of persistence and patience needed to get services and activities organized.

Serving Foreign Scholars

Many American educational institutions are employing or hosting larger numbers of visiting foreign scholars. That fact, along with the requirements set forth in the 1993 USIA regulations for the Exchange-Visitor Program, has led schools to pay more concerted attention than some formerly did to services for those scholars. The USIA regulations require that certain information be sent to scholars in advance of their arrival in the United States and that sponsoring schools provide orientation to them and their dependents. The regulations, with which responsible officers are required to be familiar, also encourage sponsoring schools to involve scholars in cross-cultural educational activities.

Foreign scholars are well served by modified forms of the same things that serve foreign students:

- Clear and concise prearrival information on topics that one would expect to be important to adults who are moving temporarily to another country—transportation, housing, financial matters (living costs, banking services, taxes), health insurance, schools for children, and so on

- On-arrival information about important logistical concerns—payroll procedures, social security numbers, housing, transportation, health insurance, English-language instruction, employment permission for the spouse, schools for the children, sexual harassment policies (which might be novel for many scholars), culture-learning opportunities, recreational facilities, and so on

- Postarrival programs, services, and activities intended to make the scholars' lives easier and/or to capitalize on their presence (and that of their spouses) for culture learning

NAFSA's working paper "The Foreign Scholar's Experience: A Concern for Quality" includes an "Institutional Checklist for Foreign Scholar Services." The USIA prints a brochure sponsoring institutions can furnish to J-1 scholars to explain the requirements of the J-1 program. My *Manual for Foreign Scholars* addresses the cross-cultural issues foreign scholars are likely to confront on an American campus.

On my own campus, systematic interviews with large numbers of foreign scholars revealed a high level of satisfaction with the professional aspect of their lives, but, in many cases, a low level of satisfaction with the personal or social aspect. Many scholars said they felt isolated and lonely, often because their supervisors and colleagues were too busy to spend social time with them. Such a needs assessment on other campuses might or might not reach a similar conclusion; in any case, a needs assessment could help an FSA determine what programs or services to offer foreign scholars.

Promoting Culture Learning

In order to approach their culture-learning responsibilities with an appropriate frame of mind, FSAs must understand the many factors that disincline people to attend their programs and workshops. Among them:

- Many Americans are simply not interested in culture learning, or at least not interested enough to work it into their crowded schedules.

- FSAs do not usually have faculty status and so cannot usually offer grades or academic credit for any teaching or training they might do.

- Most people are not interested in other people's ideas about how they could become better human beings—better informed, more sensitive, more aware, etc.

- Confirmed quantifiers that they so often are, Americans have not seen any hard evidence that culture-learning activities will benefit them.

- When foreign students or scholars are incorporated into culture-learning activities, the natives' ethnocentrism can lead them to disregard or discount their contributions, which are often seen to be coming from people who are "biased" or "too emotional."

In the face of these obstacles, what can FSAs do to promote culture learning on their campuses and in their communities? They must begin with the characteristics of patience and perseverance, and they have to develop knowledge about intercultural communication (see chapter 5) and skills in intercultural training (see chapter 6), or find someone who has them. Then begins the painstaking effort to find interested audiences, to sell those prospective audiences what they have to offer, and to develop formats suitable for the audiences.

Interested audiences might be found where there are problems in intercultural relationships, where something noteworthy and positive involving intercultural relationships has captured people's attention, or where people or organizations are looking for a cause or activity in which to invest themselves. Is there difficulty between foreign and American students in a residence hall, where staff members want help in improving the situation? Is the residence hall staff itself having some difficulty with the foreign students? Or, on the contrary, has a group of students from abroad aroused other students' interest in learning about other cultures? Is there a student honorary or service club seeking a project? Or a community service or church group or a parent-teacher organization looking for an activity in which to invest some effort? Are local businesses encountering misunderstandings in their dealings with students from abroad, or are they interested in serving that clientele more effectively?

There might be U.S. students preparing to go abroad or studying in a field where skill in intercultural relationships would help. There might be a committee seeking staff development topics. Maybe there is an academic department with a concentration of foreign students about whose educational and cultural backgrounds the faculty would like to learn more.

FSAs, if they look around carefully, can usually find people who have an interest, at least an incipient one, in intercultural relationships. Some people might be interested in developing awareness or an improved understanding of cultural differences and their effects on people's behavior; others might be interested in learning and practicing specific skills that would enable them to engage in intercultural relations more constructively.

Finding formats suitable for these different audiences is a matter of considering how much time is available, what the audiences' specific learning objectives are, their level of intercultural sophistication and sophistication in general, the forms of instruction most likely to hold their attention, and the skills and materials FSAs or other trainers have at their disposal. References given in chapter 6 can help with program planning, execution, and evaluation.

It seems to me that a mystique has developed around cross-cultural training. The term conjures up the image of highly trained specialists cleverly using an array of refined exercises to lead participants to some form of enlightenment. While I do not by any means wish to minimize the quantity of knowledge and skill needed for effective cross-cultural training, I want to suggest that a more accurate image is this: Intercultural learning begins when people with different cultural backgrounds can begin to *talk* with each other about topics that are not superficial. The trainer's job is to get the people together, provide an environment conducive to talk and a stimulus to conversation (an exercise, perhaps, a tape or a film, or just a set of interesting and pertinent questions), and offer some help in overcoming culturally based problems that interfere with the discussion. The latter might include assumptions and values that are not shared, differences in communicative style, or differences in patterns of thought.

Seen in this way, culture learning is something most FSAs can readily seek to promote, at least at the level of increasing awareness and understanding. Helping people to deal with the emotional responses to having their basic values confronted and to develop skills in intercultural interaction does require more special knowledge and training.

Most recommended formats for campus-related culture-learning programs call for the participation of foreign students and scholars. Panels, discussion groups, role plays, and intercultural workshops are clearly more effective if they include participants from diverse cultures. FSAs who arrange culture-learning programs will normally want to be sure that foreign students are included.

At the same time, FSAs should avoid assuming that all foreign students are by definition interested in culture learning, either for themselves or for the natives. Some foreign students want to minimize their involvement with the local people. They do not want to share rooms with them, join them on picnics, show them dances from home, or join intercultural workshops. FSAs ought to respect these wishes, realizing that they may stem from a reasonable desire to be left alone or to minimize the problems of reentering their own societies.

ADMINISTERING AN OFFICE

Some FSAs have almost no administrative responsibilities. Others have many. Those who have many will have to look to other, more specialized publications to learn about management philosophies and techniques, administrative practices, and leadership. This section offers a few general ideas that are intended to give some perspective to the administrative aspect of foreign student advising.

The first requisite of efficient administration is to have clear goals and priorities.[13] As was suggested in chapter 6, FSAs will want to establish a routine for periodically reviewing goals and setting priorities. Developing plans and budgets is contingent on this goal setting.

Efficient administration also requires well-organized procedures for handling routine business. In a foreign student office, this might mean preparing printed handouts responding to the most frequently asked questions. Immigration procedures (such as applying for practical training permission or reentering after a trip abroad) and routine institutional procedures (for example, getting a letter certifying full-time enrollment) lend themselves to this kind of treatment.

Having sheets for students to fill out when requesting immigration forms or emergency loans also saves time. Instructions for completing routine forms can be posted.

We have already recommended providing written policy statements concerning financial aid and other arrangements for students in financial difficulty.

A foreign student office needs a good filing system. Papers in student files are often referred to again and again, so they need to be filed promptly and accurately. Information on a wide array of topics has to be retrievable. Some institutions are using automatic data processing (ADP) for information storage, and FSAs should try to

---

[13] I am using the term "goals" in a broad sense. A more refined treatment would distinguish among "vision statements," "mission statements," "goals," "objectives," "strategies," and perhaps even "standards of performance." I confess some ambivalence about this degree of refinement. On the one hand, it seems like an example of the American preference for analysis (breaking things down into small pieces) run rampant. On the other hand, it can help clarify one's thinking if one is forced to address all these different levels. For our purposes the point is that administrators need to think clearly about what they are trying to accomplish, lest their attention and energy be dissipated in random directions. The use of "goals" is intended to convey that notion.

take advantage of these systems. There is particular value in using ADP to retrieve statistical information about the foreign student body—size, nationality and gender composition, fields of study, and so on.

In offices where there is noticeable personnel turnover, even if only at the level of student assistants, it is prudent to write an office procedures manual for training and guiding employees. Serious problems can develop when information about too many of an office's procedures and policies is stored only in the head of one person.

Much of what happens in a foreign student office is routine, as has been said, and clerical employees can handle it, leaving FSAs free to work on longer-term projects.[14] Giving clerical staff these responsibilities often improves their morale and dedication, since it makes them partners in carrying out office responsibilities.

At institutions where the foreign students have been conditioned to believe they must see the FSA personally about every single matter, the students can be reconditioned.

CULTIVATING INFLUENCE

In part to summarize ideas that have been advanced already and in part to introduce a few new ones, let us list some of the suggestions Richard W. Brislin presents in *The Art of Getting Things Done*:

- Build a network of people who embody a variety of areas of expertise. This networking is more effectively done by people who show a positive attitude, are "charming and gracious," and can get along with people they dislike.

- Build a strong knowledge base in a particular area, so you have something to offer others.

- Improve your ability to write.

- Improve your public speaking.

- Develop a "thick skin."

- Make as few enemies as possible. Strive to maintain others' goodwill.

---

[14] In visiting campuses as a consultant for NAFSA, I have been struck by the number of instances where intelligent, capable clerical people were doing nothing but the most menial of tasks, while the FSA was (1) personally talking with every foreign student who came in, no matter how routine the matter was, and (2) complaining about not having enough time to work on a better orientation program, better relationships with staff in other offices, or whatever.

- Project "an aura of confidence, social smoothness, and a 'can-do' attitude."
- Work hard.

MAKING WISE DECISIONS

FSAs make decisions every day. Most are routine, requiring no particular thought, but some are difficult—the kind that find their way into the case studies, critical incidents, or ethical dilemmas that are a staple of NAFSA conference sessions.

Effective FSAs generally make wise decisions. Faced with a difficult issue, FSAs can make a tentative decision and test it with the following set of questions.[15] Not all these questions will suit all issues, but, in my experience, at least some of these questions will help assess the wisdom of a potential course of action:

1. Is the proposed decision in harmony with the letter of relevant laws, regulations, and institutional policies?

2. Is it in harmony with the spirit of pertinent laws, regulations, and policies?

3. Does it comply with the NAFSA code of ethics?

4. Is it in accord with cultural norms?

5. Does it avoid duplicity?

6. Is it consistent with decisions previously made in comparable cases, and/or distinguishable from previous cases in which a different decision was reached?

7. Does it establish a desirable precedent?

8. Does it avoid lines of thought that can lead off the correct path:

   a. If I don't do it, someone else will.

   b. It's not worth the hassle.

   c. I could lose my job if I did (or didn't) do what has been asked.

   d. No one will ever know.

   e. Sometimes the end justifies the means.

   f. It's not really illegal or unethical.

9. Will it help in the long run?

---

[15] This list draws lightly on *CareerTracking*, by Jimmy Calano and Jeff Salzman.

10. Would the world be a better place if this decision is taken? If more people made this decision?

11. Does it feel right? Would it bring me more self-respect?

12. Considering my personal feelings toward the person or group that would be affected by my proposed decision, would I make the same decision if it affected someone I liked, or disliked?

13. Would I want my mother to know I made this decision?

14. Could I credibly defend this decision in public?

15. If I were the one affected by the proposed decision, would I consider it fair and reasonable?

16. Would I want to read about my decision in the newspaper?

17. Is this the right thing to do now?[16]

PURSUING PROFESSIONAL DEVELOPMENT

The seventh of Stephen R. Covey's *The Seven Habits of Highly Effective People* is "sharpen the saw." That designation comes from a story Covey tells:

Suppose you were to come upon someone in the woods working feverishly to saw down a tree.

"What are you doing?" you ask.

"Can't you see?" comes the impatient reply. "I'm sawing down this tree."

"You look exhausted!" you exclaim. "How long have you been at it?"

"Over five hours," he returns, "and I'm beat! This is hard work."

"Well, why don't you take a break for a few minutes and sharpen that saw?" you inquire. "I'm sure it would go a lot faster."

"I don't have time to sharpen the saw," the man replies emphatically. "I'm too busy sawing!" (287).

Successful FSAs take time to sharpen the saw. They can always benefit from acquiring more knowledge, sharper insights, broader

---

[16] This question draws on *First Things First*, by Stephen R. Covey, A. Roger Merrill, and Rebecca R. Merrill. Covey believes that asking this and related questions gives people access to their conscience, which is their guide to what he calls "principle-centered" decisions (and living).

perspectives, and improved skills. FSAs need to devote conscious attention to their own professional development.

The most accessible means of professional development is reading. Many useful books and articles are cited throughout this *Handbook*. Jimmy Calano's and Jeff Salzman's *CareerTracking* is particularly useful, offering twelve concise, practical suggestions in each of twenty-six chapters, which address such topics as managing time, dictating, improving powers of concentration, negotiating, overcoming procrastination, and taking initiative.

The authors of *CareerTracking* run a business called CareerTrack, which offers an array of professional development products. Their address is in Appendix C.

Many educational institutions offer professional development courses or sessions for their employees. These usually concern communication skills or management practices, training in both of which can help FSAs. Participating in professional development activities offered by one's own institution also provides opportunities to nurture contacts among colleagues. Sometimes FSAs can contribute to staff development programs by teaching about or training on topics related to foreign student affairs or intercultural communication. Teaching, as the cliché says, is an excellent way to learn.

In my office, we organize weekly professional development sessions, sometimes inviting people from other student service offices to join us. We do a variety of things in these sessions: read and discuss books, talk with invited guest speakers, view and discuss videos, set up our own training situations, and visit FSAs at nearby institutions. Visits with other FSAs can result in useful information, new ideas about ways to handle particular problems, suggestions for administrative improvements, plans or ideas for cooperative activities, and supportive, collegial relationships.

Of course, FSAs can enroll in regular classes at their own or nearby institutions if they prefer the structure that a class provides.

NAFSA publications and conferences have been mentioned repeatedly in this *Handbook*. In my view, membership in NAFSA and use of its publications are vital to responsible foreign student advising, not to mention professional development. One component of NAFSA, called the Field Service Program, is specifically concerned with the professional development of FSAs and others in the international educational exchange field.

NAFSA conferences provide countless opportunities to **acquire** useful information, get a new perspective on one's work, **and estab**lish relationships with helpful colleagues.

NAFSA's success depends on the volunteer efforts of hundreds of members who work on various committees, task forces, teams, special-interest groups, and specific projects. I have benefited inestimably from active involvement in NAFSA, and I heartily recommend it to anyone who is willing to volunteer and follow through on commitments. Knowledge, skills, helpful acquaintances, and expanded opportunities for professional development will result. And fun, too, in the company of a remarkably interesting and concerned group of people.

From time to time FSAs can find seminars, workshops, or short courses designed for foreign student advisers and perhaps others who work in intercultural situations. NAFSA periodically offers such programs, as do SIETAR, the Intercultural Communication Institute, and the School for International Training, all of whose addresses are given in Appendix C.

International travel is often considered the ideal form of professional development for foreign student advisers. My impression is that such travel can be quite beneficial, but is not necessarily so. Travel will help FSAs do their jobs better to the degree that it gives them the experience of being a foreigner, provides information about other cultures or educational systems, and acquaints them with the viewpoints of some people who see the world differently from the way they see it themselves.

Writing is another constructive approach to professional development. Writing an article, whether for a scholarly journal, the newsletter of NAFSA or one of its regions, or the local newspaper requires research or other information gathering, along with systematic thought and reflection. Writing can help FSAs examine ideas or information they might otherwise overlook or consider only superficially.

Research projects on aspects of foreign student affairs are more than welcome if they are carefully done and well reported. In the eyes of many academics and high-level administrators, people in foreign student affairs are inadequately rigorous in their approach to their work. FSAs are often seen to lack basic data about foreign students—data about such things as enrollment trends, academic performance, the incidence of particular problems or issues, and many other matters. FSAs will do themselves credit if they routinely keep and analyze basic data about their clients. Beyond that, they can conduct and report on research projects on dozens of interesting topics related to foreign students and scholars and to intercultural relationships. See *Needs of Foreign Students from Developing Nations at U.S. Colleges and Universities*, by Motoko Y. Lee and others, for a lifetime supply of ideas for research topics.

Professional development for foreign student advisers does not require traveling abroad, going to conferences, or extensive reading. Conversations with foreign students and scholars can provide FSAs with an immense amount of useful information and insight. All that is needed is intelligent questions and respectful attention to answers. FSAs can learn useful things from foreign students virtually every working day.

Effective FSAs include professional development in their yearly plans and on their daily to-do lists. They identify topics they could benefit from knowing more about and make plans for learning them, and identify skills they need to improve and make arrangements to improve them. They allow time and allocate funds—if possible—for attending NAFSA or other conferences and meetings. They know they cannot stay abreast of changes in their complex and rapidly unfolding field unless they devote a significant amount of time to professional development.

Appendix K can help FSAs determine where to go next for this purpose.

8

Conclusion

I sometimes remark to foreign students on the number of expressions in everyday American speech that come from baseball. Strike out, throw him a curve, take a rain check, have two strikes against, out in left field, off the wall, touch base, pinch-hit, heavy hitter, play hardball, batting a thousand—these and many other phrases come from a game that is unfamiliar in most parts of the world.

Stories from baseball (and other sports) are also common among Americans, and I want to tell one now. Maybe what I am about to relate did not really happen. I did not witness it. But if it did not happen, it could have. You can ask anyone who watched Roberto Clemente play.

Clemente was the Pittsburgh Pirate right fielder from 1955 until his death in 1972. Among Pirate fans he was known as "The Great One." His lifetime batting average was an outstanding .317. Shortly before his death he got his three-thousandth base hit, a feat accomplished by only nineteen major league baseball players in this country. Twelve times during his career he won the coveted Gold Glove Award for superior defensive play. The strength and accuracy of his throwing arm were legendary.

Clemente could hit, run, and throw with the very best. I once saw him pick up a ball at the base of the right field fence and throw it all the way to the catcher—at least 330 feet on the fly—to cut down a runner trying to score. He could catch balls that seemingly could not be caught and make throws that seemingly could not be made. He virtually never got picked off a base, and he almost never threw to the wrong place. When a ball bounced off the wall above him, he was always positioned to field it cleanly. He played with utter concentration and dedication, and he always tried to do better. He was awesome, in the true sense of that overused term.

The story goes that a reporter once asked Clemente why he worked so hard at playing the game of baseball. His reply: "I play this game the way it is supposed to be played."

This *Handbook* offers a great deal for foreign student advisers to think about and do. Most FSAs will not undertake them all. I hope they will undertake as many as they can. Foreign student advising can not only be the most interesting job on campus, but also a way to make a significant and constructive contribution toward solving what is in many ways the most fundamental problem of our age: people's inability to accept and work cooperatively with people who are different. The FSA's job, as Martin Limbird says, is to change the world. To do that requires dedication, concentration, and continuing effort to do better. That is the way the job is supposed to be done.

The D.I.E. Formulation

Explain to a group of participants in an orientation program or other session about intercultural relations that the purpose of the D.I.E. formulation is to illuminate three different aspects of people's responses to intercultural (and other human) interactions. Write on the blackboard or easel:

D

I

E

Then explicate, on the board or easel:

Describe—what you *see*

Interpret—what you *think* about what you see

Evaluate—what you *feel* about what you see

Get an example of something someone has said about some human behavior in an intercultural situation. An example that emerged in a session I conducted came from a Malaysian student whom I asked to describe the first university class she attended in the United States. "It was chaotic" when she entered the classroom, the student said. "The students were very unruly and very disrespectful of the teacher."

I pointed out that this description, like many people's descriptions of things they see other people do, was not really a description, but a combination of interpretation ("the students were very disrespectful") and evaluation ("chaotic, unruly"). I explained that this description told me nothing about what was happening in the classroom. It told me only what the student thought and felt about it. That might be relevant in some way, but it was not what I wanted.

After all, I would no doubt have my own thoughts and feelings about that classroom, and they would inevitably be different from the Malaysian student's, since we are different people with different—and very much culturally-based—standards. I explained that the classroom situation could be described in terms of the number of students in the room, their positions and postures, the number who were talking, the volume of their voices, the other activities in which the students were engaged (drinking coffee, looking at the student newspaper), and so on. This would be a description. Anyone seeing the classroom could, in principle, see the same things. No interpretation or evaluation is involved. Interpretation is subjective, and evaluation more so. People in intercultural situations will inevitably misinterpret some (or much) of what they see, and their evaluations will inevitably be based on standards inappropriate to the new culture. People in intercultural situations, including foreign students, scholars, and their advisers, ought therefore to learn to distinguish description from interpretation from evaluation, and then try, relentlessly, to stop, or at least delay for as long as possible, evaluating.

In conducting sessions where the D.I.E. formulation is being presented, it is even better if participants themselves point out where interpretation and evaluation are finding their way into the description. I recently conducted a session for a group of well-educated and socially conscious university staff members. I explained the D.I.E. formulation, as above, and distributed some photographs which small groups of participants were asked to describe, then interpret, then evaluate. They were instructed to agree on a description, provide at least two interpretations of the photo (making the point that more than one interpretation of the situation in the photograph could be justified), and at least two evaluations of each of the interpretations.

One of the small groups had a photograph showing three Asians standing around a cooking pot emitting steam on a stove. One of the people in the photo held a ladle. This small group was more boisterous than any of the other groups in the room, with several people talking loudly and with much interrupting. When I stood by them to listen, one group member explained to me, "We are having trouble agreeing on the description."

Finally, when I asked for their description of the scene in the photo, their spokeswoman said, "We agreed on only one point. It shows three ethnic minorities."

"Wait a minute!" shouted a participant from another group. "That depends on where the picture was taken!" Indeed. High intelligence, education, and social consciousness do not guarantee immunity from the effects of cultural blinders. (The photograph, by the way, was taken in Taiwan.)

Some comments about the D.I.E. formulation:

- I do not know its source. I first heard it from Janet and Milton Bennett.

- The formulation is quite useful in debriefing intercultural training exercises such as *Bafá Bafá*.

- Completely objective descriptions are probably not possible. We can say, though, that description is the *most objective* aspect of our responses to other people and to social interactions. As such, description is least likely to be contaminated by personal and cultural bias.

The Intercultural Meeting[1]

A common source of frustration for administrators of foreign student programs is the international student club, or whatever the local organization of foreign (and sometimes U.S.) students is called. "We sent out a notice about an organizational meeting," an FSA might report, "and a reasonable number of students showed up. But the meeting went on and on and got nowhere." Or, "We have an international student club, but it doesn't do much. The meetings are exercises in frustration."

From the viewpoint of the adviser who believes it would be salutary to have an active international student club on a campus, it is usually the club's meetings that are the focus of the greatest discontent. The meetings tend to be long, unproductive, and often disputatious. Why should this be? A look at people's culturally based ideas about meetings might suggest some answers to that question. Before looking at those ideas, though, it is important to mention other possible explanations for the problems advisers face in fostering the development of international student clubs. These have to do with the adviser's and students' divergent assumptions concerning such clubs.

An adviser who decides to call an organizational meeting for an international student club is probably making most, if not all, of the following assumptions:

- It would be constructive to have an international student club, to foster interactions between foreign and U.S. students and/or to provide social activities for foreign students.

---

[1] This essay, without the footnotes and some editorial refinement, originally appeared in the *NAFSA Newsletter*, November 1981.

- It is possible to have an international student club that is divorced from the political interests and viewpoints of the students.
- Students view the staff of the foreign student office as benevolent, apolitical, and capable of organizing situations that benefit most foreign students.
- Students from diverse countries see themselves as having important interests in common. They will be able to agree upon objectives for an organization and will willingly cooperate with each other in seeking those objectives.

All of these assumptions are open to question, but even if they are accurate, and the international student club gets to the point where meetings are held, the problems are only beginning. People with differing cultural backgrounds bring such diverse assumptions and behaviors to meetings that their gatherings are often rife with misunderstandings.

In *Beyond Culture*, anthropologist Edward T. Hall offers the notion of "action chains." An action chain is a series of behaviors that people who grow up in a particular culture are taught (usually implicitly) to view as appropriate for a particular situation. People follow their action chains without having to think about what they are doing or why they are doing it. The situation evokes the behavior.

One situation that evokes certain behaviors is a meeting. What does the concept of "meeting" mean to people of different cultures? What behavior is appropriate at a meeting?

To Americans, it seems quite sensible to summon interested people to an organizational meeting for an international student club. It is also sensible to assume that these people will appear at the appointed time and place and that there will be a leader, probably elected in some way or appointed for a temporary period by someone in authority. The leader will moderate the discussion, recognizing people who wish to speak, summarizing people's comments, and keeping speakers on track.

There will be discussion at the meeting. Everyone who wants to talk will have an opportunity to do so. People attending the meeting will seek common ground (that is, they will compromise), establishing a foundation for subsequent joint action. Agreements will be ratified, probably by means of a vote. If the group is large or the issue complicated, Robert's Rules of Order will be employed to manage the discussion. Otherwise, informality will prevail.

Not everyone has this same action chain concerning meetings. There can be diverse assumptions about several aspects of meetings: why they are held, the means of selecting a leader, the leader's role, and the role and behavior of those attending the meeting. Some of the various assumptions that people from different cultures make about these topics are discussed here.

Why Meetings Are Held

Americans typically hold meetings in order to share information or make decisions. People from elsewhere might, more often than Americans, hold meetings in order to ratify or formalize decisions that are made elsewhere, or to give people an opportunity to air their views in the absence of an intention to make any decisions. Of course, people who go to a meeting with the assumption that some decisions are to be made will be frustrated if there are others there who are at the meeting merely to express their opinions.

Means of Selecting a Leader

Most people make the assumption that a meeting needs a leader, although there are people who do not assume that. Among those who do suppose there should be a leader, there are diverse views about the means by which the leader should be designated. In some cultures, a person's age and/or social standing would automatically make him or her the leader in the eyes of all those present.[2] In other cultures a formal nomination and election procedure would be employed. Other possibilities for selecting a leader include having someone volunteer to be the leader, waiting for a leader to emerge from the proceedings, or having the leader appointed by someone in authority.

---

[2] I have devised an exercise to help people learn about the dynamics of intercultural meetings. It entails having a multicultural group conduct a meeting, based on a scenario they are provided, while the other participants in the session sit around the outside (in what is called a "fishbowl") and watch for aspects of the interaction that are listed on an observation sheet. After some time is allowed for the mock meeting, there is discussion among all participants. One question that is asked is, "Who was the leader?" Then, "How was the leader selected?" And, "In your own country, how would a leader be selected in a situation such as this?" In one of these discussions, a participant said that in her country, the oldest mother in the group would automatically be the leader.

At a meeting of students from different countries, especially one held for the purpose of organizing an international student club, these diverse ideas about leadership selection are likely to cause problems. The leader chosen by some people's method may not have legitimacy in the eyes of others. In fact, the others might not even realize that some of the people at the meeting believe a leader has been recognized.

THE LEADER'S ROLE

Americans typically suppose that a leader who is acting appropriately in the context of a meeting will serve as a moderator—keeping order, calling on speakers, preventing anyone from dominating the proceedings, assuring that everyone who wishes to speak has the opportunity to do so, keeping people's remarks on the subject, and helping the group reach decisions. It is often expected that the leader will be neutral with respect to topics of disagreement that arise during the meeting.

In many other societies, the leader is expected to exercise much more authority, and even to make important decisions on behalf of the group. In the eyes of people from such societies, the "democratic" style of group leaderships that Americans tend to idealize is likely to seem unsatisfactory. It may give members so much opportunity to present diverse comments that the result seems like chaos. Or the leader's presumably greater wisdom may be seen as getting too little attention.

On the other hand, in societies where it is the norm to reach decisions by consensus, a U.S.-style chair might seem too obtrusive.[3]

---

[3] In the course of another session like that discussed in the preceding footnote, some students from Japan said they would not vote to make a decision, but would continue talking until consensus was reached. "How long would you keep talking?" I asked. "One hour?"

"Sure."

"Four hours?"

"Yes."

"Eight hours?"

"Yes."

"Can you imagine a group of American students discussing something for eight hours in order to reach an agreement?" I asked.

The students burst into laughter.

ROLE AND BEHAVIOR OF MEETING PARTICIPANTS

It is probably the culturally influenced differences in group members' action chains for meetings that account for most of the difficulty at international student club meetings. First, there is the question of the role of people who attend meetings. In general, when a person comes to a meeting, he or she makes some assessment of his or her status in the group, because one's status within the group does much to determine how one is supposed to behave during the meeting. Determining one's status in a meeting of students from diverse countries is essentially impossible because there is no agreed-upon criterion or set of criteria for deciding where group members stand vis-à-vis each other. Possible criteria include age, sex, period of time as a student at the school, previous leadership position within the group, being from a rich or large country, being from the country or region with the largest number of foreign students at the particular school, being an officer in a nationality organization at the school, having charisma, or having some special affiliation with the foreign student office.

With all of these (and no doubt other) criteria being used by different people at the meeting to determine how they fit in, and with these determinations being made in the absence of conscious thought, discrepant conclusions are inevitable. Some people at the meeting will think that others are out of line.

Second, there is not likely to be a shared assumption about the overall function of the meeting. For Americans, as has been said, the unspoken assumption is that people at a meeting will "give and take" to reach compromise agreements that serve as the basis for action. For others, though, compromise is not seen as natural or desirable. And there is less of an orientation to action. Their purpose may be to win all arguments, or to block the progress of those with opposing views, or to display their rhetorical talent. Engaging in what Americans are likely to consider "mere talk" may be, according to some people's assumptions, the basic function of the meeting. People who behave according to these assumptions often seem dogmatic, insensitive, and obstructionist in the eyes of those who want to find compromises and make decisions.

A third source of disharmony in meetings of foreign students is differences in what Dean C. Barnlund calls "communicative style."[4]

---

[4] See his *Public and Private Self in Japan and the United States.*

Only two aspects of communicative style will be discussed here. They are the general manner of interaction in a discussion, and the means by which people reach conclusions in their arguments.

Americans generally prefer a style of interaction that Barnlund labels "repartee." According to that style, no one speaks for very long. A speaker gets to the point quickly, then gives way to another speaker. A person who talks for too long gets a disapproving reaction.

A style prevalent in many other societies encourages much longer presentations from each speaker. Students from those societies are likely to view American-style presentations as superficial and perhaps lacking in rhetorical skill.

Meetings of foreign students nearly always include some students who, from the viewpoint of others present, talk too long. Impatience results.

People from different cultures are likely to manifest different ways of presenting their arguments. In a meeting of foreign students, one student's logic is likely to be another's nonsense. Some speakers will cite what they consider to be objective evidence to support their views. Others will invoke authorities of some kind. Others will make appeals to sentiment or emotion. Still others will endorse philosophical principles they wish the group to follow.

With two or more different ways of arguing occurring at once, failures to understand are inevitable. Impatience and frustration result.

There are things advisers can do to make intercultural meetings more productive. At a minimum they can foster learning about cultural differences. If the students attending the meeting can be helped to understand the ideas that appear here, they will have learned a good deal about themselves, about other cultures, about the influence of culture on their own and other people's behavior, and about the difficulties that beset intercultural encounters. They might be able to work together to surmount those difficulties.

Advisers could use various approaches to helping students learn from the cultural differences that are manifest in intercultural meetings. They could attend the international student club's meetings and offer observations about culturally based behavior they see taking place. They could have students from a particular country describe for others their action chain for meetings. Better yet, students from particular countries could conduct brief mock meetings that other students could observe, and then there could be discussion of what has been seen. Such an exercise might sharpen students' ability to observe and analyze manifestations of cultural differences.

Another possibility is to have students from a particular country describe and show how they customarily conduct meetings and then have all students use that action chain for the meeting. Different groups' action chains could be used at different meetings.

Still another possibility is to have the club's leader explain his or her conception of the leader's role and his or her expectations of group members. Making these conceptions and expectations explicit can reduce the amount of frustration and anger that result from behavior that others do not understand.

A relatively common approach to the problem of unsatisfactory international student clubs is to try teaching the students the usual American action chain for meetings. This often takes the name of "leadership training" or "organizational behavior consulting." Such training is best accompanied by explicit acknowledgment of the U.S. cultural assumptions and values on which it is based.

Given all the cultural differences that manifest themselves in meetings of international student clubs, it is to be expected that such meetings will be unsatisfying for many who attend them. If they are used as occasions for learning about cultural differences, they can be made more productive. If those in attendance are able to find ways to overcome the difficulties that their diverse cultural backgrounds cause them, some important lessons will have been learned.

C

Organizations from Which FSAs Might Want Information

American Association of Collegiate Registrars and Admissions
Officers (AACRAO)
One Dupont Circle N.W., Suite 330
Washington, DC 20036-1171

CareerTrack, Inc.
3085 Center Green Drive
Boulder, CO 80301-5408

Federal Publications (publishers of *Interpreter Releases)*
1120 20th St. N.W., Suite 500 S.
Washington, DC 20036-3484

Institute for Rational Living
45 East 65th Street
New York, NY 10021

Intercultural Communication Institute
8835 S.W. Canyon Lane, Suite 238
Portland, OR 97225

Intercultural Press, Inc.
PO Box 700
Yarmouth, ME 04096-0700

Microtraining Associates, Inc.
Box 641
North Amherst, MA 01059

NAFSA: Association of International Educators
1875 Connecticut Ave. N.W., Suite 1000
Washington, DC 20009-5728

Nightingale Conant Corp.
7300 N. Lehigh Avenue
Niles, IL 60714

Sage Publications
    2455 Teller Road
    Newbury Park, CA 91320

School for International Training
    World Learning Inc.
    Kipling Road, PO Box 676
    Brattleboro, VT 05302-0676

SIETAR International
    808 17th St. N.W., Suite 200
    Washington, DC 20006

Toastmasters International
    PO Box 10400
    2200 N. Grand Ave.
    Santa Ana, CA 92711

D

List of Institutional Personnel FSAs Will Want to Know

Chief executive officer
Chief academic officer
Chief student affairs officer
Chief business officer
All people in own chain of command, up to the chief executive
People responsible for each of the following:
  admissions
  foreign admissions
  new-student orientation
  registration
  student record keeping
  student accounts
  financial aid
  housing
  student activities
  student health
  student counseling
  campus security
  public information
  alumni affairs
  fund-raising
  institutional relations with state and federal governments
Heads (deans, chairpersons) of all academic units where foreign students are enrolled
As many faculty as possible
Academic advisers (if different from faculty)

E

Outline for a Session on Students from Country X

The session's leader can explain its purpose and provide general background:

1. Location of the country (having a map posted is a good idea)
2. Number of students from Country X at the institution—with breakdown by gender, level and field of study, marital status, source of financial support, and type of housing (on- or off-campus)

Members of a panel of students from Country X can then give brief comments on the following points:

1. Educational background of students from Country X
   a. Characteristics of Country X's educational system
      i. Selectivity
      ii. Teaching methods
      iii. Mental skills rewarded
      iv. Daily life of a secondary or university student
   b. Reasons for coming to the United States and to the particular U.S. institution
   c. Educational and occupational aspirations
2. The experience of Country X students at the particular institution
   a. Initial experiences and reactions
      i. To the United States in general
      ii. To the particular institution
   b. Comparison of the institution's academic system with the one at home
      i. Curriculum

    ii. Academic advising

    iii. Selecting courses

    iv. Class attendance

    v. Behavior of teachers

    vi. Behavior of students in class, toward the teacher and toward other students

    vii. Assignments

    viii. Examinations

    ix. Use of library

    x. Grades

  c. Comparison of local student life with that at home

    i. Student services provided by the institution

    ii. General administrative procedures (admission, registration, paying bills, getting a residence hall room, etc.)

    iii. Social life

3. Things about the local situation that commonly seem unpleasant to students from Country X

4. Things students from Country X need to learn in order to accommodate themselves to the local situation

5. Things North Americans are advised to keep in mind when interacting with students from Country X

6. Questions and answers

A session following this outline will usually take at least ninety minutes. It is best if the panelists have seen the topics beforehand and have prepared their remarks. Without fairly directive leadership from the chair, the session might go well beyond ninety minutes.

The Communicative Style of Americans[1]

According to the communications scholar Dean C. Barnlund, communicative style refers to:

1. the topics people prefer to discuss,

2. people's favorite forms of verbal interaction (ritual, repartee, argument, self-disclosure),

3. the depth of involvement people seek from each other,

4. communication channels people tend to rely on (vocal, verbal, physical), and

5. the level of meaning to which people are generally attuned (the factual or the emotional content of messages) *(Public and Private Self,* 9).

When people with differing communicative styles interact, they frequently feel ill at ease and misjudge or misunderstand each other. To help understand why that happens and to try reducing the communication problems that arise, it is helpful if foreigners know something about the communicative style of the local people and the way it compares with their own.

Here are some generalizations about the communicative style of Americans:

1. *Preferred topics.* In casual conversations ("small talk"), Americans prefer to discuss the weather, jobs, mutual acquaintances, and past experiences, especially ones they have in common with their conversation partners. Men are likely to discuss sports, and women, their jobs or their children. As they grow up, most Americans are warned *not* to discuss politics or religion, at least not with people they do not know rather well, because politics and religion are considered controversial topics, discussion of which might lead to argu-

---

[1] This is adapted from the *Handbook for Foreign Students and Scholars*, published annually by the Office of International Education and Services, University of Iowa.

ments, which Americans are taught to avoid. Sex, bodily functions, and perceived personal inadequacies are traditionally considered personal topics, and are likely to be discussed only between people who know each other very well. Younger people may discuss these topics more freely than older people do, more so in the company of members of the same sex. Another "personal" area is that of finances—how much something cost, or how much income a person receives.

By contrast, people in some other cultures are taught to believe that politics and/or religion are good conversation topics, and they may have different ideas about what topics are too personal to discuss with others.

2. *Favorite form of verbal interaction.* In the typical conversation between Americans, no one talks for very long at a time. Participants in conversation take turns frequently, usually after the speaker has spoken only a few sentences. If argument is unavoidable, Americans prefer it to be restrained, carried on in a normal conversational tone and volume. They are generally impatient with ritual conversational exchanges. (Only a very few ritual expressions dependably occur in their verbal interactions: "How are you?" "Fine, thank you. How are you?" "Fine." "It was nice to meet you." "I hope to see you again.")

People from other countries may be more accustomed to speaking and listening for longer periods when they are in conversation; they may be accustomed to more ritual interchanges (about the health of family members, for example) than Americans are. They may enjoy argument, even vigorous argument, of a kind that Americans are likely to find unsettling.

3. *Depth of involvement preferred.* Americans do not generally expect very much personal involvement from conversation partners. Small talk—without long silences, which provoke uneasiness—is enough to keep matters going smoothly. It is only with very close friends (or with complete strangers whom they do not expect to see again) that Americans generally expect to discuss personal topics.

Some people from other countries prefer even less personal involvement than Americans do and rely more on ritual interchanges. Others come from countries where much more personal involvement is sought, since one wants to learn as much as possible about another person in order to open the possibility of developing a close relationship.

4. *Channels preferred.* Americans like being verbally adept, speaking in moderate tones, using relatively few and restrained gestures of the arms and hands. They touch more than in the past, especially in the form of hugs when greeting or saying good-bye to one another, but they still touch less than people from more emotive cultures.

By contrast, others might prefer even quieter conversation, less talking, and even more restrained gestures. Or they might be accustomed to louder voices, many people talking at once, vigorous use of hands and arms to convey meanings or add emphasis, and/or more touching between conversation partners.

5. *Level of meaning emphasized.* Americans are generally taught to believe in the scientific method of understanding the world around them, so they look for facts and physical or quantifiable evidence to support viewpoints. (Underlying this search for facts is the assumption that there are truths about people and nature that can be discovered by means of objective inquiry carried out by trained people using scientific means of measurement or observation.)

Compared to Americans, people from other countries might pay more attention to the emotional content or the human feelings in a message and be less concerned with what Americans would call facts. (They may not assume the existence of an objective truth, but may suppose that facts are relative, depending on who is observing them.)

Many misjudgments and misunderstandings can arise from interactions between people who have different communicative styles. Here are some examples:

- Foreign visitors in the United States might hear little but small talk among Americans and erroneously conclude that Americans are not intellectually capable of anything more than simple conversation about such subjects as the weather, sports, teachers, or social activities. The conclusion that Americans are intellectually inferior is also reached by those who regard argument as a favorite form of interaction and who find that Americans are often not adept at arguing.

- Responding to people who customarily speak little and who rely heavily on ritual conversation, Americans might use the labels "shy," "too formal," or "too polite."

- Vigorous arguing (with raised voices and much use of hands and arms, and perhaps more than one person talking at a time) of the kind that is natural to some people may alarm Americans, who expect violence, or at least long-lasting anger, to follow from loud disagreements.

- What Americans might regard favorably as keeping cool— that is, not being drawn into an argument, not raising the voice, looking always for the facts—might be seen by others as coldness and a sort of lack of humanness.[2] Conversely, Americans are likely to see those who do not keep cool as being too emotional.

- Embarrassment or unease almost always result when someone raises a discussion topic that the other person thinks is inappropriate for the particular setting or relationship.

- Americans are likely to view a highly articulate person with suspicion.

These are but a few of the many misjudgments that arise between Americans and people in the United States from other countries. It can be helpful to be aware of the communicative style differences that produce them. Talking about differences in communicative style, when such a difference seems to be causing problems, is usually a good way to reduce the negative effects of the differences.

---

[2] In *Black and White Styles in Conflict,* Thomas Kochman argues that many Black Americans share the view of many foreigners that keeping cool on the part of white Americans reflects a devious, insincere, or less-than-human stance.

F-1 Student Regulations and the Role of the Designated School Official[1]

by Margaret B. Brooke and Gary Althen

In the past ten years, foreign student advisers (FSAs) have lived through several major changes in F-1 regulations. These changes create turmoil as FSAs try to understand and apply new regulations at their institutions.

Before the May 22, 1987, regulations took effect, the Immigration and Naturalization Service (INS) was very involved in the life of the F-1 student. Transferring schools, continuing for a second degree after completing the first (at either the same or a higher level), and engaging in practical training (summer or postgraduation) all required INS permission.

We were enormously frustrated that few students could engage in practical training during the summer, since the INS usually took the entire summer to adjudicate the applications. When the INS denied a student an extension of stay to complete a new degree program or to transfer to a new school, we were furious (or at least disturbed), and the students were traumatized by their voluntary departure dates.

Very often decisions depended on individuals at district offices and their interpretation of the regulations. When a new examiner replaced an old one, or when I-538s were "remoted" (that is, sent to some other INS or customs location to be processed), we had to educate the new examiners as to our interpretations, and they had to educate us as to their requirements and understandings.

We complained to NAFSA, GRAC, INS, and our congressional

---

[1] A slightly different version of this article originally appeared in the *NAFSA Newsletter*, April/May 1992.

delegations. The INS, we said, did not understand academia or even its own regulations. We wanted the INS to let us decide what was best for our students and for our institutions. This was the sentiment behind NAFSA's deregulation campaign of the mid-1980s. The 1987 regulations, the result of hard work by GRAC, were a step in the right direction. Designated School Officials (DSOs) were allowed to authorize practical training, to effect school transfers, and to approve new degree programs. The old I-20ID copy (an INS form in use for some years) was discontinued, the I-538 shortened, and the I-20 revised and changed from a seven- to a two-page form.

Some NAFSAns, however, were chagrined by the 1987 regulations, which represented not just a change in the requirements and procedures, but a change in the INS and DSO roles regarding the immigration status of F-1 students. Some NAFSAns could not believe that DSOs were suddenly given the power to make decisions previously made by the INS. NAFSANET (on Inter-L) was full of questions and worries expressing uncertainty about this new decision-making power. The primary question asked was, what would the INS want us to do in a given situation?

Since the next round of new regulations that took effect on October 29, 1991, we have been going through this uncertainty again. The 1991 regulations put even more distance between the INS and academia. The only contact that an F-1 student needs to have with the INS is to obtain an EAD for postcompletion practical training. Everything else is up to the FSA.

This puts us in a unique position, particularly regarding employment for F-1 students. The regulations for curricular practical training are unclear and puzzle many FSAs.

NAFSANET is full of questions about employment of F-1 students, and GRAC reps struggle to answer questions from DSOs in their regions. It is very important for GRAC and the membership to remember that the regulations are vague at our request. We are the ones who complained about INS overregulation of F-1 students. We are the ones who sought deregulation. We are the ones who wanted the authority to assess our students' applications.

Now that we have been given the authority we were seeking, we must use it wisely. If we ask the INS too many questions about what they want from us instead of asking ourselves what we can do within the language of the regulations, more regulations will follow.

Many of us have had the opportunity to ask questions of...the INS staff member currently in charge of the F-1 student regulations.

She responded to some question with, "Do you really want me to answer that question?" She has strongly suggested that we look to the regulations for the answers.

If we don't find the exact answer we want in the regulations, it's because writing regulations that fit every academic institution in the United States and every academic requirement is nearly impossible. Some of our institutions are private, some are public, some are colleges, some are universities, some are specialty schools, and some are liberal arts schools. We need to devise procedures and criteria that fall within the broad framework the new regulations establish—procedures and criteria suitable for our own institutions.

In general, the F-1 regulations seem intended to ensure that people who come to the United States as foreign students are indeed students, and not, for example, workers or tourists. Thus, there are requirements for full-time study. The INS wants to know the whereabouts of aliens in the United States. Thus, there are address-reporting and school-transfer reporting requirements. The INS wants to know what aliens in the United States are doing. Thus, there are requirements for reports (on Form I-20) when F-1 students undertake a new course of study.

While the Department of Labor is concerned about the possibility of foreign students occupying jobs that would otherwise be occupied by American workers, the INS does not appear to want foreign students to be deprived of on-campus and curriculum-related employment opportunities that are available to domestic students. Foreign students pay tuition to our institutions just as American students do, and so they ought to have access to the same curricular practical training opportunities as their domestic counterparts. What those opportunities are varies from institution to institution. Thus the need for each institution to determine its own procedures and criteria related to employment for F-1 students.

Consider the situation of music students in a large university. Such students sometimes have opportunities to perform, for pay, in community and semiprofessional orchestras and bands. This kind of activity is not required of all music students because only the most talented are offered the opportunities. But the educational value of the experience has long been recognized in music schools. Often the students' major professors are principal players, and sometimes the university symphony conductor is also the community orchestra conductor. There is no doubt that this kind of employment is curricular practical training in the essential sense of that term. It is of great educational value to music students at our institution. When those students happen to be in F-1 status, we ask them to obtain a departmental statement attesting to the value of such experiences for music students and an adviser's letter attesting to the value of the experiences for the particular student at his or her stage in the music program. With these documents, we authorize part-time curricular practical training for them.

DSOs must learn to be confident of their ability to understand government regulations. We must not depend on the INS for answers. We must show the INS that we can stand on our own. The NAFSA *Adviser's Manual* will give us some guidance; GRAC reps can help confused FSAs think through their own questions and find answers that are in keeping with their schools' requirements and expectations of its students. We must not let our fear of making a mistake bring about a return to greater INS regulation of F-1 students.

H

Taking A Meeting's Pulse

Instructions: Give 3 or 4 copies of this form to *each* meeting participant before the meeting starts. At the signal of the person responsible for giving the signals, STOP the discussion and immediately fill out the form. Time limit: 3 minutes for each administration.

Meeting:_____ Date:_____ Form #:_____

	Strongly Agree	Agree	Neutral or No Opinion	Disagree	Strongly Disagree
1. I know what topic is on the floor.					
2. I know why we are discussing this topic (i.e., I know the ultimate objectives of this discussion).					
3. I feel involved in the discussion.					
4. My time in this meeting is being used wisely.					
5. I believe something constructive will come out of this discussion.					
6. The meeting's leader is effectively guiding the discussion.					
7. I am constructively contributing to the discussion.					

Suggestions for improvement: _____

_____

_____

_____

_____

Programming Considerations

Some questions to ask yourself in setting up a program might be:

1. **Identifying needs**—What do the people involved want and need?

    a. Who is the audience? Consider age, year in school, major, previous experience and knowledge of the area or subject of the program, sex, cultural background, motivation, likes and dislikes.

    b. How large is the audience?

    c. What does the audience need? To be better students? To be better people? To be better citizens? To relate better to others? To manage their lives better?

    d. What do the members of the audience want?

    e. What do we, the programmers, want from the program? To learn about ourselves? About others? Skills development in programming and leadership? A feeling of success? Recognition?

    f. What do other groups (staff, faculty, parents, etc.) want the audience to gain from their experience?

2. **Developing goals and objectives**—What do we want to do?

    a. Which of the needs identified are most important to the audience?

    b. Which aspects of those needs do we want to address?

    c. What do we want the audience to get out of the program?

3. **Organizing program plans**—What must we do to fulfill our objectives and goals?

    a. *Scheduling.* When do we want to do the program? When will most people be able to come to it? What else is going on then? Do we have time to make the arrangements? Do we have enough time to carry out the program and fulfill our personal commitments?

b. *Facilities.* Where do we want to do the program? How big is the audience? What kind of setting do we want (informal, formal, indoors, outdoors, etc.)? What room or hall is available?

c. *Budget.* How much money do we have to work with? How much will facilities, refreshments, publicity, speakers, equipment, etc., cost? How can we get more money if we need it? Do we want to charge admission? How much will the audience be willing to pay?

d. *Methods and resources.* What method (lecture, film, party, discussion group, etc.) will best help us achieve our objectives? What method will best be accepted by the audience? Where can we find needed resources (bands, speakers, equipment, films, etc.)? Are there contracts to be signed, arrangements to be made for resource people?

e. *Publicity.* What information do people need to have about the program? How can we best get that information to our audience? What can we do to attract attention? Do we need help in developing publicity and where can we get it (artists, writers, printers, etc.)?

f. *Cleanup and follow-up.* What must be done before, during, and after the event? What equipment will we need?

4. **Implementing plans**—How do we put our plans into effect?

    a. Who will do what task?

    b. Who will serve as overall supervisor?

    c. What is our timetable for doing different steps?

5. **Evaluation**—Did the program do what it was intended to do?

    a. *Methods.* What do we want programmers after us to know about this program? What methods can we use to get the information we need? When is the best time to conduct an evaluation?

    b. *Content.* Did the program run smoothly? Was sufficient time allowed for planning and implementation? What should we do next time that we didn't do this time? Who came to the program? How did the people who came respond? Did we achieve our goals? What need does the audience still have that we can plan a new program for?

International Programming: A Personal View[1]

by C. Wayne Young

Most international programming is a waste of time and money. Almost every foreign student office I know devotes a fair amount of both those precious commodities to the development, maintenance, and support of various social and educational activities intended to increase knowledge, understanding, and appreciation among people of different nations and cultures. This is a laudable goal. But few of us have really thought about why (or whether) we should even be doing international programming, what our goals should be, what kind of programs lead to those goals, or how to measure our programming effectiveness. As a result, too many of our programming efforts do not contribute significantly either to international understanding or to student development (a contemporary jargon term meaning "individual student learning and growth"). The purpose of this article is to offer an assessment of the present state of international, especially student-related, programming and to suggest some ways to improve the effectiveness of our programming.

Programming as we do it

The state of international programming is, to my way of thinking, pretty dismal. Just as most offices, in this period of expanding foreign student enrollment and proportionately shrinking budgets, have felt constrained to limit their offerings to only the most essential student services, many of us have felt compelled to limit our pro-

---

[1] This article originally appeared in the *NAFSA Newsletter,* February 1984. While the situation Young describes has perhaps improved somewhat, his basic ideas and questions still seem pertinent.

gramming to the most traditional, tried and true activities—international dinners and festivals, "culture nights," intercultural communication workshops, and the like—activities which have been done so often and which require so little thought, as they are usually done, that most of us programmers could do them in our sleep.

Not surprisingly, such somnambulistic programming has long since ceased to arouse enthusiasm on the part of the FSAs or the participants. Not that the programs themselves are faulty, unimaginative as they are; it is, rather, the way most of us go about programming that causes too many of our programs to be competent but uninspired at best, boring and counterproductive at worst. Most of them are carried out in an ad hoc, aimless way. FSAs, with minimal advice, consent, or active participation by interested students, put together formulaic, isolated events that go nowhere. FSAs dragoon reluctant foreign students (or "international," for those more comfortable with euphemisms) into engaging in time-consuming, one-shot social or "cultural" events such as international dinners or talent shows from which nobody—not the FSA, not the foreign students, not the American students or the community members who come and watch—gains much but an evening of pleasant entertainment. Well-intentioned FSAs cajole American and foreign students into participating in intense cross-cultural exercises which neither the planner nor the participants are convinced are really needed. Earnest FSAs persuade department heads to encourage their teachers to use foreign students as resources in classes, then the teachers, not really committed to internationalism themselves, gradually forget to use these resources, and the FSAs turn to other, equally temporary, enthusiasms. Nobody really expects much to come from any of these programs, and nobody is truly surprised or disappointed when nothing does.

Few of our programs fit into any long-range plan. Few are consistently worked at, evaluated, or aimed toward any goal beyond the events themselves. Most of them end up inadvertently teaching the FSA, foreign and American students, faculty, and community members that international activities are mildly agreeable or mildly dull, but essentially ephemeral expenditures of time and energy.

International student programming ought not be reduced to such a listless, intellectually debased state. Developing educational and social programs that bring together foreign students and Americans is, I believe, an important part of an FSA's role, and it can be interesting and challenging work. We do have a responsibility to try to help foreign students learn about the ambient American culture and the values of the people who make it up. We do have a responsibility to try to help Americans learn about the people and cultures of the rest of the world. And we do have a responsibility, as educators, to find ways to develop the knowledge, character, and skills of the students at our institutions. A good way to meet these responsibilities is to bring people together in carefully planned programs.

Standards for good programming

If we decide that we are going to do programming, then we need to try to set some standards for what we consider good, successful, effective programming. Each of us will have to come up with his or her own standards, I suspect. I have mine.

First, as I see it, good programming touches a significant number of people. It is an axiom of student programming that the success of programs is to be judged by the quality of the students' participation, what they gained from it, and not judged by the number of people who participate. Even so, I think it is fairly reasonable to consider a program less successful if only a very small number of people benefit from it, especially if we count as possible beneficiaries the FSA and the student organizers as well as the target audience. Many good programs may involve only a few people at any given time, but over the years a significant number of people may benefit from them.

Second, good programming touches those participants in a significant way. How we define "significant," of course, depends on just what it is we want to do. Many FSAs, myself included, are committed to two sometimes contradictory goals which we try to balance. On the one hand, we want to increase foreign students' and Americans' awareness of the diversity of ideas and behaviors found in other cultures. We want to help people understand and appreciate other peoples' values, beliefs, customs, and ideas. We want to help them gain some recognition of how their own societies look from other vantage points. We often refer to this rather vaguely as "increasing international understanding," although there is no good reason for leaving it so vague.

On the other hand, we want to be enlightened, non-directive practitioners of student development. We want to help students build their characters and their skills while letting them do pretty much what they want to do.

Both of these are worthwhile goals. The first, "culture learning," is admittedly hard to measure or judge, but a programmer who works closely with an individual or a group over time can see differences as people learn to respect the behavioral and mental habits of people from other cultures, learn how those habits make sense in other contexts, learn that their own habits make sense in their own contexts. Small, intensive, active programs such as host family programs, student conversational partnership programs, and similar ones are probably effective ways to promote culture learning; so are intercultural living situations, and ongoing task- or interest-related groups with intercultural memberships.

Mass-oriented, participant-passive events such as most international festivals, talent shows, and fashion shows probably do not move much beyond the lowest level of cross-cultural awareness, the level (as Robert Hanvey wrote in a 1977 essay titled "An Attainable Global Perspective") of tourism, textbooks, and the *National Geographic*. The best we can hope for from such events is that a few members of the audience will have whetted their appetites to learn more about other cultures and other peoples.

Even those mass-oriented events, though, can provide excellent student development-type opportunities for student organizers. FSAs can often see such things as students' enhanced self-confidence, decision-making ability, leadership and organizational skills, and maturity as the fruit of these otherwise fruitless undertakings, so even these events deserve an FSA's support, if they are student-oriented.

Third, good programming usually meets a need felt not just by the FSA but also by the participants. The participants, not just the FSA, must want the program.

Fourth, good programming serves the *long-term* best interests of the students, the community, the nation, the world, and the FSA. "Long-term," of course, requires that we take a long view. Most Americans are not accustomed to doing that.

Finally, good programming is cost-effective, figuring the costs in terms of money, psychic energy, and time, and figuring the benefits not only in terms of cross-cultural learning gained, friendships made, an estimated gain in consciousness of global interconnectedness and interdependence, but also development of leadership and organizational skills. These and other intangibles, are, of course, measured by the yardstick of judgment, based on one's experience, knowledge, and concern.

Where do we start?

Having established criteria for good programming, how do we produce good programs? The first thing we have to do is some *thinking*. Nobody can do good programming hastily or by rote; it is the fruit of much serious reflection, discussion, and argument. It cannot be done piecemeal, event-by-event. A thoughtful programmer will have, at least in embryonic form, a master plan which is itself based on a philosophy of action. Each event, each activity builds (ideally) toward a stated objective.

Goal-oriented international student programming is, I think, the product of a certain state of mind. What are some characteristics of that mental state? First, the thoughtful programmer has some appreciation of the "big picture," a measure of global awareness and a sense of how what we do fits into that larger scene. As I see it, for example, the world is becoming increasingly interdependent and increasingly wracked by conflicts born of international and intercultural misunderstandings—and, often enough, born of a very clear understanding of very different values. Our nation's people and leadership (with the possible exception of the federal executive branch) seem to be on the verge of a new understanding of our position in the world vis-à-vis other countries, other economies, and other cultural values. The large and growing number of foreign students in the United States presents us with unparalleled opportunities to learn about other peoples' values, beliefs, customs, ideas, and behaviors, and to learn more about our own in the process. We have a wonderful opportunity to teach those educational sojourners about our culture, in the hope that greater understanding will lead toward international peace and cooperation. And we FSAs have a central role in all this.

In addition to having a global perspective, I would argue that truly effective programming requires some measure of personal vision and moral fervor. I am challenged, at this point, to make explicit my own philosophy of programming. Unsophisticated as it may be, it is this: I want to make the world a saner, safer place for my children and their cohorts and descendants. I think I can do something to make it so. I am still strongly committed to working toward the three goals I adopted some years ago as a Peace Corps volunteer—to help people in developing nations, to help those people understand Americans, and to help Americans understand other peoples of the world. I see my role as an FSA—advising and counseling students and developing programs to facilitate cross-cultural learning—as an expression of my concern for other people and as a logical continuation of my Peace Corps service. I believe that the best way to help other people is to help them learn to help themselves, so I am a strong advocate of student development as a part of human development. My philosophical position is, naturally, evolving as I gain experience and maturity.

Third, the effective programmer must also be able to appraise realistically all the factors that will be involved in a particular program, and then try to design the program to fit the realities of the place, the time, and the people. Inadequate assessment and unrealistic expectations probably account for more program failures than insufficient publicity, bad weather, or any other individual factors. Perhaps the FSA should begin with some hard self-study: Do you have the kind of personality that can work effectively with student groups? Are you really interested in doing programming, or are you being directed to do it? Do you have the time or budget to do it yourself? Do you have help? What are the priorities of your office? How much do you know about the students, the university, and the community? And the students: Do they have the time to participate actively in planning and coordinating programs? What student organization or individuals can you count on to participate? How old are the students? What are their interests and priorities? Is the university or college president committed to an "internationalized institution?" Are the administration and faculty? And the community: Is the city leadership interested in encouraging international events? Are foreign students seen as a negative presence, merely tolerated in the community, or are they seen as assets? How are these community attitudes manifested? No one can make intelligent decisions about programming without considering these matters.

Next, good international student programming requires that the FSA often, perhaps usually, take a back seat to the students. Such a suppression of ego may not come easily to all of us, but the first advice I received as an FSA-to-be, and the first I will give to any new or aspiring one, is that the FSA should not try to do everything for the students, not try to solve their problems for them or to run their programs for them. Advice and assistance, yes; decisions and control, no. I venture a strategic suggestion from time to time, to be sure, but students make the decisions, do the work, and get the credit. I think this is important and I stand by it, although I am challenged fairly often when an international talent show receives less than rave reviews in the local paper or when an international dinner runs out of food. So it goes.

Students have their own interests, and student programming that does not center on student interests ends up as an ego trip for the FSA or as a failure. Students often do not know what their options are, what possibilities are open to them. FSAs can and should come up with brilliant ideas for programs, and should share them with students. When the idea catches, when students adopt the idea and proceed as if it were their own, then the program has a good chance of being successful. And students, not the FSA, should take the limelight.

Last, a good programmer is a patient planner. Both patience and the ability to make long-range plans are crucial to effective, goal-oriented programming. Five-year plans or even longer-term ones are not unreasonable if we take our objectives and our professional roles seriously. Where do you want your overall international student program to be in five years? What are your plans for specific areas? I want, for example, at least three foreign students in the student senate, with foreign students voting in student elections at least as frequently as U.S. students do. To reach this objective, I have encouraged foreign students to volunteer for various committees, I have encouraged the student senate to create a special seat for foreign students, and I have encouraged foreign student organizations to vote in the elections. Eventually, I hope to see foreign students participating fully in student government, having a say in the spending of their student fees and in the making of policies that affect them, and gaining the university leadership experience that has stood so many American public servants in good stead.

Developing international programs

A proper mindset, of course, is not all we need for good programming. We are being paid to act, to do things, to develop programs. What kinds of programs can we develop?

It is not difficult to come up with a variety of ideas for specific programs. They can be cribbed from other international student services offices' newsletters or from other FSAs, or colleagues, or students. They can even be original. Ideas are legion. Ideas are cheap. Ideas are not the place to begin. It is far better for the international programmer to start with the question of just what it is that he or she wishes to accomplish, based on a thoughtful consideration of the major issues of international educational exchange, his or her personal vision, and a critical appraisal of the situation with a focus on both the students' interests and on what we think to be their best interests. *Then*, with a goal in mind, the FSA can think about a coherent program with component activities and projects that build toward that objective.

The result of such thinking can be new programs that are tailor-made to our situations and needs. At my campus, for example, student activism appears to be on the increase. Some foreign students are desirous of knowing what civil rights they have as educational sojourners here, and at least one law school professor and the school ombudsman (as well as one FSA) think they should know, so we may soon try to put together a small seminar on the subject.

My role in instigating this seminar is less clear than my role in coordinating it: I had been thinking about civil rights for foreign students for a couple of years and even had discussed the matter with a representative of the state civil rights commission, but I had not felt the time was right to push for a program. I am sure I dropped some hints to students. Even so, the foreign students who approached me to suggest a civil rights session obviously thought it was their idea. That is fine with me.

The civil rights workshop (if it comes off) will be a small, low-budget, fairly intensive participant-active affair. That kind of activity makes a larger, longer-lasting impact than flashy, mass-oriented participant-passive ones (I contend), although it makes poor copy. I am realistic enough to admit that my office can benefit from the publicity generated by an international festival or talent show, and so I go along with student-initiated mass events more readily than some of my colleagues do, but I am convinced that more learning goes on in quieter programs such as this.

The FSA can also make programs possible even when he or she does not take a direct role in organizing them. For example, a student in our college student-personnel program did a practicum in our office. Under my supervision, she succeeded in reviving the Latin American Student Association, which went on to procure a grant for a Spanish-language radio program, to establish a scholarship program for Latin American women, and to bring in speakers on Latin American politics and literature. None of this could have been done by my office directly, given our limited resources. With an FSA's advice, support, and encouragement, student organizations have offered language courses, published cookbooks, coordinated sports events, and hosted film festivals. None of the above programs was consciously copied from other institutions and some may be unique to our campus, but, innovative or not, the programs are appropriate by my criteria set forth here and have generally been considered successful.

It is quite possible that "old" activities as well as new ones are compatible with thoughtful, goal-oriented programming. Even international festivals and "culture nights" can have a place in a goal-oriented, philosophically-based international program; they do in mine. But I am prepared to explain and justify (cynics will say I rationalize) my support of certain mass-oriented programs according to my own goals and criteria of success. Our international festival, for example, is run by students, not by an FSA. I support it because the foreign students, American students, and community members (we often have it in a shopping center) find it a satisfying experience, and their interest and enthusiasm override my lack of faith that Americans learn very much about other cultures at such an event. The festival gives students a chance to practice and develop leadership and organizational skills, provides students of different cultures an unusual chance to work together, gives them a chance to teach Americans some aspects (although superficial ones) of their cultures, and encourages other university offices and community organizations to take an active role in an international activity.

Many foreign student service offices and FSAs do take a direct part in organizing and managing international festivals, talent shows, and other mass-oriented, and usually observer-oriented, events. They do so, apparently, because of their belief that these activities "increase international understanding." Thus, it is more important for them to maximize the chance of those activities being successful—in terms of wide publicity, large attendance, quality of entertainment, and succulence of food—than it is to promote the development of the students who staff the booths and do the dancing.

I do not include "increasing international understanding" among my reasons for supporting international festivals or any other events, although I am certainly in favor of it as an ideal. Many people talk about the putative "increase" as an objective, but it is, as far as I know, inherently unmeasurable by any tool of hand or mind. What does "international understanding" mean? Increasing *whose* understanding? Of what? How does one judge whether any change in understanding has taken place? How deep an understanding are we talking about? Until I find some sensible definition of that term and some way to measure or estimate the before-and-after levels of understanding, I will continue to consider "increasing international understanding" a hopelessly simplistic bromide, unworthy of use by people who take international programming seriously.

It is time for FSAs to put some thought into international programming, an area which most of us profess to believe important but in which few of us have bothered to invest much mental energy. Or so it appears to me; this highly personal and perhaps idiosyncratic view of the state and possibilities of international student-related educational and social programming stems from my observations at my campus and from my reading and listening to others. Being where I am and doing what I do, my opportunities for observing, reading, and listening are not unlimited, so some of the foregoing may not be universally relevant.

From where I stand, though, international programs can be made much more exciting and cross-culturally productive, in terms of both student development and increasing the level of cross-cultural awareness, than they usually are. What is needed is an application of disciplined thought and planning based on a global consciousness, a vision of what a better world would be like, a realistic appreciation of situational limitations and possibilities, and a commitment to the development of our students. Having these may not guarantee a successful international program, but little of permanent value can be produced without them. With so much at risk, and with so much to gain, it would be a shame to give it less than our best effort.

Do-It-Yourself Professional Development

INVENTORY OF CURRENT PROFESSIONAL DEVELOPMENT ACTIVITIES

1. On a separate sheet list the periodic publications related to your field that you know about. After you have done that, draw a *circle* around the titles of the publications you read regularly, and a *square* around the titles of the publications read from time to time.

2. How many professional conferences have you attended in the past year?

3. What professional organizations do you belong to?

4. Within the past two years have you:

   a. held any office in any professional organization?   YES   NO

   b. attended any professional development workshop?   YES   NO

   c. written any articles for publication?   YES   NO

   d. planned any workshop or conference session?   YES   NO

   e. traveled abroad other than as a tourist?   YES   NO

   f. conducted any studies related to educational exchange?   YES   NO

   g. taken any course related to your work?   YES   NO

5. Name two books related to your work that you have read during the past six months.

   a.

   b.

6. Name two books related to your work that are on your to-read list or on your to-read pile.

   a.

   b.

INVENTORY OF PROFESSIONAL DEVELOPMENT NEEDS

SKILLS RATING

Use a check mark to show whether you consider your level of skill with respect to each item to be *low, medium,* or *high.*

	Low	Med	High
1. Using work time efficiently	____	____	____
2. Writing clear letters and memos	____	____	____
3. Explaining things clearly when talking	____	____	____
4. Giving clear instructions	____	____	____
5. Making public presentations	____	____	____
6. Keeping accurate records	____	____	____
7. Listening to others, hearing not just the words but the underlying feelings	____	____	____
8. Motivating subordinates to perform well	____	____	____
9. Working constructively with your boss	____	____	____
10. Planning: setting objectives and assessing your progress toward them	____	____	____
11. Setting priorities	____	____	____
12. Withholding judgment about other people's values	____	____	____

	Low	**Med**	**High**
13. Making decisions	___	___	___
14. Implementing decisions	___	___	___
15. Avoiding procrastination	___	___	___
16. Conducting lively, fruitful meetings	___	___	___
17. Networking	___	___	___

Knowledge Rating

On a separate sheet, list the five subject-matter areas you think it is most important for people in your area of specialization to *know about*. Then indicate whether your own level of knowledge in each of these five areas is *low, medium,* or *high*.

Professional Development Plan

Look over your ratings of your knowledge and skills. Mark the two skills and the two areas of knowledge in which you think it is most important for you to improve. Write your selections here:

Skills:

a.

b.

Knowledge:

a.

b.

List under the headings below at least two (three or four would be better) ways in which you could improve in the areas you have just listed.

Skill (a)   **Skill (b)**   **Knowledge (a)**   **Knowledge (b)**

In each of the four columns on the preceding page, circle two activities to which you could realistically commit yourself during the next year.

Write down the two professional development activities you have decided you could begin within the next four months. Beside each of them write down the *first step* you would have to take to start that activity (for example, check a book out of the library, get information about registering for a course). Then write down the *date* by which you plan to take each of those first steps.

Activity	First Step	Date
a.		
b.		

References

Althen, Gary. *American Ways: A Guide for Foreigners in the United States.* Yarmouth, ME: Intercultural Press, 1988a.

——. "Counseling Malay Students." In *Building the Professional Dimension of Educational Exchange,* edited by Joy Reid. Yarmouth, ME: Intercultural Press, 1988b. (Out of print.)

——. *Learning with Your Foreign Roommate.* rev. ed. Iowa City: Office of International Education and Services, University of Iowa, 1991.

——. "The Americans Have to Say Everything." *Communication Quarterly* 40, no. 4 (Fall 1992): 413-21.

——. *Manual for Foreign Scholars.* Iowa City: Office of International Education and Services, University of Iowa, 1993.

——, ed. *Students from the Arab World and Iran.* Washington, DC: National Association for Foreign Student Affairs, 1979.

——, ed. *Learning across Cultures.* rev. ed. Washington, DC: NAFSA: Association of International Educators, 1994.

American Council on Education. *Foreign Students and Institutional Policy.* Washington, DC: American Council on Education, 1982.

Andreasen, Nancy C. *The Broken Brain.* New York: Harper and Row, 1984.

Archer, Carol M. *Living with Strangers in the U.S.A.: Communicating beyond Culture.* Englewood Cliffs, NJ: Prentice-Hall, 1991.

Arum, Stephen, and Jack Van de Water. "The Need for a Definition of International Education in U.S. Universities." In *Bridges to the Future: Strategies for Internationalizing Higher Education,* edited by Charles B. Klasek. Carbondale, IL: Association of International Education Administrators, 1992.

Barnes, Gregory A. *The American University: A World Guide.* Philadelphia: ISI Press, 1984.

Barnlund, Dean C. *Public and Private Self in Japan and the United States.* Tokyo: Simul Press, 1975. U.S. edition Yarmouth, ME: Intercultural Press, 1989.

Barr, Margaret J., and Lou Ann Keating, eds. *Establishing Effective Programs.* (New Directions for Student Services, No. 7). San Francisco: Jossey-Bass, 1979.

Bates, Jefferson D. *Writing with Precision: How to Write So You Cannot Possibly Be Misunderstood.* Washington, DC: Acropolis Books, 1978.

————. *Dictating Effectively.* Washington, DC: Acropolis Books, 1981.

Bellah, Robert N., et al. *Habits of the Heart.* Berkeley: University of California Press, 1985.

Bennett, Janet Marie. "Student Development and Experiential Learning Theory." In *Building the Professional Dimension of Educational Exchange,* edited by Joy Reid. Yarmouth, ME: Intercultural Press, 1988, 105-19. (Out of print.)

Bennett, Milton J. "Intercultural Communication." In *Building the Professional Dimension of Educational Exchange,* edited by Joy Reid. Yarmouth, ME: Intercultural Press, 1988, 121-36. (Out of print.)

————. "Towards Ethnorelativism: A Development Model of Intercultural Sensitivity." In *Education for the Intercultural Experience,* edited by R. Michael Paige. Yarmouth, ME: Intercultural Press, 1994, 21-71.

Berlo, David K. *The Process of Communication.* New York: Holt, Rinehart & Winston, 1960.

Bernstein, Albert J., and Sydney Craft Rozen. *Dinosaur Brains.* New York: Ballantine Books, 1989.

————. *Neanderthals at Work.* New York: Ballantine Books, 1992.

Bhawuk, D. P. S., and Richard W. Brislin. "The Measurement of Intercultural Sensitivity Using the Concepts of Individualism and Collectivism." *International Journal of Intercultural Relations* 16, no. 4 (Fall 1992): 413-36.

Bliss, Edwin C. *Getting Things Done.* New York: Charles Scribner's Sons, 1991.

Block, Peter. *The Empowered Manager: Positive Political Skills at Work.* San Francisco: Jossy-Bass, 1991.

Bolton, Robert. *People Skills.* New York: Simon and Schuster, 1979.

Brislin, Richard W. *Cross-Cultural Encounters: Face-to-Face Interaction.* New York: Pergamon, 1981.

———. *The Art of Getting Things Done: A Practical Guide to the Use of Power.* New York: Praeger, 1991.

———. *Understanding Culture's Influence on Behavior.* Fort Worth: Harcourt Brace Jovanovich, 1993.

Brislin, Richard W., Kenneth Cushner, Craig Cherrie, and Mahealani Yong. *Intercultural Interactions: A Practical Guide.* Beverly Hills: Sage, 1986.

Brislin, Richard W., and Tomoko Yoshida. *Intercultural Communication Training: An Introduction.* Thousand Oaks, CA: Sage, 1994.

Bryson, John D. *Strategic Planning for Public and Nonprofit Organizations.* San Francisco: Jossey-Bass, 1988.

Buzan, Tony. *Use Both Sides of Your Brain.* rev. ed. New York: E. P. Dutton, 1983.

Byrd, Patricia, ed. *Teaching across Cultures in the University ESL Program.* Washington, DC: National Association for Foreign Student Affairs, 1986.

Calano, Jimmy, and Jeff Salzman. *CareerTracking: 26 Success Shortcuts to the Top.* New York: Simon and Schuster, 1988.

Carroll, Raymonde. *Cultural Misunderstandings.* Chicago: University of Chicago Press, 1988.

Clark, Burton R. *The Academic Life: Small Worlds, Different Worlds.* Princeton, NJ: Carnegie Foundation for the Advancement of Learning, 1987.

Clark-Oropeza, Barbara A., Maureen Fitzgibbon, and Augustine Baron, Jr. "Managing the Mental Health Crises of Foreign College Students." *Journal of Counseling and Development* 69, no. 3 (January/February 1991): 280-84.

Coffey, Margaret. *A Guide to Cross-Cultural Counseling and Advising at the Applied English Center.* Lawrence, KS: Applied English Center, University of Kansas, 1992.

———. "Assisting ESL Students in Need of Counseling," *Wide Open Spaces* (Fall 1993): 1ff.

Condon, John C., and Fathi Yousef. *An Introduction to Intercultural Communication.* Indianapolis: Bobbs-Merrill, 1975.

Covey, Stephen R. *The Seven Habits of Highly Effective People.* New York: Simon and Schuster, 1989.

Covey, Stephen R., A. Roger Merrill, and Rebecca R. Merrill. *First Things First*. New York: Simon and Schuster, 1994.

Csikszentmihalyi, Mihaly. *The Evolving Self: A Psychology for the Third Millennium*. New York: HarperCollins, 1993.

DeVita, Philip R., and James D. Armstrong. *Distant Mirrors: America as a Foreign Culture*. Belmont, CA: Wadsworth Publishing, 1993.

Doyle, Michael, and David Straus. *How to Make Meetings Work*. New York: Jove Books, 1976.

DuBrin, Andrew J. *Winning Office Politics*. Englewood Cliffs, NJ: Prentice-Hall, 1990.

Educational Testing Service. *TOEFL Test and Score Manual*. Princeton, NJ: Educational Testing Service. Annual.

Ellis, Albert. *Reason and Emotion in Psychotherapy*. New York: Lyle Stuart, 1972.

———. *Executive Leadership: A Rational Approach*. New York: Institute for Rational Living, 1978a.

———. *Humanistic Psychotherapy: The Rational-Emotive Approach*. New York: Institute for Rational Living, 1978b.

———. *Anger: How to Live with and without It*. Flushing, NY: Asia Book Corp., 1987.

———. *How to Stubbornly Refuse to Make Yourself Miserable about Anything*. New York: Carol Publishing Group, 1990.

———, ed. *Growth through Reason: Verbatim Cases in Rational Emotive Therapy*. Palo Alto, CA: Science and Behavior, 1971.

Ellis, Albert, and Robert Harper. *New Guide to Rational Living*. North Hollywood, CA: Wilshire Books, 1977.

Ericksen, Robert, and Dogan Cuceloglu. "The FSAs Must Be Crazy." Presentation at the Region II conference of NAFSA: Association of International Educators, Sacramento, CA, 7 December 1993.

Evans, Nancy J., and Vernon J. Wall. *Beyond Tolerance: Gays, Lesbians, and Bisexuals on Campus*. Alexandria, VA: American College Personnel Association, 1991.

Fieg, John, and John Blair. *There Is a Diifference: 17 Intercultural Perspectives*. Washington, DC: Meridian House, 1980.

Fisher, Roger, and William Ury. *Getting to Yes*. Boston: Houghton Mifflin, 1981.

Goodwin, Craufurd D., and Michael Nacht. *Absence of Decision*. New York: Institute of International Education, 1983.

Gordon, Thomas. *Parent Effectiveness Training.* New York: Peter H. Wyden, 1970.

―――. *Leader Effectiveness Training.* New York: Peter H. Wyden, 1977.

Grove, Cornelius R. *Orientation Handbook for Youth Exchange Programs.* Yarmouth, ME: Intercultural Press, 1989.

Gudykunst, William B. *Bridging Differences: Effective Intergroup Communication.* Newbury Park, CA: Sage, 1991.

Gudykunst, William B., and Young Yun Kim. *Communicating with Strangers.* Reading, MA: Addison-Wesley, 1984.

Gudykunst, William B., and Stella Ting-Toomey. *Culture and Interpersonal Communication.* Newbury Park, CA: Sage, 1988.

Hall, Edward T. *The Silent Language.* Garden City, NY: Doubleday, 1959.

―――. *The Hidden Dimension.* Garden City, NY: Doubleday, 1966.

―――. *Beyond Culture.* Garden City, NY: Doubleday, 1976.

―――. *The Dance of Life.* Garden City, NY: Doubleday, 1983.

Hammer, Mitchell. "Research, Mission Statements, and International Student Advising Offices." *International Journal of Intercultural Relations* 16, no. 2 (Spring 1992): 217-36.

Hanson, Philip G. "What to Look for in Groups." In *Small-Group Training Theory and Practice,* edited by J. William Pfeiffer, and John E. Jones. La Jolla, CA: University Associates, n.d.: 23-26.

Hoff, Ron. *I Can See You Naked: A Fearless Guide to Making Great Presentations.* rev. ed. Kansas City, MO: Andrews and McMeel, 1992.

Hofstede, Geert. *Cultures and Organizations: Software of the Mind.* London: McGraw-Hill, 1991.

Hood, Mary Ann G., and Kevin J. Schieffer, eds. *Professional Integration: A Guide for Students from the Developing World.* Washington, DC: NAFSA, 1983.

Horner, David, and Kay Vandersluis, eds. "Cross-Cultural Counseling." In *Learning across Cultures,* edited by Gary Althen. Washington, DC: NAFSA, 1981, 30-50.

Hughes, Robert. *Culture of Complaint: The Fraying of America.* New York: Oxford University Press, 1993.

Ivey, Allen, and Jerry Authier. *Microcounseling: Innovations in Interviewing, Counseling, Psychotherapy, and Psychoeducation.* Springfield, IL: C. C. Thomas, 1978.

Jones, John E. "A Model of Group Development." In *Small-Group Training Theory and Practice,* edited by J. William Pfeiffer, and John E. Jones. La Jolla, CA: University Associates, n.d.: 38-41.

Kayser, Thomas A. *Mining Group Gold: How to Cash In on the Collaborative Brain Power of a Group.* El Segundo, CA: Serif, 1990.

Kennedy, Marilyn Moat. *Office Politics: Seizing Power, Wielding Clout.* Chicago: Follett, 1980.

Kluckhohn, Florence, and Fred Strodtbeck. *Variations in Value Orientation.* Evanston, IL: Row Peterson, 1961.

Kochman, Thomas. *Black and White Styles in Conflict.* Chicago: University of Chicago Press, 1981.

Kohls, L. Robert. *Survival Kit for Overseas Living.* 3d. ed. Yarmouth, ME: Intercultural Press, 1995.

Kohls, L. Robert, and John M. Knight. *Developing Intercultural Awareness: A Cross-Cultural Training Handbook.* 2d ed. Yarmouth, ME: Intercultural Press, 1994.

Kuhn, Thomas S. *The Structure of Scientific Revolutions.* 2d. ed. Chicago: University of Chicago, 1970.

Lakein, Alan. *How to Get Control of Your Time and Your Life.* New York: New American Library, 1973.

Lanham, Richard A. *Revising Prose.* New York: Charles Scribner's Sons, 1979.

Lasch, Christopher. *The Culture of Narcissism.* New York: Warner Books, 1979.

Lebra, Takie S. *Japanese Patterns of Behavior.* Honolulu: University of Hawaii Press, 1976.

Lee, Motoko Y., Makhtar Abd-Ella, and Linda A. Burks. *Needs of Foreign Students from Developing Nations at U.S. Colleges and Universities.* Washington, DC: NAFSA, 1981.

Leki, Ilona. "Twenty-Five Years of Contrastive Rhetoric: Text Analysis and Writing Pedagogies." *TESOL Quarterly* 35, no. 1 (Spring 1991.)

Levine, Deena R., and Mara Adelman. *Beyond Language.* Englewood Cliffs, NJ: Prentice-Hall, 1993.

Mackenzie, Alec R. *The Time Trap.* New York: AMACOM, 1990.

Martin, Judith N. "Intercultural Communication: A Unifying Concept for International Education." In *Learning across Cultures.* rev. ed. Edited by Gary Althen. Washington, DC: NAFSA: Association of International Educators, 1994: 9-29.

Matthews, Christopher. *Hardball: How Politics Is Played—Told by One Who Knows the Game.* New York: Harper and Row, 1988.

McKay, James T. *The Management of Time.* Englewood Cliffs, NJ: Prentice-Hall, 1959.

Mestenhauser, Josef A. "Are We Professionals, Semi-Professionals, or Dedicated Good Guys?" *NAFSA Newsletter* 27, no. 8 (May 1976): 9-11.

Miller, Richard M. "Looking Back, Looking Forward at the INS." *Interpreter Releases* 71, no. 18, 9 May 1994.

Moore, Paul L. *Managing the Political Dimension of Student Affairs.* New Directions for Student Services, No. 55. San Francisco: Jossey-Bass, 1991.

Moore, Thomas. *Care of the Soul.* New York: Harper, 1994.

NAFSA: Association of International Educators (Washington, DC). *Standards and Responsibilities in International Educational Interchange.* (Guideline Series 1). Washington, DC: 1979.

———. "The Foreign Scholar's Experience: A Concern for Quality." 1986a.

———. *Handbook for Community Organizations Working with Foreign Students.* 1986b.

———. *Optimizing Health Care for Foreign Students in the United States.* 1989.

———. *Orientation of New Foreign Students.* (Working Paper 13). 1990.

———. *Adviser's Manual of Federal Regulations Affecting Foreign Students and Scholars.* 1993a.

———. *Risks and Realities: A Guide to Health Insurance for FSAs.* 1993b.

———. *Mandatory Insurance for International Students at U.S. Educational Institutions.* (Working Paper 49). 1994a.

———. *Standards and Policies in International Educational Exchange: A Guidebook for Policy Development, Professional Conduct, and the Continuing Growth of International Education.* 1994b.

Nash, Dennison. *A Community in Limbo.* Bloomington: Indiana University Press, 1970.

New York Times. "Chaos at the Gates." 11-15 September 1994.

Paige, R. Michael, ed. *Education for the Intercultural Experience.* Yarmouth, ME: Intercultural Press, 1994.

Parker, Orin. *Cultural Clues to the Middle Eastern Student.* Washington, DC: American Friends of the Middle East (AMIDEAST), 1977.

Pedersen, Paul B. *A Handbook for Developing Multicultural Awareness.* Alexandria, VA: American Association for Counseling and Development, 1988.

———. "Counseling International Students." *Counseling Psychologist* 19, no. 1 (January 1991).

Pedersen, Paul B., and Allen Ivey. *Culture-Centered Counseling and Interviewing Skills.* Westport, CT: Praeger, 1993.

Peter, Laurence J., and Raymond Hull. *The Peter Principle.* New York: Bantam Press, 1970.

Peterson, Norman. "Pulling Public Policy Levers for International Education." In *Building the Professional Dimension of Educational Exchange,* edited by Joy Reid. Yarmouth, ME: Intercultural Press, 1988, 81-86. (Out of print.)

———. *Advocacy and the International Educator.* Washington, DC: Liaison Group for International Educational Exchange, n.d.

Pusch, Margaret. "Cross-Cultural Training." In *Learning across Cultures.* rev. ed. Edited by Gary Althen. Washington, DC: NAFSA: Association of International Educators, 1994: 109-43.

———, ed. *Multicultural Education: A Cross-Cultural Training Approach.* Yarmouth, ME: Intercultural Press, 1979.

Reid, Joy, ed. *Building the Professional Dimension of Educational Exchange.* Yarmouth, ME: Intercultural Press, 1988. (Out of print.)

Renwick, George. *Evaluation Handbook for Cross-Cultural Training and Multicultural Education.* Chicago: Intercultural Press, 1979.

Rhinesmith, Stephen H. *Bring Home the World.* New York: AMACOM, 1975.

Rico, Gabriele Lusser. *Writing the Natural Way.* Los Angeles: J. P. Tarcher, 1983.

Rogers, Carl R. *On Becoming a Person.* Boston: Houghton Mifflin, 1961.

Samovar, Larry A., and Richard E. Porter. *Intercultural Communication: A Reader.* 7th ed. Belmont, CA: Wadsworth, 1994.

Sanford, Nevitt. *Self and Society.* New York: Atherton Press, 1966.

Senge, Peter. *The Fifth Discipline.* New York: Doubleday/Currency, 1990.

Shen, Fan. "The Classroom and the Wider Culture: Identity as a Key to Learning English Composition." *College Composition and Communication* 40, no. 4 (December 1989): 459-66.

Siletz, Ari B. *The Mullah with No Legs and Other Stories.* Yarmouth, ME: Intercultural Press, 1992.

Simons, George F. *Working Together: How to Become More Effective in a Multicultural Organization.* Menlo Park, CA: Crisp Publications, 1989.

Simons, George F., Carmen Vazquez, and Philip R. Harris. *Transcultural Leadership: Empowering the Diverse Workforce.* Houston: Gulf Publishing, 1993.

Slater, Philip. *The Pursuit of Loneliness.* rev. ed. Boston: Beacon Press, 1976.

Stewart, Edward C., and Milton J. Bennett. *American Cultural Patterns: A Cross-Cultural Perspective.* rev. ed. Yarmouth, ME: Intercultural Press, 1991.

Storti, Craig. *The Art of Crossing Cultures.* Yarmouth, ME: Intercultural Press, 1989.

————. *Cross-Cultural Dialogues: 74 Brief Encounters with Cultural Difference.* Yarmouth, ME: Intercultural Press, 1994.

Story, Katheryn E. "The Student Development Professional and the Foreign Student: A Conflict of Values?" *Journal of College Student Personnel* 23, no. 1 (January 1982): 66-70.

Sue, Derald Wing, and David Sue. *Counseling the Culturally Different: Theory and Practice.* 2d ed. New York: John Wiley and Sons, 1990.

Summerfield, Ellen. *Crossing Cultures through Film.* Yarmouth, ME: Intercultural Press, 1993.

Thomas, Kay, and Gary Althen. "Counseling Foreign Students." In *Counseling across Cultures.* 3d ed. Edited by Paul B. Pedersen, et al. Honolulu: University of Hawaii Press, 1989: 205-41.

Thomas, Kay, and Teresa Harrell. "Counseling Student Sojourners: Revisiting the U-Curve of Adjustment." In *Learning across Cultures.* rev. ed. Edited by Gary Althen. Washington, DC: NAFSA: Association of International Educators, 1994: 89-107.

Torbiörn, Ingemar. "Dynamics of Cross-Cultural Adaptation." In *Learning across Cultures.* rev. ed. Edited by Gary Althen. Washington, DC: NAFSA: Association of International Educators, 1994: 31-55.

United States House of Representatives, Government Operations Committee, Subcommittee on Information, Justice, Transportation, and Agriculture. *The Immigration and Naturalization Service: Overwhelmed and Unprepared for the Future.* 4 August 1993.

Walker, Lenore E. *The Battered Woman.* New York: Harper and Row, 1979.

Walsh, John E. *Humanistic Culture Learning.* Honolulu: University of Hawaii Press, 1979.

Weil, Andrew. *Health and Healing.* Boston: Houghton Mifflin, 1985.

Whalen, Susan, Raymond DiGiuseppi, and Richard Wessler. *A Practitioner's Guide to Rational Emotive Therapy.* New York: Oxford University Press, 1980.

Wurzel, Jaime. *Toward Multiculturalism: Readings in Multicultural Education.* Yarmouth, ME: Intercultural Press, 1988.

Wycoff, Joyce. *Mindmapping.* New York: Berkley Books, 1991.

Young, C. Wayne. "International Programming: A Personal View." *NAFSA Newsletter,* February 1984.

Zinsser, William. *On Writing Well.* 4th ed. New York: Harper Perennial, 1990.

Index